THE FREE PRESS

New York London Toronto Sydney Singapore

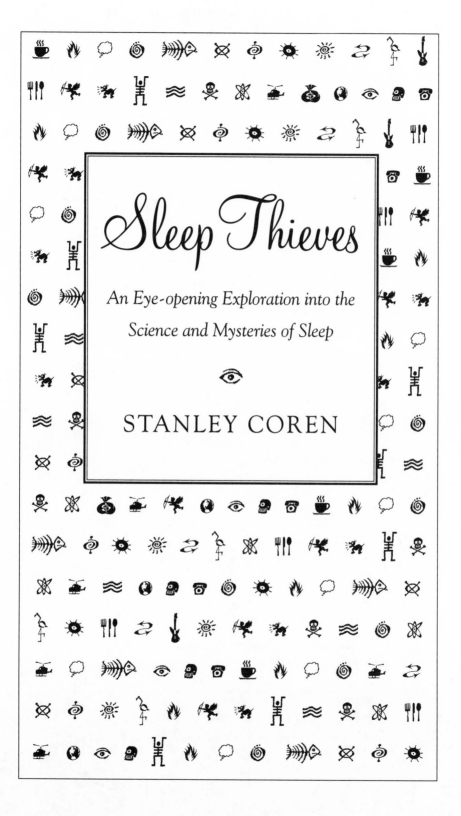

Sleep Thieves

An Eye-opening Exploration into the

Science and Mysteries of Sleep

STANLEY COREN

THE FREE PRESS
A Division of Simon & Schuster Inc.
1230 Avenue of the Americas
New York, NY 10020

THE FREE PRESS and colophon are trademarks
of Simon & Schuster Inc.

Designed by Carla Bolte

Manufactured in the United States of America

10 9 8 7 6 5 4 3 2 1

Library of Congress Cataloging-in-Publication Data

Coren, Stanley.
    Sleep thieves : an eye-opening exploration into the science
and mysteries of sleep / Stanley Coren.
        p.   cm.
    Includes bibliographical references and index.
    ISBN 0-684-82304-7
    1. Sleep—Physiological aspects.   2. Sleep—Psychological
aspects.   I. Title.
QP425.C62   1996
612.8'21—dc20   95-51549
                                                          CIP

To my parents

BENJAMIN AND CHESNA

and to my brothers

DENNIS AND ARTHUR

Contents

Preface ☕

What do the nuclear accident at Chernobyl, the near meltdown at Three Mile Island, the environmentally disastrous oil spill by the *Exxon Valdez*, and the loss of the space shuttle *Challenger* all have in common? They were all caused by people who were making mistakes because they had had too little sleep.

This is a book about sleep. It deals with some interesting and fascinating facts associated with sleep, as well as with the serious implications of a society that is running on too little sleep. I try to answer questions like "What is sleep?" and "Why should we spend one-third of our lives at this unproductive activity?" During this exploration it will become clear that sleep is a process that is so important to the physical and psychological well-being of living things that evolution has gone to great lengths to allow sleep. Some birds can sleep while in flight. Some fish sleep while swimming. Some animals sleep with one-half of their brain while using the other half to keep themselves alive.

Human beings seem to be fighting the evolutionary pressure to sleep. Despite the fact that sleep plays a vital part in our health and our efficiency, we seem out to abolish sleep. The first step in this process was the invention of the electric lightbulb, which eliminated our main excuse for stopping our work at the end of the day, namely, that it was too dark to function. Next came the continuous conveyor belt, which encouraged factories to operate 24 hours a day. Now the continuous access to information provided by the Internet and other computer communication links keeps us from our beds at all hours of the night. The work ethic we have adopted today says that we should do away with sleep, or at least eliminate as much sleep time as possible. The movers and shakers of the world don't waste their time sleeping. Yet too little sleep can kill us outright or can cause a gradual deterioration in our health. Too little sleep can make us clumsy, stupid, and accident-prone. Too little sleep can destroy our psychological motivation and put us into a deep depression.

For some people, sleep gives way to the pressure of their ambition; for others, the sleep loss is involuntary. Sleep is stolen in many ways. The sources of insomnia are sometimes hidden. A cup of hot chocolate can steal half a night's sleep, and yet people often use this as a before-bed drink. A glass of cola given to a child as a bribe for going to bed can keep the child awake until midnight. Sometimes our environment steals sleep from us. Sometimes the thief is age. Some of our problems with sleep can be easily solved. Others cannot.

There are sleepy people driving trucks, cars, planes, and trains. There may be a sleepy doctor trying to decide what emergency treatment one of your loved ones must have. There may be a sleepy investment manager groggily making a decision that will affect your life savings. There may even be a sleepy person in the White House deciding the fate of a nation. Each year, sleep-related errors and accidents cost the United States over $56 billion, cause nearly 25,000 deaths, and result in over 2.5 million disabling injuries. Running up a sleep debt can be very expensive indeed. This book will allow you to directly test yourself and see just where you stand in terms of your own sleep debt.

When I wrote this book, I had many helpers. My cherished wife, Joan, went over an early version of this book. (She also made it her business to make sure that I had enough sleep to function well enough to write it!) My friend and colleague Peter Suedfeld kept me supplied with an endless stream of news items in which sleep played a role. Hilde Colenbrander, our data librarian, found me a crucial set of data tapes. David Wong and the other members of the Human Neuropsychology and Perception Laboratory of the Psychology Department of the University of British Columbia did much of the library work for me. Grants from the National Sciences and Engineering Research Council of Canada and from the Medical Research Council of Canada helped to keep my laboratory functioning. I interviewed literally hundreds of people to gather information about the effects of sleep on everyday life. Some of their stories, in their own words, appear here. Since all were promised anonymity, I can only thank them as a group. Without the insights provided by them, this book would not have been possible.

—*Stanley Coren*

Sleep Thieves

Edison's Curse

> Most people overeat 100 percent, and oversleep
> 100 percent, because they like it. That extra 100
> percent makes them unhealthy and inefficient.
> The person who sleeps eight or ten hours a night
> is never fully asleep and never fully awake—they
> have only different degrees of doze through the
> twenty-four hours.[1]

The man who wrote these words in his diary was not a
psychologist, psychiatrist, or medical researcher. It was Thomas Alva
Edison, the man who changed the world by creating over 1,300 inventions, including the phonograph, the electric typewriter, the first practical motion picture camera and projector, and the carbon microphone
(which made the telephone possible). Yet it is not Edison the inventor
who captures our interest at the moment, but Edison the social engineer who profoundly changed the psychology of the modern world. It
was his desire to be known as the man who finally eradicated the waste
of human potential represented by all those hours spent in "unproductive sleep."

Edison's reasoning was really quite simple: If sleep could be eliminated, it would add additional work hours to the day. This would improve productivity, bring prosperity to all of society, and hasten the progress of civilization. "Anything which tends to slow work down is a waste," he explained. "We are always hearing people talk about 'loss of sleep' as a calamity. They better call it loss of time, vitality, and opportunities."

His plan was fairly straightforward and involved an invention that he had worked on for many years—the electric lightbulb. This great boon to society would banish the darkness and thus make it possible for people to work continuously through the night hours. Edison believed, from personal experience, that sleep was merely a bad habit and could be done away with quite easily. "For myself I never found need of more than four or five hours sleep in the twenty-four," he claimed. His personal experience also convinced him that sleep was deleterious to health and made people lazy and stupid. "When by chance I have taken more [hours of sleep than usual]," he wrote, "I wake dull and indolent." Edison was later able to confirm his personal experiences with sleep and with the beneficial effects of the lightbulb using other observations: "When I went through Switzerland in a motor-car, so that I could visit little towns and villages, I noted the effect of artificial light on the inhabitants. Where water power and electric light had been developed, everyone seemed normally intelligent. Where these appliances did not exist, and the natives went to bed with the chickens, staying there till daylight, they were far less intelligent."

All things considered, Edison seems to have succeeded quite well in his campaign. His prediction that the lightbulb would transform society and would lengthen the workday has certainly proven true. For one thing, the lightbulb made shift work possible. An adequate source of light in conjunction with the continuous conveyor belt meant that a manufacturing plant could operate 24 hours a day. Individual workers would work 8 hours at a time, but the workforce could be split into three shifts, each taking over as the previous one checked out. The obvious advantage was that the same facility could then produce up to three times the number of items, and there would be no need to add extra equipment or increase the size of the plant. Thus, Edison made sure that at least the machines would never waste their time sleeping.

Did Edison have any effect on human sleep patterns as a result of his invention? I think he would be gratified to learn that people regularly sleep less now than before the lightbulb was invented and that he is, at least partly, responsible for that. As an example, in one study conducted in our laboratory we looked at the amount of time the average young adult sleeps today and found that this was typically a bit less than 7½ hours a day. A similar study was conducted back in 1910. The timing is important because it was in 1913 that our modern tungsten filament lightbulb was introduced. Earlier versions of the lightbulb had a carbon filament in a globe from which the air had been pumped out to provide a reasonable vacuum. These were expensive but short-lived and only provided a fairly dim light (which gradually grew dimmer as soot deposits formed on the inside of the glass). The new kind of light-bulb introduced in 1913 used a coiled tungsten filament and a globe filled with an inert gas (nitrogen, sometimes mixed with argon). This was the lightbulb that provided the cheap, bright, and long-lasting electric light we have come to take for granted. It was this lightbulb that made it possible for working people to free themselves from the darkness of night. According to Edison, once the darkness was banished, the major excuse for sleep was eliminated. Looking back at the sleep patterns that were common in the pre-tungsten-lightbulb era, we find that the average person slept 9 hours each night. This means that there has been a reduction of more than 1½ hours per day in the average person's sleep time. In other words, Edison can claim to have added more than 500 hours of waking time to every year we live.

Edison's negative feelings about sleep were the result of his strong work ethic, which associated long hours spent in sleep only with the lazy or the idle rich. This association is common throughout society. I remember growing up with a jingle that went as follows:

> Six hours sleep for a working man,
>> Seven hours for a scholar,
> Eight hours sleep for a simpleton,
>> Or a knave not worth a dollar.

The view that too much sleep is not only wasteful but actually immoral in some sense is virtually universal. The vice president in charge of computer software development for a major company put it this way:

"When I first hire them, I tell my programmers that around here we look at sleep as just a bad habit. It is unproductive and should just be considered 'downtime' for the brain. I let them know, right off, that if they are going to be successful in this company, they're going to have to do it with a lot less sleep."

In line with this philosophy, official agents of society, such as teachers, begin to indoctrinate us quite early to make sure that we avoid the evils of too much sleep. As a child I remember being warned about the bad things that happen if one gives in to the sinful pleasures of too much sleep. My first-grade teacher, one Mrs. Pasternack, seemed to have an endless supply of proverbs and aphorisms, which she used whenever she noticed one of her students dozing off. For example: "He who sleeps all morning through will end up begging in the afternoon" and "The sleepy fox seldom has feathered breakfasts." And then there was the one that was certainly guaranteed to keep a first grader awake later that night: "There will be plenty of time to sleep when you're dead and buried."

Present-day life seems to be based on a 24-hour lifestyle. The modern hero in our culture is the workaholic. Our heroes are ambitious, achievement-oriented people who fill every spare moment of the day with activities that will advance their career. No time is ever to be wasted. Leisure time is certainly expendable. I went to a theater recently and noticed this sign next to the door of the main auditorium: PLEASE BE CONSIDERATE TO OTHERS. DO NOT USE YOUR CELLULAR PHONES DURING THE PERFORMANCE. We are so used to dealing with the 24-hour workday that such a sign does not seem ludicrous to us; rather, it appears to be merely a polite reminder.

The gurus of our modern lifestyle tell us, however, that we should make time available in our busy schedule for leisure. We must have leisure and recreation if we are to maintain a healthy psychological balance. We must also make time for athletic activities to keep us physically fit so that we may live long enough to enjoy the fruits of our hard work. However, no one warns us that we must also have adequate sleep. Some people can integrate leisure and physical activities with their work requirements, for example, by taking a client to a show or playing golf with a prospective customer. In contrast, our workday is never modified to accommodate sleep; instead, sleep is simply displaced by the requirements of our job and lifestyle. I recently spoke to an ambitious young man in the business world who gave me the following example:

I was in New York at that time; they had just made me one of the managers of a mutual fund that traded in international stocks. Now, we have buyers in all of the major world centers who watch local changes, but I wanted to personally coordinate the portfolio. The international market can really be volatile and millions of dollars can be earned or lost in a few hours, so I decided to take advantage of technology to give me a little edge. I got myself a fax machine and arranged to have the opening and closing stock prices in Paris, London, Tokyo, and Hong Kong sent to me just about the instant that they're posted. In addition, if there was any major shift that the buyers wanted me to know about they could fax it to me at any time. I got an identical version of this fax machine for my home. When I left the office at night, I arranged to have the faxes forwarded to my apartment. I put the fax machine right next to my bed. It has this beeper option, and whenever some information would come in, it would beep until I took the fax. It was a really great idea, and I felt like I was really on top of things. It messed up my sleep a little, but that wasn't much of a price to pay, I thought. It just freaked Ellen [his wife] totally out. She was teaching school, and she said that waking up to this fax beeping all the time was making her psychotic. I solved the problem, though. I put the fax machine in the next room and got this little thing that was designed for TV sets. It's like a little broadcaster and it just sat right on top of the fax. Then all I had to do was to wear these earphones to bed. When the fax beeped, I could hear it and Ellen couldn't, so she got to sleep and I got the info that I needed.

We might accept the fact that sleep is often sacrificed by hard-driving businessmen and international entrepreneurs. However, we should also recognize that people whose business lives follow a 9-to-5 schedule and who have no take-home work are also willing to treat sleep as if it were an unnecessary, expendable activity. Just about everything else in life is treated as more important than sleep time. For example, suppose that you decide to relieve some of the stress in your life by adding a pet to your household. You go out and buy a lovely golden retriever puppy. The dog's breeder, however, warns you that to keep your dog happy and healthy you must give him a half hour walk each day. How are you going to fit that extra half hour responsibility into your already overcrowded daily schedule? "No problem," you say. "I'll simply set my alarm clock a half hour earlier so that I can walk the dog before I go to work." With that one act you have now reduced your weekly sleep total by 3½ hours and your annual amount of sleep by over 180 hours. Over the dog's lifetime you have committed yourself to lose around 2,200 hours of sleep.

I am certainly not trying to single out our canine friends to blame in this matter. Suppose, as another possibility, your son wants to take up the game of hockey, or your daughter wants to learn to figure skate. In many communities the only available ice arena time for such activities is in the early mornings. Now you can no longer sleep until 7 A.M. each day, as was your former habit. Now you must have your child down at the ice rink at 6 A.M., which means that you must get up at 5 A.M. Will you go to bed any earlier? Not likely. There is the evening news and maybe the late-night talk show that you feel you need to keep you aware of the events in the world. There is the Tuesday night card game, the Wednesday night self-improvement class, and the Thursday night aerobics group, none of which can be changed. So the end result is that your child's weekday practice sessions will cost you about 520 hours of lost sleep each year, and if your child's sports activities continue from the time he or she is in Grade 2 until Grade 10, you will lose a total of 4,160 hours of sleep. This is more sleep lost than if you had simply chosen not to sleep at all one night out of every week.

Many of our sleep-stealing commitments are of shorter duration but may still result in a large cumulative sleep loss. Suppose that you are working on a major project associated with your work, taking an evening course, studying for some kind of test, or preparing for a family event such as a wedding or a big party. Where do you find the time for these extra required activities? Typically, people simply add an hour or two to their day. In these instances the hour is usually added at the end of the day with a casual "You go to bed now, dear; I've got a bit of work to do" to your spouse. In this way you may shorten your sleep time by an hour or more each night until the project is finished.

Although we find that fewer people may be employed in full-time occupations when economic conditions worsen, those who are still employed tend to work longer hours. This comes about since demands on the business fluctuate and at times the smaller staff can't meet company needs during the regular workday. Any additional overtime will still be less expensive than hiring more permanent staff. For the employee, however, overtime has consequences beyond extra money. Household duties and other chores must still be completed, shopping must be done, laundry must be washed, and home maintenance must be attended to even though there are now fewer nonworking hours in which to finish these chores. Where is the extra time to come from? The easiest place to get them is to steal them from sleep time. Thus, the end result of overtime is usually a reduction in sleep time for the duration of the new schedule.

For some people there is no monetary compensation for additional hours of work. They simply end up bringing work home with them to finish at night. This is what Bernard, a middle-level manager with a large wood products company, must do. As Bernard explains:

We never have time to finish our work during the regular workday. How can we? There are always meetings to go to, phone calls to return, mail to get out, and that sort of thing. That means that when it comes to completing quarterly reports or periodic personnel evaluations, the only time I get to do them is my own time—at home. The VPIC [vice president in charge] doesn't want to hear any complaints about not having enough time during the workday. Nowadays, you don't complain about too much work for the hours in the workday or they'll start thinking that you can't handle it. Let me tell you, management jobs are hard to come by today. That means that if the VPIC wants the reports completed and on his desk exactly on schedule, they better be there. So I slip some of the work into my briefcase and bring it home with me. I can usually catch up if I put in a few hours each night after everyone else is in bed. I don't like losing the sleep. Sometimes I do get really weary. Like I tell my wife, though, it's only a few weeks each year and it keeps things going smoothly at work.

All of this is part of a pattern. One Harris poll noted that in the mid-1970s the amount of time Americans spent in leisure activities was more than 26 hours a week. In the 1990s this has been reduced to around 16 hours a week. This 10-hour reduction represents a loss of more than one-third of our leisure time. In addition, the amount of time spent in work-related activities has been steadily rising. Although the average work week, according to contract specifications, was 35 hours in the mid-1970s, the actual time spent working was around 41 hours, roughly one hour extra per day. In the 1990s work time is close to 48 hours per week, or an extension of 2½ hours per day. This time has to come from somewhere, and it is usually found by reducing the amount of time we spend in bed.

There is another recent economic force that has the potential to play havoc with sleep. This is the tendency for more and more people to work at home, connected to needed resources and clients by computer modem, fax machines, and phones. People who work at home often work odd hours. Marilyn, a commercial artist who does most of her work at home, usually awakens at 6:30 A.M. and then hurries to help get breakfast for her husband and two children. After they are off to work and school, she works for about 2 or 3 hours. Her youngest child comes home for lunch, and after she returns to school for the afternoon, Marilyn puts in another 2 hours of work. After that she does some chores around the house until her daughter returns from school. She then spends a little time with the child before preparing dinner, which is served at around 6:30 P.M. Once dinner is finished and the dishes are done, Marilyn returns to her office at around 8 P.M. to put in another 3 to 4 hours of work. She seldom gets to bed before midnight. Thus, while working at home seems to provide her with a lifestyle that allows her to integrate her employment and her family life, it does so at the cost of restricting her to an average of 6½ hours of sleep each night. Marilyn's situation is not atypical for people who work at home, whatever their occupation. People who use this strategy often end up working longer than they would in an office or shop. Since there is no separation between the workplace and the living space, it is easy to cheat on our normal activities to provide a little more time for work. Of course, the activity that we most frequently cheat on seems to be sleep.

One hard-driving young businessman gave me his view of the situation: "Look, if time were money, I would say that me, and most people like me, are suffering from a cash flow problem. Now if that is true, do you think that I am going to squander my limited resources on something with as small a profit margin as sleep?"

As a neuropsychologist, I always get a certain feeling of disquiet from such statements. In the face of technological and social changes we must ask whether human beings can keep up and adapt to the new conditions we have imposed upon ourselves. When Edison introduced the lightbulb, he was opening the door to a new technological era that had the potential to allow us to abandon sleep and work around the clock. However, the intended user of this new technology is a biological machine with a very long history of adaptive evolution. Technology has evolved at a speed that has far outstripped the rate of biological evolution. Our physiology cannot change with a flick of the switch. Human beings today are making demands on their bodies and their minds that are in conflict with their biological nature.

Our species evolved very slowly. The development of human beings can be traced back about 4 million years to *Australopithecus afarensis,* which is considered the first of the hominids, but it was only 2 million years ago that there appeared the first hominids that are sufficiently humanlike that we can classify them in the biological group *Homo,* or "man," that we reserve for ourselves. The first definitely human creature was *Homo habilis,* which means "handy man," a term that was chosen because he is also the first of the toolmakers. The chain of evolution then continues slowly, and it was only around 30,000 years ago that modern human beings (*Homo sapiens sapiens,* or "wise man") appeared.

During this slow biological evolution the lifestyle and behavior patterns required for survival were probably changing at a rate compatible with the changes attributed to physical evolution. For some 4 million years man was basically a hunter and a gatherer. Gathering such foods as nuts, berries, and roots required light and could not be efficiently done in the dark. Hunting also required light. The end result was that man slept through the dark hours because it was too inefficient and too dangerous to do anything else. After all, if there were saber-toothed tigers out there in the dark, it was safer to be asleep in a nice, well-hidden cave. Given the average light cycles in the regions of the world where man is believed to have originally developed, human beings were probably dealing with up to 14 hours of darkness, or relative darkness, each day. Presumably, much of this time was spent sleeping.

Let's compare the rate of our biological evolution (4 million years) to the rate at which our technology has evolved. The history of machines probably begins with the invention of the wheel. It often surprises people to learn that the first evidence of any use of the wheel is dated only 5,000 years ago. An early Sumerian sketch shows the use of primitive wheels, really only wooden slabs, roughly rounded at the corners and mounted on a crude cartlike vehicle. Modern technology has a short history. The first alternating current electric motor was only patented a bit over 100 years ago, in 1888. The fluorescent lightbulb, which gives us a much better approximation of continuous daylight than the incandescent lightbulb ever could, was developed in 1936. It is difficult to believe that it was only in 1951 that the computer era began; UNIVAC (an acronym for "universal automatic computer") was the first digital computer designed for commercial use. It would still be another 11 years before IBM would introduce the first hard disk drive, and it was only in 1970 that the first floppy disk drive was introduced, thus making it possible for people to carry their data and programs easily from one machine to another, instead of requiring thousands of punched cards to do the same thing. Think of it: the total time elapsed since the development of the tungsten lightbulb, which made electric light practical and universally available, is less than 100 years, and the time elapsed since we entered the computer age, where information flows continuously and can be tapped into 24 hours a day, is less than 50 years. Technology has certainly changed very quickly, but what about us?

Unfortunately, we still have the physiology of the hunter-gatherer. For 4 million years, minus only the last 100, the evolving human species was not required to deal with monitoring atomic power plants in the dead of the night, pulling all-nighters to cram for exams, writing a quarterly sales report at 2 A.M., watching late-night TV, hanging out in singles' bars, or working the midnight-to-8 A.M. shift on a production line. We were designed to fit a particular ecological niche, to fulfill particular functions under a well-defined set of fairly constant environmental conditions. Continuously available light, electrically operated equipment, and worldwide computer hookups, as well as entertainment and recreational activities that can be accessed at any time of day or night, have drastically changed our environmental conditions. These new conditions have tempted us to think that Edison was right. Perhaps we might be able to function around the clock, with little or no need to waste time in sleep. Yet all of these technological changes occurred only an instant ago in evolutionary time. It was the needs of the primitive hunter that determined our evolution and thus our present physiology. Evolution has not yet responded to the needs of the night shift worker or the hard-driving, ambitious stock manager monitoring the Tokyo exchange prices from his New York apartment in the middle of the night. No matter how wasteful sleep may seem to us today, it has probably evolved for a purpose.

Just how much flexibility do we have in terms of our sleep requirements? Is sleep really a worthless time-out period that merely squanders one-third of our lives? If so, can we find some way to go without it or at least reduce its wasteful impact? If not, are there any long-term or serious consequences of our modern proclivity to do without sleep or at least to cheat as much as possible on our sleep time? The answers to these questions are becoming more important because it is beginning to look like many current problems may have more to do with too little sleep rather than with time wasted sleeping. It seems that we have not evolved fast enough to keep pace with our present technological world. It is obvious that we can and do cheat on the amount of sleep we have to accommodate to technological and societal demands. Unfortunately, such cheating can ultimately make us clumsy, stupid, unhappy, and dead.

Sleep and Consciousness ☁

I think that when most of us consider the important activities in our life, high on our list are those associated with eating and sex. If I asked you for some proof of how important these activities are, you might mention the fact that you spend a lot of time each day devoted to these behaviors (or at least thinking about them). However, the amount of time even the most amorous gourmands might spend in these activities pales in comparison to the amount of time they will spend sleeping. If, for example, you live to be 70 years of age and sleep the average amount of time that most people do, you will have actually spent over 200,000 hours asleep. Obviously, if our species has been programmed to commit such a large amount of time to this activity, it must fulfill some important, perhaps critical, function. Yet it was not until the 1950s that people actually had a reasonable understanding of what sleep is.

If one watches a sleeping human or animal, one soon discovers several common features or characteristics that seem to define this behavior:

- Sleep is usually associated with a typical body posture. It would be extremely unusual to see a human standing up while asleep. To encourage people to sleep we usually have them lie down.
- Sleep usually involves greatly reduced physical activity. Although there may be movements during sleep, one does not typically expect

a person or animal to run down the street in this state. It is also unusual for people who are not asleep to lie quietly without moving for long periods of time (especially for young children).

• There is usually a particular place set aside for sleeping. In animals this may be a nest or den while in humans it is a bedroom, or at least a bed.

• Sleep usually is a regular daily occurrence, which occurs at roughly predictable times. Thus, a human being typically sleeps during the night hours while a lion or tiger has two sleep episodes, one at night and one at midafternoon.

• When people are asleep they are usually less aware and less responsive to changes in the environment. That's why you generally remember very little about a TV show that you slept through.

If you wanted to study sleep and all you could rely on was simply observation of characteristics such as those just mentioned, you would probably learn very little (and would spend a lot of boring time watching people apparently doing nothing). Perhaps this is the reason why there was only one major scientist from the 1930s to the early 1950s whose sole interest was the study of sleep. Nathaniel Kleitman, who was a professor of physiology at the University of Chicago, entered the field of sleep study with much the same preconceptions most people seem to have today. He started with the view that the body is like an automobile, with the brain corresponding to the engine. Sleep was seen as the equivalent of parking the car overnight: during sleep, the body becomes inactive and the brain effectively shuts off. The car is then brought back into activity when someone turns on the engine in the morning. The only difference was, Kleitman admitted, that the brain didn't actually turn off completely; instead, it slowed down (like a very slowly idling engine) during the night, with an occasional quick sputter of activity that might show up as dreaming. In his 1939 book *Sleep and Wakefulness*, Kleitman described sleep simply as "a periodic, temporary cessation or interruption of the waking state, the latter being the prevalent mode of existence for the healthy adult."

When Kleitman first began to study sleep, there were few methods of gathering reliable data on this behavior. Obviously, sleeping people cannot tell you what they are feeling or experiencing, and if you wake them to find out what is in their minds, then of course they are no longer asleep. This leaves you in the odd situation of asking people for a description of a behavior state that they can't actually be experiencing while they are reporting it. This does not make the scientist feel very confident about his or her observations.

For the scientist, things get worse. You see, people are really quite bad at reporting on their own sleep patterns. I once helped to monitor a sleep investigation that involved briefly awakening a young adult every 30 minutes. The young man was shaken awake and then, just to be sure that he was no longer asleep, asked some simple question like "What day is today?" or "If you add the numbers 6 and 3, what do you get?" After a total of 15 such wakenings, he was finally allowed to sleep through the night until he woke up naturally. In the morning he was asked to describe how well he slept that night.

"It was really a good night's sleep," he said.

"Do you remember anything about last night?" we asked.

"Not much. I may have had some dreams, but they're hard to remember. I think one of them had to do with being here in the lab and somebody talking to me, although I don't remember what they said. I may have awakened once, when I thought I heard you guys adding up some numbers, but other than that I didn't wake up at any time after my head hit the pillow last night."

This may sound somewhat bizarre, but it is quite typical. Some people with sleep problems (for example, *sleep apnea*, which we'll encounter again later) may actually awaken several hundred times each night. Although they may feel sleepy and not well rested the next day, they frequently do not have any recollection of having awakened before their alarm went off in the morning.

In the same way that you can have the false sense that you slept well, you can also have the erroneous belief that you slept poorly or not at all. A series of studies (many done at Stanford University) have looked at the sleep patterns of people who feel that they are suffering from insomnia. When such people are tested in the sleep laboratory, researchers usually find that although they do get less sleep than people who feel they sleep normally, the difference is not as great as their personal impressions suggest. Groups of insomniacs typically report that it takes them an hour or more to fall asleep at night, but actual measurements of their brain waves show that almost all of them are asleep in 20 to 30 minutes. This means that their estimates are two to three times as long as the real state of affairs. Most insomnia sufferers also tend to underestimate the amount of time they actually are asleep during the night by nearly half.

I have a personal example that illustrates how we can have a perception that we are awake when we are actually sleeping quite soundly. During my graduate school years at Stanford University in California, my wife and I were living in married student quarters, which were actually old army barracks that had been divided into apartments. One morning I was lying in bed bemoaning the fact that I had just spent a totally sleepless night.

"I didn't sleep a wink last night," I complained to my wife. "I just lay there staring at the ceiling for hours."

"Actually, I didn't sleep so well myself," she groaned back at me.

The clock radio was insisting that it was time for us to get up, however, so I pushed myself to a sitting position only to find myself staring at a layer of white, pebbly material that covered the blanket and most of the floor surrounding the bed. The words from the radio announcer now began to enter my consciousness. "We are still getting reports about last night's earthquake," he said. "Some windows broken, shelves emptied, and the usual cracks in the wall plaster, but no major damage or injuries." Now I understood. Although I felt that I had been awake all night, I had actually been so soundly asleep that I had completely missed an earthquake that had brought down a large quantity of plaster from the ceiling of our bedroom onto our bed. In fact, as I got up, two large chunks of plaster, each the size of a tennis ball, rolled off of my chest, where they had apparently been resting for the hour or more since the earthquake. So much for my experience of a completely sleepless night!

Obviously, if people can't even accurately tell us how long it takes for them to fall asleep or how many hours they remain asleep or whether their sleep was interrupted or continuous, then simply asking them about their sleep behaviors is not going to yield much useful data. Clearly, we need some objective way to monitor a person's sleep. Before we do this, however, it would probably help if we had a definition of what we actually mean by the term *sleep*. To do this we may also need to understand what we mean by *consciousness*.

Sleep is generally viewed as the opposite of wakefulness. At first glance, the difference between these two states seems to have to do with how we interact with our environment. When we are awake we are actively processing information from our senses, monitoring the world, and engaging in complex interactions with the environment. To the average person, being awake is the same as being conscious. How-ever, for the psychologist, both sleep and wakefulness represent con-sciousness, just different states of consciousness. So, you ask, what is consciousness? While this is a tough question to answer, there is actu-ally some agreement about what consciousness is.

Consider this situation: suppose that your best friend has just walked up to you and asked you for some advice on whether he should marry the woman he has been dating. Your consciousness of this event would include a number of aspects. First, you are aware of the world around you, including the sight of your friend in front of you, the words in his question, his tone of voice, the expression on his face, and so forth. Second, you are aware of your internal sensations, including perhaps the fact that your heart is racing, you are starting to sweat, and you are twitching your fingers. Next, you are aware of yourself at a higher level: you know that you are a unique individual who is actually experiencing this situation. In this case it might simply be the feeling of "Why me? I don't want to answer this question." Then, at the highest level, you are aware of your own consciousness; that is to say, you know that you are thinking about these experiences. This may be in the form of specula-tion and predictions, such as "If I say what I think, I'm going to make a fool of myself this time." Some people describe this highest state as being like a conversation with themselves that goes on inside their head. Psychologists sometimes casually refer to this as "rooftop chat-ter." Note that the various aspects of consciousness just described are associated with different degrees of complexity; this is what psycholo-gists mean by different levels of consciousness.

Any of these levels of consciousness would be reasonable for a nor-mal, awake human being. However, it is possible to be awake and to still show reduced levels of consciousness. To understand this it will probably help to know what the current thinking is about the functions of consciousness. Most psychologists feel that consciousness serves two main purposes. The first we can call *monitoring*, which refers to keeping track of the state of our body and what is happening in the world around us. The second function is *controlling*, which includes planning, initiating, and guiding our actions. Controlling includes the simple activity of scratching a place on our body that itches as well as the more complex activity of preparing for a lifelong career.

The monitoring aspect of consciousness actually involves more than just being aware of events that are picked up by our sense organs. Monitoring also involves the process of screening out events that have little relevance to us at the moment. Some monitoring is *preconscious* rather than conscious. What this means is that some information is unconscious at a given moment but can easily be made conscious. For example, until I mention it, you are probably not aware of the weight of your body pressing down on your buttocks as you sit reading this book. This sensation was preconscious before I mentioned it; however, the moment that I alerted you to this source of stimulation, you immediately became consciously aware of it.

The gateway between conscious awareness and preconsciousness is attention. When you shift your attention from one source of stimulation to another, the events that come into the spotlight of your attention become conscious while those that you have turned away from begin to recede from your awareness. If we did not have this ability to limit the amount of material in our consciousness, we would be assailed by so much information that we could not function at all. For example, at this moment in time you could be aware of the pressure, feelings, temperature, position, and states of movement of each finger on each of your hands. This is a lot of information, but add to it the same kind of data about your hands, wrists, arms, shoulders, toes, feet, face, ears, tongue, and nose—and we haven't even started to talk about what you are seeing and hearing at the same time—and you can see how much data we must deal with all of the time. If we continually monitored all of this information in consciousness, we would have no mental reserves left to make plans for dinner, engage in activities to earn a living, create art, or do scientific research.

Just because you are not conscious of something does not necessarily mean it is not being noticed at some level. We can still process information without being aware of it. For example, I am sure that you have had this sort of experience: You are in some sort of crowd scene, such as a party, or standing in line waiting to get to a lunch counter. As you stand there you are talking to some friends, and for all intents and purposes the only things that you are consciously aware of are the voices of the people you are talking to. Yet suddenly the voices of the people in the line or group next to yours come into your awareness as you hear them mentioning your name. This means that even though their voices were not in your consciousness, you were monitoring them at some level. When events of relevance occur (and what could be more personally relevant than your name?), the gates of consciousness automatically open and you become aware of these events.

Conscious awareness of our surrounds is more tenacious than you might think. Even under surgical anesthesia, sensations are still processed at some level. Let me give you one such example: A patient we will call M was being operated on to remove a very painful cyst. A general anesthesia was used, and after the appropriate dosage of the gas she lapsed into unconsciousness. By all appearances this was a minor surgical procedure, and in the recovery room after the operation the surgeon was able to inform M that the operation was completely successful and that no further difficulties were anticipated. Although there were no further physical problems, over the next few nights it seemed that M was slipping into a deep state of depression. Her usual cheerfulness seemed completely gone, and she complained of nightmares, fitful sleep, and despondency. Her depressed mood was so obvious that the surgeon called on a postsurgical psychological support team to provide some treatment. This team was headed by a therapist who had dealt with this kind of situation before. His approach was to first make sure that nothing in M's life prior to the surgery was now causing the depression. Having done that, he hypnotized M and had her recall as much of the surgical experience as possible. Under hypnosis M's recollection was remarkable in that it continued well beyond the time when all her physical signs indicated that she was fully anesthetized. Here is part of what M related during the hypnotic trance:

I'm closing my eyes, and she [the anesthetist] *is saying, "I'm just adjusting your face mask. Okay, now start with the number fifty-seven and count backwards." Fifty-seven . . . fifty-six . . . fifty-five . . . fifty-four . . . It's get-*

ting warm. I'm feeling fuzzy, like being wrapped in a blanket made of rabbit's fur. It's getting dark.

I can hear people talking. It's like they're in the next room. It's kind of like listening to the radio in my old car. The sound keeps getting louder and softer and sometimes I can make out the words and sometimes I can't. A man keeps saying "Give me" and a woman keeps saying "Doctor" and there are other words.

The man just said my name. I can hear him a little better now: "I've got it open now. Look at how ugly that is. It's as big as a lemon and looks rotten as hell. This damn thing is probably malignant." I don't feel good. I feel really frightened, I think, or maybe I'm falling. I think I'm wetting myself, but it feels cold, not warm there; they don't seem to notice. The man is saying "Give me" a lot again. "Give me a bye." He just said, "Cancer"; now he's saying, "Where's my bye?" They're talking a lot but it's soft, like I'm hearing it through a pillow, and now a different woman is saying, "Clean, doctor . . . clean, doctor."

Even in the depths of her anesthesia M was able to process scraps of conversation during the operation. While she was not consciously aware of why she was depressed, she had clearly been frightened by the words "ugly," "cancer," and "malignant." The surgeon was later called in to talk to M. He remembered being startled by the size of the cyst during the operation and speculating that it might be cancerous. "I was concerned about it because of the size and color," he said, "so I ordered a rush on the biopsy. We kept her on the table until it came back, just in case it had been malignant and in case we had to do a more drastic operation, like removing the nodes in the vicinity. I'll bet that that was the 'bye' that she heard me asking for—you know, bi as short for biopsy. One of the surgical nurses came in with the lab report. I'm not fully sure, but I think that her words were something like 'It's clean, doctor,' meaning that there were no cancerous cells."

When M was shown the biopsy report and assured that the tissue was fibrous but completely benign, her mood began to improve. Within 24 hours she was sleeping better and showing her usual optimistic out-look.

The case of M shows that some patients who are sufficiently anes-thetized to allow surgical procedures to be performed can still process information from their environment. This case is not unique or even all that unusual, since there are many reports of instances in which patients have picked up fragments of conversations from the operating room while they were under anesthesia. Some researchers have suggested that if negative comments made during anesthesia can induce anxiety in patients, perhaps positive or encouraging messages can produce more optimism in the postoperative period. A few research reports have suggested that patients who are exposed to positive communications during their surgery require shorter postoperative hospitalization. Such patients recover more quickly, require lower dosages of pain-reducing medications, and complain less about postoperative discomfort.[1] For our purposes, however, the important fact to note is that even in a state of unconsciousness that we consider to be deeper than natural sleep, individuals still can have some awareness of their environment and can still process information about events going on in it. Given this fact, it should not be surprising to find that sleep itself is not a case of total insensitivity or temporary death but, rather, represents a condition of reduced ability to monitor events in one's world.

Actually, it should be obvious that some form of monitoring of the environment must go on during sleep. If we did not have some awareness of bodily sensations during sleep we would have long ago died out as a species. If our ancestors were so insensitive during sleep that they could not feel a saber-toothed tiger gnawing on their legs during the night, today's world would be ruled by buck-toothed felines rather than hairless apes. At the very least, we must be sensitive to changes in the environment that might signal danger. A watch dog would not do us much good if we could not hear its bark in the night, nor would the signal of a smoke alarm save our lives if we completely turned off our sense of hearing while we slept.

It is certainly clear that when we sleep we are screening out a lot of sensations. However, if the stimulation is strong enough, such as a loud sound or a strong slap, we do process the information and leave the sleep state. Stimulation does not have to be excessive to cause some reaction during sleep, though. Even very subtle changes can be detected by a sleeping person. We all know that light is only partially screened out by our closed eyelids and that it is easy to tell if a light has just been turned on even if our eyes remain closed. One reason that we may awaken automatically each morning at about the same time may be due to the fact that we are keeping track of the level of light in the room that filters through our closed eyelids while we sleep. As the sun rises and light floods our bedroom, we process its intensity until it reaches some level that triggers our morning awakening. You can test this for yourself some weekend. Leave your curtains or shades in their usual setting and don't set your alarm clock. If you go to sleep at your usual time, you will probably find that you awaken the next morning at a time that will be within 30 minutes (plus or minus) of the time your alarm is usually set for (although you'll probably go back to sleep when you remember that this is not a workday). For the next night draw your curtains and use some heavy material to block off all of the incoming light; cardboard or aluminum foil taped to the window works well for this purpose. (Don't worry; since it's only for one night, the neighbors probably won't even notice.) Now if you go to sleep at your usual time, you will probably find that the next day has you awakening 45 minutes to several hours later than you usually do. It is the absence of the increasing morning light that you unconsciously monitor that allows this oversleeping to occur.

At one time alarm clock manufacturers tried to cash in on the fact that we are responsive to light while we sleep. They developed the "silent alarm clock." The advertisements claimed that with this clock you could be "gently awakened without disturbing your partner or the people in the next room." The silent alarm was simply a clock with a luminescent frame that began to flash on and off at the designated time. The idea was that this sudden change in illumination level would gently awaken the sleeper. This silent alarm did work, but there were a few unanticipated problems, the most important being the requirement that the sleeping person face the alarm clock; otherwise, its signal did little good. Attempts were made to solve this problem by making the flashing light very bright, but when this was done it also tended to wake the bed partner (whose sleep it was designed to protect) as effectively as if the alarm had a loud sound. Nevertheless, I suppose the silent alarm clock did meet one of its advertising claims by sparing the sleep of the people in the next room.

Not only vision but also your senses of touch and hearing are active during sleep. You can again easily demonstrate this if you have a sleeping person to experiment with. The easiest experiment starts with the sleeper on his or her back. Now, very gently, slip a tennis ball under one of the sleeper's shoulders. In just a couple of minutes most sleepers will gently roll so as to remove the persistent localized pressure they sense from their body's weight on the ball. This means that, without awakening, they are processing and adjusting to changes in what their sense of touch tells them. In some cases, you can gently touch a sleeper's face with a feather or a light piece of string and he or she will swat at it or rub the face near the point it was touched without ever coming out of the sleep state.

Your sense of hearing is diminished but also still working while you sleep. This becomes painfully obvious each morning when your alarm or clock radio goes on. There is a much more subtle way to demonstrate that we are not only aware of sounds while we sleep but actually process their meaning. Again, we need our sleeper as a test subject. First make two or three chiming noises, for example, by tapping a spoon against an empty glass. These sounds should be neither loud nor soft but at about the same level of loudness that you might encounter in everyday speech. In most instances the sleeper will show little or no reaction to these test sounds. Now lean over near the sleeper's ear and quietly say his or her first name two or three times. Although the sound of your whisper may only be half as loud as the chiming sound you used before, many sleepers will now awaken or will at least show signs of activity. Our names are very special personal stimuli that we are always on the lookout for (remember the example of hearing your name uttered by someone in a group next to the one you are conversing with). Even in our sleep we will detect this special sound from all of the other noises in the world and will give it special processing and attention.

These examples and demonstrations show that sleeping is not synonymous with being unconscious, unaware, or temporarily in a death-like state. While we are asleep our bodies are still alert for changes in the world about us. Our vision, hearing, and sense of touch are still functioning, although at a lower level. We are still conscious; our brains are still working. It is just that our level of consciousness differs from that associated with being awake.

What Is Sleep? ◉

So what is sleep? Well, we've seen that it is not a complete loss of consciousness. For scientists, sleep is defined as a special set of circumstances and activities that go on within the brain. Exactly what these involve I learned on my first visit to a sleep laboratory. The laboratory belonged to William C. Dement, professor of psychiatry at Stanford University School of Medicine and one of the pioneers of the research that defined sleep. In 1967 his lab was a large metal Quonset hut that had been erected by the military behind a Veterans' Administration Hospital. My recollection is that it contained a main sleep lab up front, with lots of space for various recording machines, and I think that there were at least two tiny bedrooms beside it. Down toward the other end of the lab were an array of different-sized rooms, some of which were used to study sleep in animals, and at least two rooms that were piled nearly floor to ceiling with boxes containing miles of paper with squiggly lines on them. This was the data archive, which contained all the sleep records the lab had taken in the past few years.

I was a graduate student in Stanford's psychology department at the time. Most of my research had to do with human perceptual processes, but I was fascinated by the problem of sleep. There was a lot of talk about Dement's research, and it was causing a bit of a stir around the university at that time. Dement's theoretical orientation favored the psychodynamic theories of Sigmund Freud, who believed that dreams

23

are keys to the most secret parts of the mind. It was said by some members of the psychology department that Dement was out to "catch some dreams." This all sounded a bit strange to me. Freudian theories were not held in much regard by the neuropsychologically and behaviorally inclined faculty members of Stanford's psychology department. For this reason I didn't want to approach Dement directly lest he might quiz me about psychodynamics and I might be forced to admit my skepticism about Freud, which was based on the psychology department's indoctrination. Instead, I managed to convince the technician who was actually conducting most of the experimental sessions in the sleep lab that spring to let me be a subject and an observer over a period of a few weeks. The technician, whose name I think was Bob, complained a bit about spending those long hours in the sleep lab, and I often felt that his motivation for letting me informally join the operation may simply have been to have someone to chat with during the long night hours.

My first night in the sleep lab began when a man in his 60s arrived in the early evening. Richard was to be a part of a study that was looking at how age affected sleep. This was his first session in the lab, and I got the impression from Bob that there were to be several nights of recording. As we began to prepare Richard for the night's recording session, the technician remarked that bald men were a delight for sleep researchers since it was much easier to paste the recording electrodes on the head when there was no hair to get in the way.

The electrodes that researchers used at that time were little metal disks, indented to form a tiny cup, with wires attached to them. These metal contacts were used to detect the tiny changes in voltage that come from various regions of the brain. First, the skin was cleaned with a bit of solvent, which removed some of the fatty oils from its surface. Next, the little cup end of the electrode was filled with a cream to help maintain electrical contact and was then attached to the skin with a bit of adhesive tape. These electrodes were placed at various points on the person's skull, on the ear lobe, and next to the eyes; one was placed on the arm to measure changes in muscle tension. When you look at someone wearing this array of electrodes, each with three or four feet of wire hanging from it, the whole thing looks dreadfully uncomfortable. I even had a momentary vision of the scene from the old film *The*

Bride of Frankenstein where electrical charges are captured from lightning bolts and carried down wires and through electrodes to bring to life the brain of the horrific female creature played by Elsa Lanchester. The sleep lab electrodes, however, were designed not to carry electricity to the person but, rather, to simply record the electrical changes that demonstrate nervous system activity and bodily movements. Furthermore, while they look uncomfortable, they are actually quite unobtrusive and don't interfere with sleep in any way.

After the electrodes were put on, Richard was settled into one of the tiny bedrooms. The ends of the electrodes were then plugged into sockets that went through a panel on the wall and out to the observation room, where their activity was recorded by one of the big machines.

When you look at something like an operating electroencephalograph, or EEG, it looks quite impressive: there are banks of dials and knobs and a broad table with a set of eight or more pens that are producing jagged lines on a continuously moving strip of wide paper. The more modern versions used today often skip the paper, record directly on magnetic tape or computer disks, and show the traces on a computer monitor. The underlying principle behind this piece of equipment is, however, quite simple. In reality, the apparatus is nothing more than a big, sophisticated voltmeter, not much different in principle from the kinds of voltmeters you use to test the charge in a battery. The only difference is that the EEG is extremely sensitive; it is capable of recording changes in electrical current of the order of only a few microvolts. In addition, it makes a permanent record of how these voltages change over time.

Neuropsychologists use the tiny electrical changes picked up by the electrodes to measure the activity in the brain and the rest of the body during sleep. The advantage of this is that we can learn what is going on without actually waking the person. Small electrical changes can also signal activities in the muscles. For example, the electrodes pasted on the sides of the head enable us to record eye movements and eye position, even if the person's eyes are closed. This sounds like an odd thing to do in a sleep experiment; however, as I was soon to learn, the motions of the eyes are an important aspect of sleep.

Bob and I left Richard resting in the sleeping chamber with the electrodes already passing information through the wall. We poured some coffee while we settled in to watch the continuous flow of paper. There seemed to be miles of it, with printed green grids. As the paper moved along a table-like surface, the pens of the EEG machine marked its surface with a series of red lines. Periodically, Bob bent over the moving paper surface and marked the page with some code or time indication.

Bob pointed to several of the lines, each of which showed tiny ragged irregularities, much like lines might look if traced by a slightly shaky or palsied hand. "This is the typical low-level random electrical activity in the brain that you get when you are measuring the EEG of a person who is awake," he explained. "At one point in time we thought that we would be able to read specific thoughts by interpreting changes in these waking EEGs. Someday in the future we may, but we haven't had much success thus far." Suddenly several of the pens moved simultaneously. They swung back and forth rapidly, about eight or nine times in a second, and the tracings showed a burst of large, regular movements. "Those are alpha waves," Bob told me. "They aren't a sign of sleep but seem to be an indication that the person is relaxed. If you ask people how they feel when alpha waves are present, they tend to tell you that they weren't sleeping but just sort of drifting and at ease."

Presently, Bob said, "Ah, there we go." Pointing to one line that showed a very slow drift, he continued his explanation. "This indicates that the eyes are sort of slowly rolling around behind the lids. I always look at this as one of the signs of transition of moving into sleep itself. Now watch the brain traces. Although we tend to break sleep up into stages based on some details of the EEG pattern, the process of falling asleep really shows up mostly as a slowing of the brain waves. Notice that the traces don't look the same as they did when we put Richard in there. Now, although the voltage changes still are random, there are some larger and slower wave patterns."

We sat a while watching the pens trace their lines on the paper. The waves became more and more pronounced and slow, with swings of the pen now taking half a second or more. The time that had elapsed since Richard had gotten into bed was almost exactly one hour. "This is the deepest stage of sleep," Bob said. "We call it 'slow wave sleep' because the voltage changes are really slow as well as being large in size. Each of those pen swings represents the synchronized activity of thousands or hundreds of thousands of brain cells, all increasing and decreasing their activity levels at the same time. You know, when [Nathaniel] Kleitman and his team [at the University of Chicago] first started studying sleep, they looked at this wave pattern and assumed that this must be all that there was to sleep. They simply thought that once the brain activity had slowed to this level, it would continue like this throughout the night. Since it was boring just sitting there watching nothing much happen and since the EEG paper is very expensive, it didn't seem to make sense to continue on through the night. So they simply shut off the machines and went home or went to sleep themselves until it was time to wake their subjects. Because of this they missed some of the most important features of sleep. You'll see."

The EEG machine hummed quietly as hundreds of feet of paper seemed to flow by. It was hypnotic, and I began to find myself drifting a bit lazily toward sleep myself. Bob nudged me. "Okay, we're on our way up now," he said. I was a bit confused. Nothing seemed to have changed except that, maybe, the slow waves were not as pronounced as they had been before. Over the next 20 minutes the wave pattern became more irregular and more like the waking electrical pattern. When the EEG looked virtually like that of the waking state, I was about to suggest that Richard must no longer be asleep. Then something strange happened. Suddenly, the line that represented the eye position went crazy. Richard's eyes were moving in sharp jerks—big movements, small movements, some in one direction, some in the other, as though Richard was watching some sort of chaotic activity behind his closed eyes. "It's rapid eye movement sleep," Bob explained. "We just use the first letter of each word, which lets us call it REM for short. Let's go in and wake him up."

Bob made a quick mark on the paper flowing by and then started moving toward the sleeping chamber. When we were standing beside the sleeping man, Bob whispered in my ear, "Look at his eyes." When I looked down I was startled to see Richard's eyes moving back and forth behind his closed eyelids. You obviously can't see the eye itself under these conditions. What you see is the bulge made by the clear portion of the eye (the cornea). As the eye moves, you can see this bulge moving behind the eyelids.

Bob shook our sleeper fairly vigorously and called, "Richard, wake up. Come on, wake up, Richard." At first there was no response at all, but Bob continued to shake the sleeper and call his name. Then Richard's eyes snapped open, and after a few seconds he exhaled with a snort and rose to a semisitting position, looking quite awake. "Were you dreaming just now?" Bob asked.

Richard nodded. "Yeah, I think so."

"What were you dreaming about?"

"A party, sort of a reception. We were giving it for my old boss. He was retiring. There were decorations and crepe paper all over the room. Flora was going to make some salad and order a cake. I was supposed to bring the spaghetti. So I went down to some kind of bakery or something and asked him for my order of spaghetti. He said, 'It's ready, but what are you going to carry it in?' I hadn't brought a pot or a bowl or anything. So I gave him my raincoat and told him to wrap it up in that. I was worried that it would fall out when I carried it, so I rolled the raincoat carefully and held it like a baby. It was warm and squishy, and I think that I was dripping some of it on the floor. When I got to the party, it was dripping real bad and it was making the floor slippery. There were a lot of steps to go down and I was afraid that I would slip on the spaghetti sauce, which was dripping out of my coat and down the steps, but I couldn't grab the railing since then I would drop the coat. Some of the spaghetti was already coming out of one sleeve, and I was worried that I would lose it all before I got to the buffet table. That's when you woke me."

"Okay, Richard, you can go back to sleep," Bob said as he motioned me out of the sleeping chamber and quietly closed the door.

Once back in the observation room, Bob made a couple of notes about the dream that Richard reported and put a few more codes on the EEG paper. He turned to me and said, "It's almost always during the REM period that we find people dreaming. About eight or nine times out of ten, when we waken someone during this rapid eye movement sleep we find that they have a dream that they recall. Dr. Dement thinks that the eye movements come from the fact that we are watching our dreams as if they were projected on a screen in front of us. Because the brain waves look just like the brain waves that we see in people who are awake and active, some researchers call this stage 'active sleep.'

"You know, it's sort of funny about the discovery of dreams and REM sleep. It was all so accidental, according to Dr. Dement. Kleitman had a student named Eugene Aserinsky who was working on his Ph.D. in psychology. He had some trouble coming up with a project, so Kleitman more or less assigned him the task of looking at those slow-rolling eye movements that happen when sleep starts off. When these episodes of active eye movements first appeared on the EEG tracings, both Kleitman and Aserinsky thought that the machine was just on the blink. It was an old rickety thing, anyway. It was only after they actually looked at the eyes moving, like we did with Richard, that they became convinced that it was a real phenomenon. The funny thing is that it is so easy to see the eyes moving during the REM phase of sleep. It's amazing that all those parents looking at their kids sleeping and all of those people looking at their sleeping spouses never noticed it."

Bob was absolutely correct about how obvious these eye movements are—once you know what to look for. I have now not only seen them in my wife and children but also in my dogs and even in the ever-sleeping cat named "Willow" that Kari, my daughter by marriage, brought into the house. The REM phase of sleep occupies about a quarter of our sleep time, so it should be easy to catch. Why was it missed for so long? Part of the reason was probably that people weren't looking for it. This has happened many times in science. Scientists who pride themselves on their observational abilities are, much like the rest of us, often swayed or influenced by their expectations. Knowing what to look for helps a lot in finding it.

Richard continued to sleep. His dream episode had come at about 90 minutes after he had dozed off. Over the next hour he repeated the same pattern of the first hour of sleep. The brain waves slowed down again, becoming larger and more pronounced. He had now returned to the deepest stage of his slow-wave sleep pattern.

"Let's do it again," Bob said, and started off to the sleeping chamber. "Richard. Wake up, Richard." This time it took quite a bit of shaking and calling to rouse the sleeper. Richard sputtered and groggily raised his hands, though his eyes remained closed. "Come on now, Richard. Wake up."

Richard's eyes slowly opened, and he looked at us uncomprehendingly and muttered, "What . . . who?"

"Richard, were you dreaming just now?" When there was no response, Bob repeated the question.

The response was more slurred this time: "Uh . . . yeah . . . no . . . uh . . . sort of."

"Tell me about it."

"I think I was sitting on a bench or maybe a chair. I was thinking that it was almost time for the mailman to come."

"Was there anything else?"

"No."

"Where was the bench? Could you see anything around you?"

"Don't know. I was sitting. Maybe it was a bench . . . maybe it was a chair. I couldn't see anything. I was just thinking."

We quietly let Richard sink back to the bed and moved out of the room. "When they are deep in slow-wave sleep, they are really hard to wake up," Bob told me. "It takes a good deal of shaking to get them up out of the REM sleep, too, but once they're awake, they're in pretty good shape. The transition to the wakeful, thinking mode from REM is probably easier because their brain is already acting much as if it were awake. When people wake up from deep sleep, they often act groggy— out of it—like they were drunk. Some people even call this effect 'sleep drunkenness.' It can last for a few seconds or several minutes, it seems. During slow-wave sleep you virtually never get any dreams. The report that Richard just gave us is typical if you get anything at all. There are no visual images per se and not much detail. People often just report that they were thinking and sometimes they report sensing nothing at all."

Bob returned to making a notation, and I glanced at the ink lines on the moving paper. Over this night and several subsequent nights it became clear that sleep could be divided into two broad states: (1) the deep slow-wave phase, with its deep sleep and relative insensitivity, and (2) the rapid eye movement state, where the brain looks as if it is awake and the person experiences dreams. Between these are some transition stages.

Traditionally, sleep researchers have referred to the depth of sleep using four numbered stages (five if we call wakefulness Stage 0 of sleep). Stage 1 is the transition from wakefulness through drowsiness to real sleep. During Stage 1 sleep the person is clearly drifting in and out of awareness. This was demonstrated by giving research subjects the task of detecting some faint tones and indicating that they had heard them by simply lightly flexing or pressing their hands. Subjects in Stage 1 sleep responded to somewhat less than half the tones presented, which indicates that when we are in this transition stage of sleep, we are consciously aware of faint sounds in our environment only some of the time.[1]

Stage 2 is generally called the first true sleep state, and it is best characterized as light sleep since individuals are easily aroused from this sleep state. If we conduct the same experiment as before, where we ask people to respond to a faint tone, after about 5 minutes of Stage 2 sleep we are not very likely to get any response, indicating that the sleep is noticeably deeper now. However, EEG-indicated Stage 2 sleep is still light: if you awaken people from this stage, about 7 out of 10 will tell you that they really didn't think they were asleep, but were just dozing and thinking.

Stages 3 and 4 make up the deep slow-wave sleep. Stage 3 might be called moderately deep sleep and Stage 4 very deep sleep (which is the stage Richard was in when we had such difficulty arousing him). Not only are people hard to awaken at this time, but if you do prod them into consciousness, they may be disoriented for a few minutes. Some researchers have referred to this postawakening mental lag as "sleep inertia," although I have always had a fondness for the more picturesque (and more descriptive) label Bob used, namely, "sleep drunkenness." The important thing to note is that the stage of sleep refers to its depth. The higher the number of the sleep stage, the deeper the sleep.

Throughout the night human beings show a roughly 90-minute cycle of sleep. Each cycle starts with light sleep, goes to deeper sleep and then back to light sleep, and ends with a dream. When we awaken in the morning, we are usually breaking out of sleep during a dream episode. All told, human beings spend about 30 percent of their sleep time dreaming, and about 20 percent in deep sleep, with the remaining 50 percent of the time in light sleep.

From the EEG recordings, which show that our brain wave patterns become gradually slower and the voltage swings more pronounced as we go from wakefulness into slumber, you might think that people experience sleep as a gradual sliding away from awareness, something like riding an escalator down, with wakefulness at the top and sleep at the bottom. This is not the case. There is a simple experiment you can try

for yourself. When you go to bed, try to carefully experience the moments leading up to when you fall asleep and then try to actually capture the moment that you drift off. If sleep has a gradual onset, you
ought to experience a steady relaxation process, perhaps with your
muscles going limp, your breathing becoming slower and more regular,
and so forth. Your awareness of information from your sense of vision,
touch, hearing, and so forth, should gradually disappear. It should be
an experience something like the fade-out of a motion picture or TV
show, where the sound gradually diminishes and the screen slowly
fades to total darkness. However, for most people this is not what happens. Entering the state of sleep is more like being dropped into noth-
ingness rather than a slow slide into the land of Nod.

I have tried this experiment many times and am always amazed at
my inability to catch the moment when sleep begins. I might feel myself growing a bit more comfortable and languid in the first few minutes
after I get into bed; however, my experience of falling asleep is not similar to a gradual and steady withdrawal from consciousness. Instead,
my experience has been similar to that of most people: sleep is more
like the clicking of an on-off switch. One moment you are clearly
awake, and after what seems like only a fraction of a second you are
awakening from sleep. You might not even have any idea how long you
remained in the state of sleep, for when consciousness switches to its
sleep mode, your sense of the passage of time seems to suddenly switch
off as well.

I once decided that it might be possible to capture the gradual de-
scent into sleep if the stimulation hitting my senses was varied enough
and available for continuous observation. Usually we sleep in quiet surroundings with the lights off and our eyes closed. If everything is already quiet and dark, I reasoned, it may be difficult to see things fade
out as we grow drowsy. I decided that what I needed was a continuous
source of sound and sight that I could monitor. These requirements
were neatly met by a TV on a table at the foot of my bed. I expected
the monitoring of the sound to be easy, since ears do not have lids or
flaps that close when we relax. The problem was how to monitor my
response to visual images; if my eyes were closed, how could the signal
from the TV get to my consciousness? The solution was obvious, although a little uncomfortable. I had my eyelids carefully taped in a

half-open position. This meant that when I tried to close my eyes, I couldn't. I thought that this technique would allow me to continue to observe the TV even when I became drowsy and that it would give me the opportunity to see if my vision faded to black as I fell asleep. I tuned the TV to a program I had little interest in and instructed the research technician to waken me after I had completed one cycle of sleep. I settled down on the bed, carefully monitoring the sound level and the brightness and clarity of the picture. I was watching some silly program that had something to do with a book that had been lost by some poorly dressed person with a high-pitched voice. When next I was conscious of seeing and hearing again, the characters on the TV were sportscasters arguing about whether figure skating was really a sport and whether it could be judged objectively. Somewhere in between these programs I had fallen asleep. I experienced no fade-out and no gradual dimming of the sound but just a sort of a sudden switching off of awareness. Awakening was similarly abrupt: there was no gradual brightening of the scene, only an immediate awareness of the current sights and sounds in the room. Unfortunately, there was also an awareness of an itching discomfort in my eyes. In the absence of closed lids or frequent blinks to spread a film of tears over their surfaces, my eyes had become quite sensitive and irritated and were to remain that way for more than a week.

In passing, it is interesting to note that some animals (not just inquisitive scientists) sleep with their eyes open. Among the familiar animals who often do this are horses and cows. Not only do snakes not close their eyes when they sleep, but many species are incapable of ever doing so. It is also not unheard of for humans to keep their eyes partially open during sleep. I was reminded of this when a friend of mine complained, "I don't know if my relationship with Don is going to work out. He sleeps with his left eye open. It makes me feel like there is a spy in bed with me."

My brief stay in the sleep lab allowed me to describe some of the major aspects of the sleep process. Unfortunately, although we have managed to learn much about sleep, it is the scientist's curse to feel the need to explain every observation. The obvious question to start with is "Why do we sleep?" or "Is sleep really necessary?" Surprisingly, there are some people who say that sleep is completely optional.

Support for the notion that sleep is an elective behavior usually comes from anecdotes about very rare people. For example, there is the case of Señora Palomino, whose case came to public notice around 1974. At that time she was 51 years of age and living in Caceres, a mountain town located somewhat south of Madrid. This woman supposedly was a normal sleeper until she was about 20 years of age. She recalls when she stopped sleeping quite clearly: her sleep patterns changed at the same time she dislocated her jaw (ironically, her injury occurred when she opened her mouth while yawning). Her jaw eventually relocated itself, but for the subsequent 30 or so years she claims to have not slept at all. She reports that she leads a busy and active life, starting with a bout of housework at around 7 A.M. each day and then running a day nursery for 27 children of working mothers. She shows no signs of sleepiness and spends her night sitting awake in an armchair and doing quiet activities. Unfortunately, Señora Palomino, as in most similar cases, has never been available for actual scientific testing.

There was, however, one case where laboratory testing of a nonsleeper occurred. It involved an Englishman who claimed that he had not slept for a single night between 1970 and 1980 (the year he was tested in a sleep lab). The man was middle-aged and had been injured in an automobile accident, which resulted in a period of unconsciousness. After that he complained that he never slept again. He also had headaches and difficulty concentrating. However, a brain scan showed no perceptible pathology. When he was hospitalized a few years later, the nursing staff disagreed about whether he ever slept. Following several years of litigation, he eventually received a large financial settlement. He claimed that he could not work because he was continually exhausted owing to his lack of sleep. Because of this condition he was receiving continuous disability benefits, which allowed him to live comfortably despite being unemployed. In 1980 he agreed to be tested in a sleep laboratory, where he and his wife were given a room with twin beds. Although he did not sleep the first night, on subsequent nights it appeared that his wife was trying to keep him awake. His behavior began to show the typical deterioration associated with prolonged sleep deprivation, and he was caught several times sleeping for hours at a time. When his wife awakened him from a sound sleep (complete with snoring) on the fourth day, he seemed disoriented. He begged to be allowed to sleep and then claimed that he must have been cured by the staff at the sleep lab and that they must have given him some kind of drug injection. When the researchers insisted that he actually had been sleeping 2 to 4 hours a night, he and his wife became upset and angry and stormed out of the lab. The researchers, Drs. Ian Oswald and Christine Adam, summarized their observations of this case by saying, "He may have been always a short sleeper, who, surrounded by medical opinions, cashed in on it. Dramatic statements about lack of sleep remain unreliable."[2] Even in the face of this conclusion and his "miraculous cure" at the sleep lab, the man subsequently appeared both on TV and radio reiterating his claim that he had not slept a single night in 10 years and insisting that his sleeplessness was still present. His statements were, of course, corroborated by his wife.

Despite the absence of scientific support, some people still believe that it is possible to go without sleep. When I was going through basic training in the army, I had a drill sergeant who consistently berated the trainees about how much time they spent asleep. "Sleep is a rotten, time-wasting, and potentially deadly habit when you are a soldier," he would declare. "Part of your training will be to learn to live without sleep!"

If it is possible to live without sleep, why would such an odd habit evolve? Let us see if we can find some answers to this question.

Evolution's Mistake?

How did sleep evolve? This is an interesting question, one that might help us understand whether sleep is really necessary or not. As Dr. Allan Rechtschaffen, the perceptive sleep researcher from the University of Chicago, so elegantly put it, "If sleep does not serve an absolutely vital function, then it is the biggest mistake the evolutionary process has ever made." After all, the apparently useless time that we spend in bed reduces our active lifetimes by one-third. In other species the amount of functional life lost is even greater (for example, domestic cats spend twice as much time asleep as they do awake).

Whenever I deal with the evolutionary explanation of a behavior, I always feel that I am entering a realm that is closely related to the creation of myths. The evolutionary story we tell for any behavioral processes is really a very delicate blending of verifiable facts and speculative conjectures. It is the scientific community's attempt to make sense of the present state of affairs by creating an epic tale describing its view of the past. Like ancient Greek or Norse myths, our modern saga of the evolution of the various species and their characteristics, begins back in a misty antiquity. It is an exciting tale. It features a cast of fearsome, alien, and wondrous beasts, each of which is subjected to a series of strange and wondrous transformations. The exotic, often threatening landscape of this long-lost world, like the beastly denizens themselves, are also undergoing metamorphoses. Instead of the dreadful creatures of myth like demons, ice giants, or cyclopes, we substitute tyrannosaurs, triceratops, and pterosaurs. Instead of the classic struggle between the forces of good and evil or the struggle between greed and compassion, we substitute a cosmic principle that we call "survival of the fittest."

It is sometimes difficult for the nonspecialist to understand that, for the scientist, evolutionary accounts of behavior are not true or false in any simple sense. This is because evolutionary theories of behavior are not directly testable in the same way that we could test the theory that the gravitational pull causes objects to fall to earth at a specific speed or that the earth rotates around the sun. For the scientist, the value of an evolutionary theory of behavior is that it serves as a more or less sensible framework that allows us to organize the facts as we know them. If it works, the good evolutionary theory provides us with a coherent and organized picture of behaviors that we can observe today in our contemporary world.

For Darwin, the theory of evolution was needed to explain the differences and similarities among living species and also to provide a framework for interpreting fossils. Fossils were a real problem because they indicated that unusual creatures once roamed the earth but could no longer be found anywhere in the world. On the other hand, fossils and living animals provide incontrovertible physical evidence. From them we can determine that horses started as small, dog-sized animals with toes and gradually evolved into larger animals with hooves. We can verify the link between dinosaurs and contemporary birds by noting that some dinosaurs had bones with air pockets to make them lighter and hips that were hinged in a reverse fashion relative to other animals, both characteristics being true of contemporary birds. Questions involving structural and physical evolution can be tested against fossils and related to living animal species. That means that for physical evolution we have enough testable data to let us determine if our evolutionary theories are right or wrong. But what about theories dealing with the evolution of behaviors?

Sometimes we are lucky and can make some solid guesses about the evolutionary history of behaviors. For example, we can examine the beak of a living species of bird and relate its shape and mechanical properties to the kind of task the bird uses it for. This is usually related to the kind of food the bird eats and sometimes to certain specialized activities that it engages in. By examining the fossils of extinct birds and studying their beak structure, we can reasonably speculate about the kind of food the birds ate and perhaps about some of their behaviors as well. Unfortunately, there is no fossil record of sleep. To the best of our knowledge, there are no sleep organs that we can identify in fossils and observe across species. There are no special sleep structures, and no specific body shape or size seems related to the sleep process. There is simply no residue of sleep that has managed to survive the eons to tell us when this strange behavior first emerged.

There is another technique that evolutionary theorists use when the fossil record is insufficient. This involves reasoning on the basis of some common ancestor. The argument is this: if we find two species of animal that show a similar behavior, we can make the presumption that there was some common ancestor that both species evolved from and that this ancestor also showed that same behavior. Of course, there is another possibility, namely, that the behavior could have evolved separately in the two species. Scientists, however, have a love of simplicity and a desire to explain as many phenomena as possible with a single theory or mechanism. For this reason, scientists usually disregard the idea of separate evolution as being unnecessarily complex and will generally only return to it when all of the simpler explanations have failed.

Some scientists seem to think that sleep, as opposed to rest or inactivity, is a relatively recent evolutionary development. If that is the case, we ought to see sleep only in the more highly developed creatures and should find some simple creatures in which sleep is absent. The differences in the characteristics and behaviors of the creatures with and without sleep may tell us something about why we sleep.

There are a couple of problems with this method of investigation that are worth noting. There are somewhere around 5,000 species of mammals, 9,000 listed species of birds, 5,300 different types of amphibians, and over 50,000 catalogued species of fish. The sleep patterns of only a small fraction of these different species have been recorded. My search of the literature found that under 200 different species seem to have been tested so far. It may well be that this sample of tested species is too small to reach an adequate conclusion. Our drawing conclusions

about sleep might be equivalent to researchers claiming that no reptiles have legs simply because the only reptilian specimens they had
studied thus far included snakes and not lizards or tortoises.

The second caution has to do with the definition of sleep. We have
already seen that sleep in humans is defined scientifically on the basis
of particular brain wave patterns. If you want to start a fight among a
group of sleep researchers, all you have to do is announce that you
have found, or have failed to find, consistent sleep behaviors in any
particular species. Some researchers will insist that to have true sleep
the animal must have the same types of brain waves that humans do,
namely, slow-wave sleep and rapid eye movement sleep. Others have
argued that this is far too stringent a set of requirements. They argue
that this is equivalent to saying that before we conclude that an animal
can think, it must have the human capacity for language. For this reason, some researchers have used more relaxed definitions of sleep.
Some have insisted that there at least should be some difference in the
brain wave patterns between the animal's normal active states and its
supposed sleep states. Others have used more behavioral measures,
suggesting that if an animal becomes less active and relatively unresponsive to the stimuli around it—so that, for example, you might be
able to safely approach it or even touch it without getting some sort of
defensive response—this might well be considered sleep. We'll lean a
bit toward these more permissive definitions of sleep for the moment,
and, to be on the safe side, we'll simply note any sleep peculiarities of
particular species as we need to.

When we turn to our closest ancestors, the apes and monkeys, we
find that they sleep in a manner similar to human sleep. This is true in
terms of their brain waves as well as their gross behaviors, such as their
sleeping postures. The greatest differences between humans and other
primates has to do with the amount of sleep per day. All of our primate
relatives tend to sleep a bit longer than we do. Chimpanzees, baboons,
vervets, rhesus monkeys, and squirrel monkeys all sleep between 9 and
10 hours a night. The gorilla is a slugabed with a 12-hour average sleep
time, the longest sleep time of all the great apes. The record-holding
sleeper among all the primates is the primitive owl monkey, a New
World monkey with large eyes, a long tail, and a spherical head. In
South America it is often kept as a pet, being useful in controlling mice

and insects around the home. This little beast sleeps approximately 17 hours each day. The fact that human beings have the briefest sleep time of all the primates is an interesting observation that will be important later.

Let's move down the scale a notch and consider the other mammals. Consider some of the grazing animals, like antelope or sheep, that are always at risk from predators. Their only defense is to run at the sight of approaching danger. Nevertheless, they go through periods where they are motionless and relatively insensitive to their environment in order to sleep. Generally speaking, they sleep only a few hours a day, typically around 3 or 4 hours out of every 24. On the other hand, they may spend up to 8 hours a day in a sort of dozing state in which they are inactive but still quite aware of their environment and easy to arouse in time to get away from predators. To appreciate the risk that some animals take to get some sleep, look at the case of the giraffe. While some grazing animals, such as horses, can actually lock their legs so that they can sleep standing up, the giraffe has to lie down to sleep. The problem is that when the giraffe awakens, standing up is often quite an effort. Those lanky legs have to be uncurled, and then the animal does a slow, effortful dance as it untangles its feet and carefully lifts itself to a standing position. Naturalists have filmed this process, and it is not unusual for the giraffe to take up to a minute to get up. During this time the animal is completely unprotected. To place the giraffe in such a position of vulnerability each day, sleep must be very important indeed.

Some animals have to use very complex physical mechanisms and behaviors to get some sleep. As an example, let's look at the northern fur seal. This animal swims away from the shore on fishing expeditions and may stay at sea for several days at a time. Sleep becomes a problem since the seal is an air-breathing mammal. If it simply stopped swimming in order to take a nap, it would sink into the water and drown. In order to prevent this an extraordinary and complex system has evolved. When it is time to go to sleep, the fur seal stops swimming and hangs quietly in one place; to accomplish this it has only to slowly flap one flipper just enough to keep its nose above the surface of the water. Seals are neurologically similar to humans in that their brain is divided into two parts, or hemispheres. In humans the right hand is controlled by the left hemisphere of the brain while the left hand is controlled by the right hemisphere. In the fur seal the flippers are controlled in a similar fashion, so that if the fur seal is using its right flipper to keep itself afloat, the left hemisphere of its brain must be active. Electrical recordings of a sleeping seal's brain have shown that when the left hemisphere of the brain is awake enough to keep the animal afloat, the unused right side of its brain has actually gone to sleep. In other words, one half of the fur seal's brain is sleeping while the other is working. After 20 minutes or so the seal flips to its other side so that now the left flipper and right half of the brain are used to keep it buoyant enough to breathe and the unused left side of the brain has a chance to nap. A similar mechanism seems to have evolved in some species of dolphins.

Every species of mammal that has ever been tested has shown a sleep pattern. Some examples of the typical sleep times for some common animals are shown in Table 1. Notice that sleep times are quite variable, going from the 20 hours a day of the soporific bat to the insomnia of the grazing animals we mentioned earlier, with their scant 3 hours of sleep each day.

It was originally believed that some marine mammals, like killer whales and certain members of the dolphin family, do not sleep. The evidence for this belief was the observation that these animals never stop swimming. Consider the Indus dolphin, which gets its name because it lives off Pakistan in the Arabian sea near the muddy delta formed by the Indus River, which flows from the Himalayan mountains. Over its entire life this dolphin never stops swimming. If it did, it would risk serious injury from the extremely dangerous currents in the region and the vast quantities of debris that are carried down the river and into the sea, especially during the monsoon season. Sleep in the form that we have come to expect it (where an animal stops to rest in one position) is not found. However, despite the dangers associated with sleep in this environment, sleep has not actually disappeared. When electrical recordings of the brain of the Indus dolphin were taken, it was found that the animal actually sleeps around 7 hours a day. The trick is that the dolphin does not sleep in a continuous 7-hour block of time but instead takes very brief naps, with the longest around 60 seconds in duration and the shortest as brief as 4 seconds. (The

TABLE 1
Typical Daily Sleep Times for Various Common Species of Mammals
(Rounded Off to the Nearest Hour)

Species	Hours Sleep Per Day	Species	Hours Sleep Per Day
Donkey	3	Baboon	10
Horse	3	Hedgehog	10
Giraffe	3	Beaver	11
Roe deer	3	Fox	11
Elephant	4	Jaguar	11
Goat	4	Gorilla	12
Sheep	4	Chinchilla	13
Cow	4	Wolf	13
Dolphin	7	Raccoon	13
Humans	8	Rat	13
Rabbit	8	Mouse	13
Pig	8	Hamster	14
Guinea pig	8	Cat	15
Mole	9	Squirrel	15
Dog	9	Chipmunk	15
Chimpanzee	10	Gerbil rat	15
Rhesus monkey	10	Opossum	19
Squirrel monkey	10	Bat	20

Indus dolphin is a good example of the fact that evolution does not tolerate excess baggage in the design of animals. Over the years it has become blind, presumably because vision is not very useful in the muddy waters that it inhabits. Instead of vision it has developed an excellent sonar system, much like that of a bat, which it uses to navigate and also to find the fish and squid it preys upon.) The fact that sleep has remained, even if it has to be taken in tiny naps, suggests that it must still perform some important function for the animal.

The dolphin's larger relatives, the whales, and some of the porpoises also seem capable of sleeping while on the move. Like passenger planes circling an airport, the beautiful black-and-white killer whales and the bottle-nosed porpoises circle in a counterclockwise direction until awakened by some intense event in their environment or perhaps by a call from some inner control tower.

Before we leave the mammals, it is important to note that all mammals not only sleep but also show two major types of sleep, namely, a deep, slow-wave brain and a more active sleep similar to the rapid eye movement sleep of humans. Because rapid eye movement sleep is normally associated with dreaming in humans, its presence in mammals strongly suggests that they, too, dream.

People often ask me if there is some way to determine if their pet dog or cat is dreaming. We know that the best way to determine when an animal enters the active sleep or dreaming phase is to use laboratory measures of brain wave activity; however, behavioral signs are really quite clear in animals as well. If you are trying to determine if your pet is dreaming, you can watch for a sequence of events. When the dog or cat first goes to sleep, the slow-wave sleep always occurs first. The first sign of slow-wave sleep is slow, regular breathing. During this phase, there are only occasional body movements and the animal is generally fairly still and quiet. After a period of 10 to 20 minutes the first episode of dreaming or active sleep should start. Now you can probably catch glimpses of the eyes moving under the eyelids, thus indicating the REM phase of sleep. In addition, there will be a noticeable change in the breathing pattern. Respiration now becomes more rapid, and there may be shallow irregular breaths and occasional brief periods in which the animal looks like it's holding its breath. The ears and whiskers may visibly vibrate or twitch. If you watch the animal's face, you may also see spasms, jerks, and grimaces there. (In human babies the facial motions during REM sleep may include sucking movements as well.) Another obvious sign is that the animal's paws may also twitch. The paws of my sleeping cairn terrier often twitch in synchrony, giving me the impression that he is trying to run or jump.

In animals, frequency of these episodes of active or dreaming sleep seems to be related to body size: the smaller the animal, the more frequent the active sleep or dream episodes. Thus, we find that the tiny mouse may start an active dream state every 9 minutes while the average cat dreams every 15 minutes. In monkeys (as well as in children) the dream cycle returns every 50 minutes whereas in gorillas (and in adult humans) the first dream will occur after about 90 minutes. In elephants there may be a nearly 2-hour delay before the first dream state is entered.

If all mammals sleep, we must go lower down the evolutionary ladder if we are to find the origins of this behavior. How about birds? All of the birds studied to date seem to show sleep patterns that are similar to the sleep of mammals; that is, they show deep, slow-wave sleep and active REM sleep. Obviously, in birds that are unable to move their eyes, such as the owl, there must be some other indication of the active phase of sleep; in fact, the brain waves of birds in active sleep have been found to be exactly the same as those found in animals whose eyes do move. There is one clear difference, though, between the sleep of birds and that of mammals. The active (dreaming) sleep stage in the former is usually very brief; it is unusual to see a dream state in a bird that is longer than 30 seconds, and in most cases active sleep lasts only 5 to 6 seconds in length.

Some birds fly continuously for many days, typically while migrating during the spring and fall. Others, such as the albatross, fly far from land and must remain aloft for a week or more. These birds have evolved a sleep strategy similar to that of the Indus dolphin. Instead of stopping to sleep, they literally catch their sleep on the fly. Generally, this involves short naps of a half minute or so, with the bird gliding during the short sleep. Some researchers have speculated that there are varieties of birds that may be able to continue to flap their wings while catching a minute or so of sleep, as though they are sort of navigating on automatic pilot.

One important feature of the sleep of birds is that the amount of sleep they get seems to be directly related to the amount of light in a typical day. Generally speaking, as the days grow longer, birds tend to sleep less, although the minimum sleep duration for daylight-active birds is seldom less than around 7 hours.

An interesting feature of the sleep of birds like pigeons, which are preyed upon by other birds and animals, is something we can call the "sleep peep." This is simply a brief opening of the eyes without a full awakening. Researchers have found that the number of peeps seems to depend upon the number of predators (hawks or cats, for instance) that have been observed in the vicinity, a finding that suggests that the peeps are a defensive measure permitting the bird to maintain its vigilance against predators. Moreover, the number of sleep peeps decreases when there are other birds of the same species nearby; apparently, the sleeping bird feels that there is safety in numbers and doesn't check out the environment as frequently.

Since birds evolved from reptiles, studying the phenomenon of sleep in reptiles such as lizards, snakes, and crocodiles would be equivalent to looking at sleep mechanisms of an even earlier evolutionary origin. When we ask, "Do reptiles sleep, and if they do, what kind of sleep do they get?" we get our first glimpse of a different type of sleep. It is obvious that at the behavioral level reptiles do have inactive periods during which they close their eyes, adopt a particular characteristic body position, and perhaps even use a particular place for this behavior. During these periods it is more difficult to get them to respond to stimuli, and there are times when their muscles go quite slack and their heart rate and breathing become slow and regular. All of this is consistent with sleep. However, the problem is that EEG recordings of reptiles don't show the clear patterns we have come to expect, namely, slow-wave deep sleep regularly alternating with the dreaming-related active sleep patterns. Careful study of certain technical characteristics of the sleep patterns, though, lead to the conclusion that slow-wave deep sleep and the active sleep patterns associated with dreaming do exist. British sleep researcher Ray Meddis has offered an intriguing, but controversial, explanation of reptilian sleep. He suggests that the sleep pattern of mammals and birds (mostly slow-wave deep sleep interrupted by shorter episodes of the active sleep pattern associated with dreaming) is reversed in reptiles, with the reptile being mostly in active sleep mode with only occasional episodes of slow-wave sleep.[1]

Do fish sleep? It is certainly the case that most fish have active and quiet times that cycle regularly each day. Some fish are active during the night while others are more active during the day. One difficulty in determining whether fish sleep or not is the simple fact that, except for the elasmobranch group (which includes all of the fishes whose skeletons are mostly made of cartilage, such as the shark or the manta ray), most fish don't have eyelids. Fish often have a transparent membrane that can be pulled in front of the eye to protect it, but the opaque eyelids that we see in all land-dwelling vertebrates is absent. Although closed eyes can't be used as an indicator of whether a fish is asleep, many fish do have characteristic sleeping postures. They rest with their fins either flattened against their body or held out stiff and unmoving. At such times their gill movements slow down and become very rhythmic and regular. Some fish have habitual sleeping places, such as under overhanging ledges or among rocks or dense vegetation, and some will even burrow into the sand.

Certain tropical fishes, such as the wrasses that live around coral reefs and the colorful parrot fish, with its beaklike mouth, perform the fish equivalent of camping out in a tent. What these fish do is first find a crevice or niche in the reef; they then wedge themselves into it and soon secrete a clear mucus membrane that covers them completely and makes them look as though they have been wrapped in clear plastic. They become totally immobile and remain in what looks like a comatose state through the night. A scuba diving friend of mine reported that he observed one of these fish in its transparent tent during a night dive off the coast of Hawaii. He approached the animal and found that he could actually pick it up without disturbing it.

Just how far back must we look before we find the earliest sleeping ancestor? Well, it appears we must look quite a way back. Until about 25 years ago the invertebrates, such as worms, slugs and insects, were almost completely ignored as subjects for sleep research. The rationale for this was the recognition that their nervous systems are so different from that of vertebrates that to try to draw conclusions that apply to both groups would be difficult. Scientists could not rely upon EEG data to define sleep, given the vast differences in physiology, and some scientists were reluctant to even try to define any behaviors as being the same as what we call sleep in mammals. However, there are a few reports that are of interest to us.

Consider the sea slug *Aplysia*. This primitive animal is quite active during the daylight hours. As the light begins to dim, however, the sea slug tends to go to a very specific location and to assume a particular body posture. It then remains immobile through the night. This looks much like a sleep behavior. The slug is not completely immobile, however. At various times it spontaneously waves its tentacles for a few minutes. One scientist has even suggested that tentacle waving is the sea slug equivalent of the active REM sleep of mammals.[2]

Many flying insects have periods of activity and inactivity. Bees, for example, are active during the day, but during the night hours they become quiet and less sensitive to stimulation of any sort. For some moths, the differences between their active and their inactive periods are even more obvious. When the Mediterranean flour moth enters what appears to be its deepest sleep stage, it folds its antennae back and covers them with its wings. Once it is in this position, the moth doesn't react even if its wings are gently touched or even lightly lifted using a small paintbrush.

Can we go back further than the insects in our search for the earliest sleeping ancestor? I don't think that we really need to push this to extremes. I really don't want to get to the point of speculating as to whether the closing up at night of some flowers is the vegetable equivalent of sleep. The fact that sleep is as pervasive as it is, across so many different species and so many different levels of physical and neurological complexity, suggests that it is performing a useful and vital function. Certainly, the complex procedures adopted by certain species to get some sleep and the fact that evolution is willing to sacrifice anywhere from 20 to 70 percent of the animal's active life to this activity testify to its importance. These also seem to suggest that we may be risking grave harm to ourselves, from a biological perspective, if we ignore the evolutionary imperative to sleep and instead try to extend our active conscious hours.

No Sleep at All ⊗

We have already seen that evolution has gone to great lengths to preserve sleep. However, this does not confirm the fact that sleep is actually necessary. After all, there is a large investment in baseball and football, and it is possible, despite what some people believe, to survive without them. Is it possible to survive without sleep?

In 1959, Peter Tripp was a radio disc jockey on station WMGM in New York City. In order to raise money for charity, Tripp decided to conduct a fund-raising marathon. He would stay awake continuously for 200 hours (over 8 days) and would continue to do his 3-hour daily radio show as well.

When Tripp first announced that he intended to hold this sleepless fund-raising marathon, he was immediately contacted by a number of psychologists, psychiatrists, neurologists, and other medical specialists, all of whom advised him not to do this. There had been a number of animal experiments that had already shown that complete absence of sleep could be damaging. The first such study was conducted in France by a Dr. M. de Manacéine back in 1894. He showed that totally depriving dogs of sleep led to their death. Autopsies later revealed that there were many small hemorrhages in the brains of these animals. A number of studies showed that adult dogs tend to die after about 13 days with no sleep; the effect of sleeplessness on puppies was considerably quicker since 6 sleepless days usually led to death. Despite the specter

48

of possible death and brain damage, Tripp chose to believe a flock of unverified anecdotes from explorers and military personnel who claimed that they had remained awake for periods up to 10 days, under extreme conditions, and had shown no adverse effects. However, just to be on the safe side, Tripp agreed to have some of these psychologists and medical people monitor his attempt.

The entire "experiment" was conducted in a glass-walled army recruiting booth located in Times Square, in the heart of Manhattan. The idea was that this arrangement would allow the public to verify that Tripp was awake at all times. To confirm that he was awake, he had to perform certain simple activities, like recording the time, every 15 minutes. His only breaks, when he could get out of the booth and out of public sight, were occasional brief trips to a nearby hotel to use the toilet facilities and to change clothes.

Tripp made it through the 200 hours—but not without some signs of mental deterioration. The various specialists who continued to test him throughout the ordeal found that his thoughts became increasingly distorted and that there were marked periods of irrationality. By the end of 4 days without sleep Tripp could not successfully complete the simplest tests requiring any degree of focused attention. One of the psychologists was quoted as saying, "Here is a competent New York disc jockey trying vainly to find his way through the alphabet." In addition, Tripp began to have hallucinations and distorted visual perceptions. At one point he became quite upset when he thought that spots on a table were bugs. He thought that there were spiders crawling around the booth and once even complained that they had spun cobwebs on his shoes. He indicated that objects seemed to change size unpredictably and reported that the clock in front of him began to stare back at him and had a human face. Tripp's mood began to change as well. He became increasingly paranoid and suspicious. When he would miss one of his time checks because of his inability to keep his attention focused, he would often blame the people around him, claiming that they were "fooling around with the clock."

Surprisingly, even though Tripp was showing bizarre symptoms and reduced ability to think efficiently, each night when it came time to do his show, he seemed to hype himself up. Perhaps it was the increased motivation to present himself well that sustained him during these times. His deteriorating mental functions were never apparent to his listeners, and he did not utter profanities or make any strange remarks. In fact, during his broadcasts there were no obvious cues that might cause his listeners to suspect that he was suffering a nightmarish degree of mental strain.

For Tripp the worst events came at the end. He became increasingly subject to delusions and was convinced that the doctors who were attending to him were involved in some sort of conspiracy to have him locked up. On the last morning of his "wakathon" a Dr. Wolff, from Cornell, was supposed to examine him. Dr. Wolff typically dressed in dark, formal-looking suits that were quite a few years out of fashion and looked fairly gloomy. Tripp was initially cooperative. He undressed and lay down on the table for his medical examination. Then something must have snapped in him. Gazing up at this doctor in his dark, old-fashioned suit, Tripp came to the conclusion that this man was really an undertaker who was about to bury him alive. Once he had reached this ghastly conclusion, he was overtaken with fear. With a yell he bolted for the door and tore down the hall, half dressed, with several doctors and a psychologist in pursuit. He could no longer distinguish the difference between reality and nightmare. It was only with a good deal of persuasion that Tripp was convinced to make his last appearance in the glass booth.

At the end of 200 hours (actually 201, since the episode with the doctor and some subsequent tests took an extra hour to finish) Tripp was escorted home. He slept continuously for 13 hours. When he awakened, his thinking, memory, and perception were normal and his mood was back to the playful level that was characteristic of him.

Peter Tripp's 201 hours of sleeplessness are not the record, however. That is held by a then-17-year-old high school senior named Randy Gardner. Randy was the oldest of four children, and his father was a career military officer stationed in San Diego. Randy and two friends decided to submit an entry to the San Diego Science Fair, the subject being the effects of prolonged sleep deprivation. They decided that they would set a goal of 264 hours (11 days) so that if the project was successful, it could be submitted to the publisher of *The Guinness Book of World Records*. The idea was that Randy would be the test subject who would go without sleep, and his two friends would take alternating shifts to make sure that he stayed awake. Randy started his vigil in early January 1964. It was only after the local press began to publicize what he was doing that researchers learned about this project. Both of Randy's parents were concerned about the project and its effect on their son. Fortunately for his parents' peace of mind, there was a well-known sleep research unit run by the U.S. Navy nearby. A Navy doctor from there began to monitor Randy's condition, and he also called in a number of specialists and sleep researchers to assist him.

The world of science is as fraught with bits of folklore that are taken as truth as is the rest of the world. In the world of sleep research Randy Gardner has become one of those myths. From the time I first studied sleep in graduate school, the case of Randy Gardner has been presented as an illustration of how easily we can do without sleep. Summaries of the study usually blandly report that Randy suffered no hallucinations, paranoia, or other negative mood changes and that his motor coordination and sensory abilities were quite good throughout the entire episode. This conclusion is so widespread that it has now become a stock "fact" presented in virtually any psychology or psychiatry book that has a chapter on sleep. This conclusion seems to be based on only two items of information. The first was the observation that there were no obvious long–lasting physical problems encountered by Randy. The second was based upon a casual observation of a researcher who wandered around the city with Randy and one of his companions on Day 10 of the experiment. As the final hours of the marathon were ticking away, the researcher took Randy and his companion to a restaurant. After they had eaten, they noticed a pinball game in the restaurant and decided to play it; the researcher later noted that Randy played the game well and even beat him at it. While this observation indicates that under certain conditions, such as one where the individual is highly motivated, excited, and interested in an activity, it is possible to compensate for sleep loss for short durations, it does not mean that the loss of sleep had no deleterious effects on Randy. (Remember, Peter Tripp also had episodes of clarity and apparently normal functioning during his marathon, specifically, when he went on the air with his radio show.)

Systematic neurological and psychological examination over the course of the vigil showed that Randy actually was having quite a bad time overall, especially at the psychological level of functioning. Lieutenant Commander John J. Ross of the U.S. Navy Medical Neuropsychiatric Research Unit in San Diego systematically described the course of Randy's marathon and did a full neurological examination of him on the last day. Let's look at his findings:[1]

On Day 2 Randy was having intermittent difficulty focusing his eyes. The visual problems were bad enough that he gave up watching television for the rest of the investigation. At this time he was also showing some signs of *astereognosis*, or difficulty recognizing objects using only the sense of touch.

On Day 3 there was some evidence of moodiness, and there were some signs that Randy's physical coordination and strength were deteriorating, a condition known as *ataxia*. Randy also had great difficulty repeating simple tongue twisters.

Randy's moodiness increased, and he became quite irritable and uncooperative on Day 4. His mental abilities were also diminishing, and he showed memory lapses and difficulty concentrating. He was developing strange sensations, actually misperceptions, such as the feeling of a tight band around his head and the perception of fog around street lamps. At around 3 A.M. his first hallucination occurred: the experience that a street sign was a person. This was followed a short time later with a delusional episode in which he imagined he was a famous black football player. This delusion then melded with his negative mood, and he began to show resentment and anger about what he felt were racist statements about his ability as a football player. This appeared to be a form of delusional paranoia (paranoia is a condition in which people believe that others dislike them and are trying to do them harm in some way).

Randy's equilibrium appeared better on Day 5, but he was having low-level hallucinations. These were blandly described by one researcher as "hypnagogic reveries," which are the thoughts you have before falling asleep, probably because Randy recognized, at least after a short while, that the visions were illusionary in nature. One vision was of a path that extended from the room in front of him down through a quiet forest.

Several of the problems that had disappeared on the previous day came back on Day 6, particularly the difficulty recognizing things by touch, the mild muscular weakness, and incoordination. In addition, Randy's speech was starting to get slower and he was having difficulty naming common objects.

On Days 7 and 8 Randy was having intermittent episodes in which his speech was slurred. His speaking would continue to deteriorate until it had "a soft, slow, slurred, mush quality." Irritability and uncooperativeness, which were present earlier but which had diminished for a day or two, reappeared. Memory lapses and difficulty concentrating became more apparent.

On Day 9 Randy started to show episodes of fragmented thinking, and he frequently failed to finish sentences. His blurred vision was getting somewhat worse, and there were periods of time when his eyes would independently drift from side to side.

Evidence of a more personalized form of paranoia appeared on Day 10 and continued to the end of the study. The focus of this paranoia had to do with a certain radio show host who Randy felt was trying to make him appear foolish because he was having difficulty remembering some details about his vigil.

On Day 11, the last day, a full neurological examination was given to Randy. Physically he seemed fine: he could move his hands and legs with normal coordination and had adequate balance, although some muscle tremors were noticeable in his fingers. There was also a slight heart murmur, which disappeared two days after he resumed sleeping. His eyes were showing rotary drifts and an inability to focus well. His face was described as "expressionless." His speech was slurred and without intonation, and he had to be encouraged to talk to get him to respond at all. His attention span was very short, and his mental abilities were somewhat diminished. An example of this involved the "serial sevens" test (in which a person is instructed to start with the number 100 and count backward by subtracting 7 each time). Randy got to 65 (which is five subtractions) and then stopped; when Dr. Ross asked him why he had stopped, he informed him that he couldn't remember what he was supposed to be doing!

At the end of 264 sleepless hours Randy and his friends terminated the experiment, since they had met their goal and were assured that they had the world record for documented time without sleep. Randy then went home and slept for 14¾ hours, about 6¾ hours longer than usual. He awakened spontaneously and felt quite well and normal (although, perhaps, still a bit sleepy). All of his mental capacities seemed back to normal. He had no further difficulties with speech, his memory was fine, the paranoia and other negative mood symptoms were gone, his vision was normal, and there was no hint of any hallucinations or delusions. On his second night he slept around 4 hours longer than usual, and on his third night he slept around 2.5 hours longer than usual. After that, for all practical purposes, his sleep patterns returned to their usual length.

Both the cases of Peter Tripp and Randy Gardner are typical of a number of sleep deprivation findings. Many of these findings have come from "experiments" that were spontaneously organized by individuals or groups who had some goal other than the advancement of scientific knowledge. Sleep researchers tagged along on these experiments, taking measurements as opportunities presented themselves. Most of these experiments terminated well before the 201 hours of Peter Tripp or the 264 hours of Randy Gardner. In most instances, individuals stopped their sleepless vigil because they simply could not tolerate the mental deterioration they were experiencing.

An example comes from a Trivial Pursuit marathon that was organized by five medical students of the University of Leiden in the Netherlands. (Trivial Pursuit is a game in which individuals throw dice to move around a board and at the end of each turn are called upon to answer certain factual questions in order to progress further.) The goal these students set for themselves was that at least three of them would play for 76 hours without any sleep. They were allowed 10 minutes away from the game every 2 hours, as time for refreshments, walks, massages, cold showers, and so on. The players did not make their goal. The first player dropped out after 40 hours of no sleep; he complained that his brains felt "overheated." The second player dropped out at 56 hours, being unable to stay awake. When the third player, Liesbeth, dropped out at 65 hours, the game and the marathon ended, 11 hours shy of the goal. When she dropped out, Liesbeth was having difficulty walking and had slurred speech. Observers had noticed that her answers to questions were delayed and that questions sometimes had to be repeated to her several times. The great surprise was that most of the answers she was giving were still correct. Liesbeth offered some comments on her subjective experiences:

The distance between me and the surrounding world seemed enormous. Touching something meant pushing it down, and differentiating between colors (brown and green) became difficult. From 60 [hours without sleep], *4 hours of my memory are lacking. Jan and Jeroen were no longer present for me. I could not find my playing cup, and I obeyed commands like a marionette. . . . The soles of my shoes seemed to be of double thickness, I felt dizzy and exhausted, and panic and paranoia overcame me. The fear of losing self-control was my reason for stopping.*[2]

Peter Tripp, Randy Gardner, and the University of Leiden Trivial Pursuit players had similar symptoms. Because the sleep loss was longer for Peter Tripp and Randy Gardner, the effects of their experiment were more spectacular and included hallucinations and obvious deterioration in movement patterns, language production, and processing abilities. All of these individuals, however, were young and healthy, and all recovered quickly after their bout of sleep deprivation. What would have happened if they had gone for even longer periods without sleep? This has not been done with human beings under controlled laboratory conditions, since safety is an obvious concern. However, it has been done with animals.

What actually happens under extreme sleep deprivation was investigated by Dr. Allan Rechtschaffen. Rechtschaffen started his sleep laboratory at the University of Chicago three decades ago. Chicago already had a history of sleep research; you might remember from our earlier discussion that the first full-time sleep lab was also at the University of Chicago, under the supervision of Nathaniel Kleitman. Rechtschaffen decided to use rats as his experimental subjects. To deprive them of sleep he devised an ingenious (some might say diabolical) system. First of all, pairs of rats were selected and wired so that their EEG patterns could be continually monitored. Next, the rats were placed on a circular platform surrounded by a shallow depth of cold water. The platform was divided into halves by a vertical barrier, and one animal was placed in each half. One of the animals was designated as the sleep-deprived animal. Each time its EEG pattern showed that it was falling asleep, the circular platform would begin to slowly rotate under the barrier.

When the platform rotated both animals had to move to avoid being gently pushed by the movement into the surrounding water. Rats do not like being wet, especially cold and wet, and they would try very hard to avoid falling off the platform. Food and water were continuously available, the light was continuously on, and the temperature was at a neutral level for a rat. The only thing that was denied to the test rat was sleep.

Why did Rechtschaffen need two rats? Recall that the platform operated whenever the brain of the test rat showed any evidence of falling asleep. The other rat (called a control animal) did just as much moving as its sleep-deprived companion. It had one advantage though: when the platform was not in motion, it had a chance to sleep. Thus, it could make up a good deal of sleep time in little "ratnaps" as long as its partner did not doze off. Overall, this setup resulted in the sleep-deprived animal losing about 92 percent of its daily sleep while the control animal only lost about 25 percent of its sleep time.

What happened next was not pretty. The sleep-deprived member of each pair of rats began to look pretty scraggy. Their fur began to take on a yellowish tinge, and they began to lose weight; by the end of the experiment they had lost about 20 percent of their initial body weight. This weight loss was really quite remarkable since the animals were actually eating more than they had before the experiment began. In fact, they were eating 2½ times as much as their usual food intake. After 21 days of sleep deprivation, *all* the test rats were dead (the first actually died 13 days into the study). In comparison, the control rats, who could still steal adequate sleep in small snippets, were all still alive.

In order to find out what killed the sleep-deprived animals, very thorough postmortem examinations were conducted on all the animals. Rechtschaffen's team looked at all the important organs: the brain, kidneys, lungs, liver, spleen, thyroid, thymus, and the stomach and other sites in the gastrointestinal tract. They also looked for vitamin deficiencies and infections and did a number of complex and careful chemical analyses of tissue samples. What they found, however, was nothing. Despite careful examinations in a series of studies that extended over a decade, Rechtschaffen's lab was not able to find any obvious physiological or biochemical condition that killed the sleep-deprived animals. They just died!

There was just one possible hint as to what might have been happening. This was the observation that the body temperature of the sleep-deprived animals fell steadily during their final days. When considered together with the fact that the sleep-deprived animals were eating massive amounts of food yet losing weight, this finding suggests that the animals were suffering from an overactive metabolic rate. The tentative theory is that a short time after the sleep deprivation routine begins, the animals begin to lose body heat. They compensate for this by eating more food. This seems to work for a while, at least when combined with some additional burning of the stored body reserves (hence the weight loss). After about 2 weeks, the body of a sleep-deprived rat loses its ability to create enough heat to compensate for the heat loss and the body temperature falls. We know that death inevitably follows a few days after the rapid decrease in body temperature. In fact, a further study in the same lab showed that this temperature drop marks a sort of point of no return: once a marked loss of body heat regulation is noted, the animal will die even if it is allowed to sleep again. What we still don't know is whether the animals die as a direct consequence of the inability of the body to maintain its normal temperature or whether the crash in body temperature is due to some other factor, one that is too subtle for us to detect yet but is still calamitous enough to prove fatal.

Similar patterns have been noted in humans who have been sleep deprived. A number of studies have shown that sleep-deprived people tend to eat more and that although they gain weight initially, they tend to lose weight over prolonged periods of sleep deprivation. They also tend to show sustained decreases in body temperature of about 0.5°C (0.9°F) after about 2 or 3 days of sleep loss. In individuals who show severe effects of sleep deprivation, however, the temperature drop is considerably more marked. Thus, among the participants in the Trivial Pursuit marathon, Liesbeth, who dropped out with severe disorientation and distress, had a body temperature of only 34.5°C (94.1°F) after only 50 hours without sleep.

Even if sleep deprivation is stopped well before a person is in danger of dying, all the psychological and physical effects of sleep loss that we have examined are quite unpleasant. The psychological effects include a sensation of losing contact with the world, and people often feel as though they are losing their mind. That sensation is even more un-pleasant because of accompanying feelings of anxiety and dread, such as the fear that once one's mind is damaged by such sleep loss, it may never recover. These negative feelings, combined with a sense of loss of control, probably explain why depriving individuals of sleep is a common aspect of systematic torture in many countries. In a book that resulted from the deliberations of the American Psychological Association's Subcommittee on Psychological Concerns Related to Torture, Peter Suedfeld of the University of British Columbia noted that contin-ued disruption or deprivation of sleep has been called one of the most potent means of "softening up" prisoners. It is often used quite deliber-ately to obtain false confessions, and if it is continued long enough, the torture victims often come to believe that the false statements they make are actually true.[3] Amnesty International reports that 54 percent of the torture victims they interviewed reported being deprived of sleep for 24 hours or more and that sleep deprivation might have extended over a week or more for about half of these people.

A truly frightening picture of how sleep deprivation has been used as torture can be extracted from a series of communications that ap-peared in a torture victim's support and news group on the Internet. Let's focus on one person's account, which unfolded in several mes-sages over a period of about 2 weeks:

We were all very frightened. We expected to be beaten. They slapped us and hit us with sticks. They wrapped the sticks in wet cloths. They told us that this was so that they would not leave marks on our bodies. They took away our clothes and stood us in a room. Next they made us do plantón. . . .

For us plantón *was to stand in one place and not move and not sleep. We could not talk. If we talked they would come in and hit us. Then they would make us stand with our arms out, like a cross, with broken bricks in our hands, for weights. . . .*

The worst part about plantón *was the no sleep. I do not know how long we stood without sleep. All of the windows were covered, so I never saw day or night. There was a bright light on all the time. Sometimes they would turn on loud music that hurt our ears. I think that I got sleep while I was standing. Sometimes I must have lay down because I wakened up on the floor. If they catch you asleep, it was bad because they did* teléfono *[teléfono is a form of* physical torture where the victim is boxed on the ears with cupped hands, causing intense pain]. . . .

After we were awake for a long time, I was afraid that my mind was ruined. Once I saw white snakes come out of the floor. They were big and they bit me. I could feel their teeth in my skin. I could feel their poison burning in me. I knew I would die from this. Later I looked but there were no marks where they bit me. This made me know that they were from my mind. This scared me even more because it showed how my mind was not working right. . . .

With no sleep I think Carlos had a bad thing. He saw something. He was crying all the time and saying that they were eating him. Sometimes he would punch things in the air. Soon he started falling asleep anyway. They would hurt him to make him stay awake. It didn't work much. They had to be there all the time. Then Viejo [apparently, the nickname of one of the guards] *said Carlos was cold. When they get cold they always die, he said. Him and the doctor left Carlos on the floor. I could see that he was asleep. I thought he would be OK with sleep. After what looked like a long time sleeping, he stopped breathing. They took him away. . . .*

The hallucinations and the fear of losing one's mind that this person experienced are all part of the pattern that we have come to expect in cases of extreme sleep deprivation. But what about Carlos's death? Undoubtedly, the beatings and abuse contributed to it, but the guard's comments about Carlos being cold and about how cold sleep-deprived torture victims always die remind us of Rechtschaffen's sleep-deprived rats, whose ability to maintain their body temperature appeared to be lost a short time before they died.

The formal laboratory studies, the voluntary marathons, and the tragic accounts of torture victims all point to the same conclusions: sleep is needed to maintain our normal mental contact with the world, and when we are deprived of sleep for too long, we may actually die from as yet unknown physical consequences.

Cutting Down on Sleep ☙

We have seen that we can't completely do without sleep, but do we need *all* the sleep we are typically getting? Let me give you a personal case history that may help to answer this.

About 15 years ago there were a number of exciting reports coming from Britain and from U.S. Navy researchers that suggested that the amount of sleep we actually need is less than the 7 to 8 hours we usually get. James Horne, a very astute sleep researcher from Loughborough University in England, used data from these reports as the basis for his theory of "core" (that is, vital) versus "optional" sleep.[1] His notion was that only the first few hours of each night's sleep—specifically, the first three episodes of slow-wave deep sleep and rapid eye movement sleep, which amounts to about 4 to 5 hours of sleep—are really vital. The rest of each night's sleep is optional. Horne speculated that some of this "excess" sleep results from an evolutionary program designed to simply keep us out of trouble (such as blundering into the jaws of predators in the dark of night) and that the rest is probably due to the fact that sleep is pleasant to many people. He used the analogy that most people eat and drink more than they truly need from a nutritional standpoint and claimed that most people can cut down their food intake by around 20 percent with few negative effects, acknowledging that there will be some weight loss, until the body stabilizes at its new level of food consumption, and some hunger, at least over the short term. Horne suggested that the same is possible for sleep, with a reasonable "sleep diet" being perhaps 5 to 5½ hours each night. We might be a bit sleepy at first, he said, but should adapt well to this regime.

As evidence for this theory, Horne cited data from sleep deprivation experiments. When people are totally deprived of sleep, they do tend to sleep longer after the experiment is over. However, the amount of recovery sleep time is considerably less than the total amount of sleep actually lost. After Randy Gardner stayed awake for 264 hours, he did sleep longer than usual on the first few nights immediately following his vigil. However, if you total up his extra sleep time, he really made up only about 25 percent of the full amount of sleep he lost. Horne argued as follows: If Randy really needed the lost sleep, he would have made it up when he got the chance. If, on the other hand, extra sleep is optional, then nothing much was lost in the long term through Randy's vigil. From sleep recovery data Horne concluded that the vital "core sleep" may be as little as 3 hours per night. In any event, Horne was certain that we could slowly and systematically cut down on the amount of sleep we take each night and still continue to function quite well.

The idea of reducing sleep time fascinated me. Like many researchers, I am a workaholic, and I really hated the wasted time that 8 hours of sleep each night represented. I thought to myself, "What if I could cut back my sleep to 5 hours a night? The gain of 3 hours a night would add up to 21 hours a week (almost three full 8-hour working days gained) or 1,092 hours a year (that's 136 work days), and over the period of a decade I could add nearly 4 years of work time." The prospect seemed astounding. I became virtually euphoric about the possibilities, saying to myself, "Think of what I could accomplish in that added time—the additional books I could write, the increased research I could do, the added thoughts I could think, the extended life I could live!" On this wave of enthusiasm, I decided to immediately start cutting down my sleep time and garnering the benefits of not wasting any more time sleeping over and above the absolute core minimum.

At that point in time I was living by myself, which meant that I didn't have to adjust my schedule to meet the living patterns of others. I plotted out my strategy. I would reduce my nightly sleep time by 30 minutes for the first week, another 30 the next week, and so forth. My ultimate aim was to get down to 5 hours of sleep a night, in what I predicted would be about 6 weeks. I allowed myself some leeway: if the going got tough, I would spend 2 weeks or so at a particular sleep duration. Although the main purpose of this project was to improve my lifestyle and steal back time for additional creative work, I thought that some record ought to be kept, in the form of a diary or, at least, informal notes. I will refer to those notes as I now describe what happened during this project. I decided to start on a Sunday and reduce the sleep durations by a half hour on each successive Sunday. I started with a modest reduction of 30 minutes, which brought my sleeping time down from 8 to 7½ hours a night.

On Sunday morning, the end of the first week of 7½ hours of sleep a night, I summarized my experience:

The first week was a snap. I don't feel like I lost any sleep at all, and work seems to be going normally. Unfortunately, I think that I squandered the hours that I gained. I really didn't do much more than watch an extra half hour's worth of nightly news on the TV. On the other hand, a half hour a day really isn't enough to do much. I'm sure that when the block of time is a bit bigger, I'll be able to accomplish something more meaningful.

On Thursday of the week with 1 hour's sleep reduction, I wrote the following:

I think that hacking off an additional half hour of sleep is making more of a difference than I originally thought it would. There is a tired feeling when I get up which is vaguely present for a couple hours in the morning, sort of like my clothes weigh a few pounds more than they should. There's a bit of after-lunch sleepiness that is more noticeable than it used to be. Other than that, it doesn't seem to affect my work or anything else.

On the Sunday morning ending the second week:

I think that this week went reasonably well. I don't think that I had my usual energy level, but some weeks are just not as good as others, I suppose. I still haven't gotten the hang of how to use the extra time. The original plan was to extend the time in the evenings so that I went to bed successively later. All that I end up doing with this regimen is spending more time watching TV.

Maybe a better idea would have been to wake up earlier and to get to work a bit earlier. So for tomorrow I'll set the alarm a half hour ahead.

With my sleep time now down to 6½ hours, my Wednesday diary entry included the following observations:

I still feel that I am functioning well; however, some things are bother-some. First of all, I need the alarm clock to wake me up. I always used to get up with very little prompting, but now I lie there listening to the alarm and try to work up the motivation to get up. Waking up a half hour early doesn't seem to give me the half hour extra time at work that I thought it would. Somehow, I just poke along in the morning and only get to work 10 minutes earlier than I used to.

The diary entry for Friday, after 6½ hours of sleep:

Damn, I missed a meeting today and had to be reminded after everyone was already assembled. I never miss meetings because I have this calendar thing on the wall that I always check each morning. What's worse is that I had organized and called this meeting! Then when I got there, everyone in the PCE group was waiting, and I had to blunder around and try to remember why I had called the thing in the first place. I've had the sense that I'm for-getting things—no, overlooking things is closer to the truth. Details just seem to go astray. Maybe I'm pushing this sleep reduction thing a bit too hard.

Sunday, ending Week 3 (with 6½ hours of nightly sleep):

This was not a great week. I'm not getting the full half hour benefit of get-ting up earlier. Usually I get there [the office] a couple of minutes before the usual time, but not better than about 10 minutes early. I'm really getting tired in the afternoon. Maybe it's the work load. Memos that I usually quickly clear from my desk just seem to pile up. I just don't seem to have the motiva-tion to move them. At night it's just TV till sleep time. I think that I may be reducing the sleep length too quickly. I'll stay at 6½ for another week.

Sunday, ending Week 4, the second week with 6 ½ hours sleep:

I'm still not getting into the office much earlier and just don't feel as if I'm benefiting from the extra time. Some people have said that I look a bit washed out and not as energetic as I usually do. I have had this sense that the work is getting out of hand, and, worse, I have a feeling that I just don't care. I'm going to go to the next level, however. Once I cut the sleep time to 6 hours, I'll have 2 extra hours a day. I intend to really use that time. I'll set the alarm forward another half hour. This will definitely get me into the office earlier and it will allow me to clean up the logjam on my desk.

Wednesday, Week 5, after sleeping only 6 hours a night:

I just can't figure it out. I used to get up at 7 A.M. and make it to the office by 8:30. When I started to wake up at 6:30, I was just making it to the office by 8:20 or so. Now I am getting up at 6 A.M. and reach the office by about 8:10. I just must be moving slower in the mornings. I know that getting out of bed is getting to be really hard. I almost cheated this morning by hitting that alarm delay button that lets you sleep an extra 10 minutes before it goes off again. I realized that that would defeat the purpose of this training plan. Instead, I made some heavy-duty coffee, which dissolved my taste buds and woke me up. The hour at the end of the night is a loss. It's always the same: sit on the sofa, stare at the TV. I've got to figure a way to turn that into productive time. It's just that come the evening, I don't seem to care.

Thursday, Week 5:

This was embarrassing. I fell asleep in the middle of a research talk. There I was, sitting right up near the front so that I could hear better, and there was VSR talking about research that I really care about. The lights are dimmed, he starts to show some interesting slides, and the next thing I know PS is poking me in the ribs. "Sorry, Stan," he says, "but I didn't think that you wanted to be left snoring in the second row, right in front of the speaker."

Sunday, ending Week 5, with 6 hours of sleep at night:

I'm not sure that this is working out. First of all, I seem to be micro sleeping at night. I was watching the Letterman show the other night, where he gives this list of the worst something or other and then counts backward. I heard him start out saying, "Number 10 is . . ."; then I heard "Number 9 is . . ." and then "Number 4 is . . ." That jolted me. It meant that I had missed 8, 7, 6, and 5, maybe 15 seconds or so. I just blanked out and probably slept for those seconds. In addition I'm not feeling psychologically terrific. I got a letter about a manuscript that wanted a lot of revisions before the journal would publish it. I got really dejected. CP said that I was moping around as though it had been rejected when it was clear that the editor meant that he *would take it if the changes were made, and I realized that she was probably right. Even realizing that didn't lift my spirits very much. I just don't seem to be getting anything done and don't seem to care much if I do or not. I think that I better stay at this 6-hour sleep length for another week to see if I adapt to it any better.*

Thursday, Week 6, with sleep length remaining at 6 hours:

LMW wanted to know if I was feeling all right. He told me that I looked "gray" and seemed to be lacking in any enthusiasm. "You don't even stop to tell stories anymore," he said. You know, he's right. I always tell jokes and funny stories, but I can't remember doing it in the past few weeks. Nothing much seems very funny, so there is nothing much to tell to other people. It's not that I'm sick, physically, though. I've been charting my running times every day that I jog, and I'm making my times and distance OK. This means that there hasn't been any deterioration in my physical performance. My running time always goes bad when I get sick, so I'm physically OK.

Friday, Week 6:

LMW wanted to know what I thought of the manuscript. I didn't know what he was talking about. He reminded me that we had a conversation yesterday and that he was worried about my health. He had given me a section of the manuscript that we were coauthoring at that time. I was sure that he was wrong. When I went to my office, though, the computer disk with the manuscript, plus a folder with the rough drawings of the figures, was lying next to the phone. I don't remember him giving them to me. When I finally looked at the manuscript text, I felt that it didn't make much sense. It was more that the content felt trivial, and it was as if I was asking myself, "Why would anyone want to read this kind of junk?" This is not right. I do like this area. When I sat back down at my desk to think about this state of affairs, I think that I must have dozed off because when the phone began to ring, I became startled and couldn't remember what I had been doing a moment before.

Sunday, end of Week 6, with 6 hours of sleep a night:

This is just plain annoying. I know that I can do this. It's just a matter of bulling my way through it. I am simply not adapting to schedules quickly enough. Maybe if I were younger, it would go better. I know that the sleep that

I am getting is good. There is no lying awake when I get into bed. My head touches the pillow and I am gone. There is something almost bovine about it. Without the alarm, though, there isn't a chance that I could wake up in the morning. Although sometimes things feel the way they used to, I have these waves of sleepiness. The first comes in the middle of the morning, the second an hour or so after lunch. At night though, it's sometimes hard even to watch the TV. I find myself glancing at my watch, counting off the minutes to bed. I spoke with JD briefly. She is away for the summer, somewhere in Alberta, and I haven't seen her since I started this project. She sounded really concerned. She said I sounded really "blue," and she must have asked me three or four times if I was sure everything was OK. I told her I felt a little down but it was nothing that a little sleep couldn't cure. After I hung up the phone, I recognized that I had just cracked the closest thing to a joke that I could remember in weeks, but since JD didn't know about the project, there was no way that she could see the humor in it. Tonight I move the alarm back another half hour so that I sleep 5½ hours. I think that I'll hold at this sleep length for as long as necessary, until I can work out how to distribute my time with this schedule. I just don't seem to be using all this extra time very well.

Monday, Week 7, with current sleep length at 5½ hours:

Really hard to get up this morning. I felt like I had a hangover. Got to campus and went to my office. Dumb! I went to my old office in the Angus Building, not my new office in the Kenny Building. I stood there in the hallway looking stupid for 3 or 4 minutes before I realized what was wrong. Good thing it was before 8 A.M. and nobody was around to look at the lost dummy.

Tuesday, Week 7, still at 5½ hours sleep:

Tried to work on the chapter LMW gave me. His interpretation of the data was all wrong, but I didn't know where to start to change it. One of the best things I do is write. Why can't I get my writing straight? WW came in to ask me something about the lab. I was still at the computer looking at that mess of words. He asked me what was wrong. I asked what made him think something was wrong. He said my eyes were all teary. I felt my face and it was wet, like I had been crying. I lied to him and said it was allergies.

Wednesday, Week 7, 5½ hours sleep:

I'm ending it tonight. It's not working. It's dangerous. It's making me stupid. Today I showed sequencing and memory problems. For all purposes, I became dyslexic at moments. I took a phone number from my answering machine and wrote it down. It ended 6427. When I called, it was a wrong number. I checked the message again against what I wrote—6427. Called again. Wrong number again. Checked again; I wrote 6427, only the person said 4627. I'd missed the transposed numbers twice. Later on took a message to call a number ending 6881. Called but wrong number again. Checked the phone message again. I had written 6881, the person had said 9881. I inverted the number when I wrote it. Just like a dyslexic. What if I have been inverting numbers or mixing up their sequence in my manuscripts? I could be getting all of these numbers wrong. This scares me. I have to check the stuff I've been writing very closely now. What if it doesn't get better?

Driving home tonight. Stopped at corner of 16th and Arbutus for red light. Next thing I know the guy behind me is blasting his horn and the light is green. I must have dozed off. Slapped my face, pinched my temples, paid careful attention to the traffic. Stopped for a red light 16th and Oak. Next thing I hear a bang on the back of the car. Guy on a motorcycle yelling, "Move it, man!" The light was green but was turning to yellow. I must have slept through a whole cycle. Really scared then. I knew that I had to stop this damn thing. It's too dangerous. Hell with dinner. Going to sleep now. No alarm. End journal entry 7:55 P.M.

I undressed; turned off the alarm clock, which had become my hateful taskmaster for 7 weeks; and went to bed. My guess is that I fell asleep instantly, which means that I probably began my recovery period at about 8 P.M. When I awakened the next morning, it was 8:05. I had slept almost exactly 12 hours, or about 4 hours longer than before my sleep diet began and 6½ hours longer than the night before. I got up very slowly, feeling a little light-headed but good. The sun was shining. It looked particularly beautiful. It reminded me of a line in some song from my college years that went, "The sun shone in like butterscotch and stuck to all my senses." Now, with a full quota of sleep, I recognized that I had been ploughing my way through massive feelings of depression, anxiety, and helplessness but that I was now okay. I knew that I wanted a cup of the strongest coffee in the history of humanity and then I wanted to go to work and clear up that mess that I'd left in my office.

I got to my office feeling enthusiastic and energetic for the first time in weeks. One of my colleagues stopped me in the hallway and noted, "You're looking a lot better. You seemed a bit off your stride recently." I smiled and I think I told some sort of joke in response. It felt good to want to say something funny again.

When I walked into the office, I was immediately struck by the mess that things were in. My office has never been noted for its neatness. However, generally speaking, the apparent chaos is under a reasonable degree of control. This was not the case any longer. There was a 3-inch-high pile of unanswered memos; a half dozen unreviewed manuscripts, which appeared to have simply been dropped randomly around the room; and manila folders with data sheets poking out of them piled on chairs. There didn't appear to be a square foot of table or desk space that was not covered by some file, bit of correspondence, or other piece of paper. Remarkably, it took me only about 3 hours to clean up the backlog of memos and administrative correspondence.

I next entered my word processing program and retrieved the manuscript that I had been working on. It was in really bad shape. There were hundreds of trivial errors, many of them grammatical. Articles and other short words, like pronouns, were randomly missing in sentences. On the other hand, in the first few pages there were instances of repeated words (like "the the"). However, those errors were details. What was much worse was the structure of the text and the pattern of reasoning. It was just poor. It read like an undergraduate student essay rather than the work of a professional scientist. I was horrified and wondered to myself, "How much of this garbage have I sent out?"

My answer was to come back over the next several months. Of the three manuscripts I sent out during the course of my sleep reduction experiment, only one (the one completed during the first week, when I had only a 30-minute per day sleep reduction) was accepted for publication. The other two were rejected and had to be completely rewritten before they were acceptable for publication anywhere. Some comments by the reviewers about these rejected manuscripts were very telling. One wrote, "I am surprised at the shoddy quality of the writing. He is normally one of the clearest writers in this field." Another wrote, "The main arguments don't appear to be thought through. There are gaps in the discussion, almost as if whole sentences had been left out." Yet another wrote, "He seems to jump from point to point without connections. Sometimes he repeats whole analyses as if he forgot that he had discussed that point only a few pages earlier." What was most distressing is that these reviewers were absolutely correct. I had been writing, but in the absence of my usual sleep diet the words I had been putting down on paper were not worth much. I had lost my creative edge.

It is interesting to note that sometime later a member of my department and I were discussing what happened to me during my sleep reduction regimen. She laughed and said, "It happened to me, too. When I had my daughter, I was nursing her, which meant that my sleep was disrupted every few hours. I don't know how much I was actually sleeping each day, but it was a lot less than usual. Anyway, I was still doing my scientific writing, which at least I could do at home. After I finally got back to sleeping regularly, I looked at the material that I had written during that period. It was some of the worst writing that I have ever done. It was also some of the worst thinking. I really felt ashamed of myself." I understood her feelings exactly, since I had felt the same way about the work I did while I was on my sleep diet. I had reduced not only my sleep but apparently also my creativity and precision in the process. This was, of course, only my own experience; however, its effects were such that I was convinced that cutting back on sleep was not an effective way for anyone to improve either the quantity or quality of his or her work.

A Little Bit of Sleep

$\mathcal{M}$ost of us will never be in a situation where we, like Peter Tripp, will be asked to go completely without sleep for many days. On the other hand, many of us will go with less sleep than we need for periods of time. If we have to prepare for a major social event, such as a holiday gathering of the family or a wedding, we will steal time from sleep by staying up nights, just an hour or two longer, to finish our preparations. If we have a family crisis or our child gets sick, we find that we sleep less for a week or two. If we must finish some extra work or meet some deadline, we will do without a few hours of sleep a night for a few weeks at a time. Will such sleep losses make any difference in our lives, other than, perhaps, causing some feeling of fatigue during the day?

Depriving yourself of sleep is very much like depriving yourself of food. Most weight loss diets are based on the idea that you don't starve yourself but, rather, reduce the number of calories you eat to less than what you typically burn on any one day. If you take in 500 calories less than what you normally metabolize, you will slowly lose weight because the effects are cumulative. If you are 500 calories short every day, at the end of a week you end up being 3,500 calories short; if these are burned from your existing fat supply, you would reduce your body weight by a pound. When we deprive ourselves of

70

sleep, the total amount of sleep loss accumulates over days in the same way. If you lose one hour of sleep each night, at the end of a week you will end up with a sleep debt of 7 hours. This is almost the equivalent of losing a full night's sleep. You may then start to show some of the symptoms that people show when they lose a full night's sleep all at once.

It is important to remember that there are other ways to build a sleep debt besides not going to bed early enough for several nights or rising too early. It can also result from having your sleep disrupted or fragmented. If, for instance, your dog decides that the sound of the branches of the trees brushing against your house in a summer breeze is really the sound of an army of burglars trying to break in, his bursts of barking may awaken you. With each awakening some sleep is lost. Under such conditions it is harder to accumulate the refreshing slow-wave sleep, since it may take a half hour or more to sink back into that deepest level of slumber. You'll lose more sleep if you do things when you awaken, such as getting out of bed, shouting at the dog, or getting angry and complaining to your bed partner. It is not unusual for each awakening to cost you the equivalent of 10 minutes or more of useful sleep. This means that a half dozen attacks from imaginary burglars can cost you a full hour or more of actual sleep time.

It is not just Fido that is at fault. Any of the following can awake you and rob you of needed sleep: a restless child who needs reassurance or care, street noises, a restless or snoring bed partner, an environment that is too hot or too cold, lumps in a mattress, or night clothes that bind. Every night that you get less sleep than you really need will add to your sleep debt. The good news is that a single long night's sleep can pay back most of the debt in one installment, in much the same way that Peter Tripp recovered almost completely after a long night's sleep. Two or three uninterrupted nights of sleep can bring you to virtually 100 percent recovery.

It may surprise you to learn that even a modest sleep debt of 7 or 8 hours over a week has a noticeable effect. You may occasionally experience such symptoms as itching or burning eyes, blurred vision, feeling chilled, and, understandably, waves of fatigue or sleepiness. Many people say that they get really hungry and find it difficult to avoid high-fat and -carbohydrate foods when they have built up about one night's worth of sleep debt.

Generally speaking, individuals with a total sleep debt of 3 to 8 hours will show very few obvious changes in their physical and athletic ability. When the first studies on this issue were performed, neither the aerobic nor anaerobic exercise performance of athletes seemed to be affected by sleep loss. However, more recent research shows that some athletic activities are impaired. For instance, Thomas Reilly and Mark Piercy of the Centre for Sport and Exercise Sciences at John Moores University in Liverpool tested weight lifters whose nightly sleep had been reduced to 3 hours.[1] By the second night it was found that their maximum ability to bench-press, leg-press, and dead-lift weights had all deteriorated. As the sleep debt built up over several nights, the performance went down even more.

Some of the effects of sleep debt on physical performance are more subtle. For example, a team of French researchers tested cyclists who had been awakened during the night and deprived of only 3 hours of their normal sleep.[2] When they were tested the next day, their performance appeared generally unaffected if they were working at normal (not their maximum) levels of exertion. Even though things looked normal, the researchers found that the athlete's bodies were working much harder. Their heart rate was higher, and their ability to take in oxygen was reduced. In addition to these more common tests, the concentration of lactates in the blood (which are responsible for feelings of muscle fatigue) was also measured. When the cyclists were operating with a sleep debt, the lactate buildup was much faster. This means that the athletes fatigued faster. Some other studies have shown that with a sleep debt equivalent to losing one night's sleep the work time to reach total exhaustion is reduced by about 11 percent.

Sleep debts of around 8 hours will also cause a nosedive in your mood. Obviously, you will feel more fatigued, less vigorous, and more lethargic, but the data are quite clear in showing that with increased sleep debt people begin to become more depressed. It first shows up as a loss of their sense of humor. Jokes no longer seem as funny, and most of the sense of playfulness that they may have started with seems lost (this was true of my experience on my sleep diet). The ability to experience things as being pleasant and desirable is also rapidly diminished.

As the sleep debt gets larger, people no longer show any desire to socialize and they care less about the food they are eating. People with a significant sleep debt don't look forward to the entertainment they used to enjoy, such as films, theater, music, or sports. There is also a noticeable increase in irritability and snappishness with other people.

Some of the mood changes associated with sleep debt can have a direct impact on people's ability to do their job. As their sleep debt goes up, people begin to feel overwhelmed and they become indecisive. Some people begin to feel worthless and guilty about not being able to keep up, even though their productivity might not have really changed very much. There is also often a loss of motivation. When you are carrying a sleep debt, you just don't care much about the job you are doing. You feel that you can't be bothered with details, so you don't double-check your work, regardless of how important it might be. The obvious result of this is that errors creep in and go unnoticed. When they are finally found, these discoveries tend to add to your feeling that things are out of control.

Running a sleep debt also has direct effects on thinking ability and mental efficiency. In the past 10 years there have been around 50 studies that have looked at mental performance and sleep debt. They have produced a remarkably clear pattern of results. First of all, with sleep debt there is a general slowing of mental processes. Reaction time studies have been used to determine how quickly people can process basic information (for example, being presented with simple signals like a tone or a light flash) and respond. Losing only 4 hours of sleep in a single night can make a person's reactions 45 percent slower. Losing the equivalent of a full night of sleep can double the amount of time it takes for a person to react.

Sleep debt really demolishes your ability to keep your attention fixed on a task for a reasonable amount of time. Many experiments have used vigilance tasks to test this. Some of these tasks are much like that required of a radar operator, who must continually scan a screen for small changes in the patterns that represent the positions of aircraft. In a vigilance task the important bits of information come only intermittently, but you must be alert all of the time to detect them, which means that your attention must be on the screen at all times. This is where sleep debt takes a major toll. It is very difficult for sleepy participants in a vigilance study to keep their attention fixed. They often miss important information. It is as though their consciousness is flickering on and off. In the real world such lapses in attention can be disastrous. A momentary lapse in your attention while driving can result in a motorist's not seeing a pedestrian emerging from between parked cars. If the attention of a doctor wanders, he or she might miss a sudden change in the vital signs of a patient during an operation. A flicker in sustained attention can cause a number in a column to be missed and a series of calculations to be wrong, resulting in a wrong order being placed or in a mistaken conclusion being reached about the soundness of an investment. The number of times a person's attention momentarily switches off and the duration of those time-outs are directly related to the amount of sleep debt.

Memory processes are also impaired when there is sleep debt. While it may be possible to retrieve information from our long-term memories with only a modest degree of error, it is our short-term, or immediate, memory that is strongly affected. This makes it hard for us to keep details in our mind. If we are dealing with a task that has many parts that must be considered in relationship to each other, impaired short-term memory will make this difficult. This could have drastic effects on tasks such as political negotiations, where various parts of a complex agreement must be kept in mind and considered in relationship to each other.

In some instances there appear to be losses in logical reasoning ability as well. Routine problem solving involving familiar techniques and procedures may be undamaged by moderate amounts of sleep debt. It is when the problem is difficult and novel and creativity is needed to solve it that the impairments caused by sleep loss are most likely to be noticed. As sleep debt increases, we act more and more like a machine or an airplane on autopilot. We can respond to simple changes and relatively moderate demands on us, but we do so using a preprogrammed or mechanical set of responses. Anything out of the ordinary will cause us to start to make errors.

It may be surprising (and somewhat disturbing) to learn that some professionals find that the loss in thinking efficiency associated with sleep loss can be used to their advantage. We often hear about labor contract negotiations that go on deep into the night. I used to think that this simply indicated that the parties were near agreement and didn't want to stop the negotiations when things were going well. However, over a number of years I began to notice that these marathon sessions, involving long sleepless meetings, only seem to occur if there is a professional mediator present. This aroused my curiosity, and I decided to get in touch with a well-known labor mediator in my area. He agreed to talk to me about it ("as a courtesy to a university professor") as long as I did not reveal his name. His story shows a deliberate use of sleep debt in an effort to lower the mental abilities and motivation of contract negotiators in order to reach an agreement:

You have to understand that most labor contracts involve a lot of different issues. To people looking at negotiations from the outside, the only thing that they might see is the question of wages. Believe me, there is a lot more on the table. In addition to salaries there are health benefits, vacation provisions, time off for holidays, maternity and paternity leaves, sick days, and all that. There are a flock of matters about the workplace, like designated lunch or coffee areas, issues about smoking, workplace noise and light—even exercise and shower areas. Then there is the relationship between union and management. You've got questions about the chain of command and job descriptions, and we're just talking generally. When you get to specific industries, there are always special issues. If I am working on a contract for teachers, you can bet there will be the matter of the number of students in the class, the number of teaching days in the school year, teacher input into the curriculum, requirements for extracurricular supervision (like coaching teams). . . . Well, you get the idea. This means that every contract is really a package. There are demands for a lot of things in a lot of areas, and some are important and some are trivial.

The first step is to get everybody's package proposal on the table. Then let everybody fool around with the other side's demands or offers. There are so many parts to each package that you don't make much progress at all in the beginning. Before we all sit down together, I might meet with each side alone a few times to get a feeling about what is really important to each team.

Next I wait until we are staring some important deadline in the face. It could be a deadline for the actual strike, lockout, or government intervention. With a deadline looming up, I have the leverage to pressure both sides to stay at the table for longer periods. I then try to whittle away at the time the negotiators spend sleeping. The trick is to do it in a way that sounds natural.

Suppose that we're negotiating a contract and it has reached twelve midnight. I can say to both sides, "Look, it's midnight. Let's knock off so that we can get some sleep and be fresh in the morning. Why don't we meet again right here at nine in the morning." It sounds like I've given them a generous nine hours to go home to sleep, but that's not really so. First of all, most of the teams will want to meet among themselves for an hour or so to work out their strategy for the next day. Then most have to travel to get home. What with time to undress and dress, shower, shave, and eat breakfast, I figure that if they have four or five hours in bed, that's a lot. Even if they get that much sack time, they'll find it hard to sleep. That's because I keep lots of coffee available during the night sessions. Most of them are so wired on caffeine that it's got to take them an hour to fall asleep. I avoid the travel problems that they have by taking a room in the same hotel that we are using for the talks, if possible. I don't drink any coffee at all. This means that I can just walk out of negotiations, take the elevator to my room, tumble into bed, and get eight hours of solid sleep.

I try to keep up this routine for a couple of days, if possible, before the big push. Now, that is the night that I say to them, "You know, we're awfully close, and I know that it's late; but I think if we go on just a little while longer, we'll be able to work it all out tonight." Then I push things straight into the morning. The extra hours of that session, added to the sleep that they've already lost, takes most of the rough edges off the negotiating teams.

There is a psychological point to all of this. You see, when they get really tired, they can't keep all of the pieces of their own negotiating package straight in their heads, let alone the package that the other side is offering. Things get blurry for them. They don't really remember whether we have reached agreement on particular items or not. Sometimes, small items that might have some symbolic or emotional value and that could be a sticking point can just be swept under the carpet without anybody noticing until later. They also get very sloppy and don't check things carefully, which means that details that might cause friction disappear since nobody is checking on them. In addition, something seems to happen to their motivation levels. Everybody gets a bit flat. There are some things that I know they might have fought for really hard when they were well rested, but when I've got them this tired, they seem less willing to exert themselves over anything except the really major issues. Sometimes during the big push I can even say things like "Okay, now that we've agreed on that point, let's move to the next one," when, in fact, there might still be objections or unresolved issues with the item on the table. In their foggy mental states most are not sure as to whether the issue is resolved or not and are often too tired to object. If they are tired enough, all that they really want is for things to be finished quickly so they can get out of that room and get some sleep. Very often they will end up agreeing to whatever compromise seems most likely to end the discussion.

If it works, then come morning we break up. If it's a big deal, then there may be a press release or press conference where both sides say that negotiations were difficult and complex but that they reached an agreement and are going to recommend the contract to their constituency. I take an hour or so and then send them all a written copy of the tentative agreement. Sometimes it's based on a framework that I've drawn up days before, when the negotiations were moving slowly. I make whatever changes and insertions that I need in that draft, so I finish it pretty fast. On the issues that weren't fully settled (the ones we glossed over or I pushed from the table) I try to write some compromise wording, or I just drop them. When the teams get some sleep and then go over the document in detail, they might find some item or another that they are really unhappy with. Usually, they don't even remember how the discussions went over that issue the night before. Then they have to decide whether to scuttle the whole deal over that one issue. There is also the matter of appearances. They are bound to look stupid and incompetent if they say in the morning that the deal is highly recommended and then that afternoon say that the deal, which they agreed to and helped work out, is inadequate. Most just presume that the issues were decided in the negotiations but that they don't remember the details of the discussion. Sometimes that's true; sometimes . . . Well, everybody ends up with a contract that they can at least live with, and there is always the hope that things will be better next time.

I sometimes think that it is impossible to work out any kind of complicated agreement between smart, motivated people. That's why international bodies like the United Nations don't work so well. But if you can steal enough sleep from both sides to make them dumber, less detail oriented, and less motivated, I think that a negotiated contract is always possible. No matter how far apart the parties are at the start of the process, if they get tired enough they'll find some compromise just so that they can end the discussion and go home to sleep.

The deliberate use of sleep loss to wear down negotiators is not a strategy that all mediators will acknowledge. A government mediator I spoke with simply told me that sleep loss on the part of the union and management teams might be "a secondary benefit of round-the-clock negotiations." He went on to say that "some pretty dumb things begin to sound logical when you've been negotiating all night and it's now 5 A.M."

Most typically, however, the poor decisions and the lack of attention to details simply happen without anyone planning it and without anyone consciously anticipating any gain from the poor thinking involved. More often, the lowered reasoning ability of people with a sleep debt leads to embarrassing, silly, or just plain dumb decisions. A city councillor from Toronto, the largest city in Canada, describes one such instance:

The city of Toronto grew up in an odd way. There was a central city and a set of municipalities and townships around it. I think that it was in the 1950s that the Ontario Municipal Board recommended a unique kind of federated municipal government that would put thirteen municipalities under the control of a Metropolitan City Council. The members of the council included the elected mayors, aldermen, and controllers of the various municipalities. In the late 1960s the number of municipalities was reduced to six. So, really, Toronto has not only a unified city council, which handles most city services, including sewage, transportation, schools, and such, but it also has six mayors.

Each year the city's budget has to be completed by a certain date and filed with the appropriate provincial authorities. This is one of the jobs done by the council. If we have had a rough political year or if funds are tight and there are competing priorities, negotiations concerning the city's annual budget can run pretty late into the night on the week before the budget figures have to be submitted. That happened one year when I was on council. We had had several back-to-back late sessions that week, maybe about eighteen hours each, and just about a day before the law said that we had to have the budget done we pushed our deliberations well into the early morning. We were dead tired but we were really under the gun to get things done and I think that it was around 3 A.M. that we actually voted on the salary allocations for city officials. Now we all knew that we were tired, and some people were having a hard time staying awake, but we thought that we were doing a good job and attending to all of the details before we took any actions. A few days later someone in the government was looking over the budget and noticed what we had actually done. We had set the annual pay for the six municipal mayors at exactly zero in the final vote! I still don't know how it happened, and nobody who was there at the time can figure it out, either.

Probably just another example of sleep-debt-ridden minds at work.

The Clocks Within Us   ☀

When you first look at the effects of sleep debt and sleep deprivation, you probably come to the conclusion that the only important consideration is the total amount of sleep that has been lost by the person. This is far from true. A person with 8 hours of sleep debt may function perfectly well at 10 A.M., feeling few effects of the lack of sleep at that time. However, by 2 P.M. that person may feel quite dopey, fatigued, and out of sorts. At 4 A.M., with no more than the 8 hours of sleep debt that would go unnoticed in the midmorning, that same person may feel a virtually irresistible urge to sleep and a major inability to concentrate on his or her work. The reason for this is that we have an internal clock that wakes us up and puts us to sleep. When the clock is indicating a period of wakefulness, the fast pace that it gives to bodily processes and the resulting boost in energy lessen the effects of any sleep debt. However, when our internal clock indicates that we are entering a low point, the slowing of our bodily processes and the reduction in energy may actually exacerbate the effects of our sleep debt.

Many of our behaviors are cyclical in nature. The cycle that seems most obvious to us is the repetitive 24-hour cycle. If you go to sleep at around 11 P.M., you repeat this behavior every 24 hours at around 11 P.M. The same goes for awakening: if you awakened at 7 A.M. today, it is likely that you awakened at roughly the same time yesterday and will awaken at that hour tomorrow—even without the assistance of an alarm clock. Some cycles are longer than a day. Women have the 28-day menstrual cycle, which involves changes in the body associated with fertility and also with psychological changes, particularly in emotionality and feelings of well-being. It may surprise you to learn that men also have a similar 28-day cycle of mood variation, but it is much less marked. The first evidence for the male monthly cycle came from a 17th-century doctor named Sactorius. By systematically weighing healthy men over long periods of time he was able to show a rhythmic variation of 1 to 2 pounds that followed the lunar month, much like a woman's menstrual cycle. Since then, it has been shown that a man's emotional state and energy level seem to follow the monthly cycle as well.

There are even longer cycles, including a yearly rhythm that influences such things as our interest in sex. The popularity of June weddings seems to be a reflection of this annual cycle, which peaks in May and June and makes us all feel a bit more romantic or sensuous or, perhaps more accurately, lustful. This probably also explains why there have been reports suggesting that sex crimes are more frequent in the spring. There are also cycles that are shorter than a day: some are only 4 hours long, others as short as 90 minutes, and still others about 12 hours in length. These cycles reflect changes in bodily processes and, often, psychological status.

Our daily sleep–wakefulness cycle reflects a number of changes that go on internally. For example, pulse, blood pressure, and body temperature show day-to-night variations in humans and most other animals. In humans there is a more than 2°F (1°C) difference in body temperature between the coolest point, which occurs during the night, and the warmest point, which occurs during the afternoon. All of these fluctuations are examples of a circadian rhythm (the word comes from the Latin *circa*, meaning "around," and *dies*, meaning "day"). Thus, a circadian rhythm is one that varies with a cycle length of around 24 hours.

The regularity of the cycles affecting our behavior and physiological functioning seems to suggest that there must be some kind of internal biological clock. Of course, this is not the only possibility. It may well be that cyclical changes over the 24-hour day are simply the result of external timers, that is, cues from our environment. The regular changes in light and temperature that occur daily as the earth rotates in relationship to the sun would work as such an external timer. An animal might become active in the presence of daylight when it can see more clearly and the temperature is a bit higher, and it may slow down when things cool off and there is too little light to safely navigate through the world.

Is there any real evidence that we have some sort of internal timer that is capable of monitoring 24-hour cycles and that may also control our sleep and waking patterns? The method of determining the existence of internal timers actually first came from plant biologists. The Greek Androsthenes, who accompanied Alexander the Great on his march through India around 330 B.C., was fascinated by the fact that the tamarind plant regularly closes its leaves at night and opens them during the day. Charles Darwin was also interested in this and referred to it as "plant sleep."

This kind of plant behavior really doesn't require an internal timer since, as we mentioned above, it could be the result of external factors, such as changes in light levels (that is, when the light brightens the plant opens it leaves, and when the light dims it folds them). The alternative is, of course, that there is some internal timer in the plant that monitors time. In 1729 a French researcher, Jacques d'Ortous de Marian, tested for this by using a relative of the tamarind, the common mimosa plant, which also has a daily cycle of opening and closing its leaves. He tried to see if light might be serving as an external timer by simply putting the plant in a closet for several days. What he found was that the plant continued to unfold its leaves in the morning and close them in the evening even though there was no change in the light level to tell the plant when morning and evening had come. This experiment clearly suggests that the clock that controls the plant's daily cycles is internal, and it seems to prove that there are biological timers that can keep track of the 24-hour cycle we call the day.

Not too long after these studies, Carolus Linnaeus turned his attention to the daily cycles of plants. Linnaeus was a Swedish naturalist who performed a magnificent service to science by developing the first rational systems for classifying and naming plant and animal species. However, his first love was flowers. When he was only 8 years of age he had already been nicknamed "the little botanist." He observed the regular opening and closing of flowers in many species of plants. He also noted that different plants tended to do this at different times. For example, in the region around Uppsala, where he lived, the rough hawk-bit flowers opened regularly at 4 A.M. and closed their flowers at around 8 A.M. White waterlilies opened at 7 A.M. and closed much later, at 5 P.M. whereas the ice plant's flowers were late risers, opening at 11 A.M. and closing again by 3 P.M. In 1751, in his book *Philosophia Botanica,* Linnaeus provided information about the opening and closing times of dozens of plants. He then went on to suggest that it might be possible to create a fairly accurate "flower clock." His notion was that plants that opened and closed their flowers regularly could be planted in a circular garden and that time could be told by which plants were open at any given time. Before you start petitioning Timex or Seiko to create a flower clock for your own personal use, I think I ought to alert you to a few problems with this concept. First of all, not all of these plants flower at the same season. Thus, you might end up with a clock where 3 P.M. could be read only in June and July and 6 P.M. in July and August. In addition, the opening and closing times depend upon latitude, since weather and day length seem to influence the exact characteristics of the flower cycle. Thus, a flower clock that would be accurate in Sweden might be hours off in Greece.

Since those pioneer experiments by de Marian and Linnaeus, researchers eventually discovered internal clocks in almost every living thing studied. Daily rhythms are found in all complex animals, in simple organisms such as worms and insects, and even in single-celled algae.

To discover more about the biological clock in human beings, such as how such a clock might affect sleep, scientists adopted a version of de Marian's experimental method. The idea was to isolate individuals from all outside time cues and let them sleep and wake at times dictated by their bodies. The first such study was provided by sleep researcher Nathaniel Kleitman in 1939. He and a colleague isolated themselves in an unused but continuously lit chamber in Mammoth Cave, in Kentucky. The reason they went to the trouble to run this experiment in a cave was to remove the influence of as many daily changes in the environment as possible: As the earth rotates and we face toward and away from the sun, there is a cyclic increase and decrease not only in light but also in electromagnetic forces and even cosmic rays. The moon affects the earth in a 24.8-hour cycle, producing variations in gravity that we see as changes in tides and also in wind patterns. Since Mammoth Cave is a quarter of a mile (0.4 km) underground, the participants hoped they would be somewhat shielded from the various electromagnetic and geomagnetic fluctuations that occur daily. More recently, Jürgen Aschoff and Rutger Wever created specially built shielded underground laboratories at the Max Planck Institute near Munich. Their aim was to accomplish the same effect of shielding individuals from many daily electromagnetic variations but without forcing researchers or their subjects to live in a cave for a month.

"Free-running" studies are designed to examine our internal time clocks. In these studies people are deprived of clocks, light changes, and anything else that might indicate the passage of time. Participants are allowed to sleep or engage in any activities they desire, but they never know what time it is. In the Max Planck studies, research subjects were also isolated from other people and were required to spend an entire month free of any external influence that might affect their daily cycling. Under such circumstances, whether they are in a cave or in a high-tech shielded laboratory, people do show a circadian rhythm of sleep and wakefulness. Their activities regularly cycle over the course of a day, thus confirming the existence of an internal biological timer. The internal clock, however, is not exactly synchronized with our 24-hour day. In fact, for most people the day is around 25 hours long. Thus, on the first day of free-running, people go to bed around an hour later than they usually do; the next day their bedtime is moved back another hour, and so forth. After about 2 weeks of this routine the participants in these studies might be half a day out of synchrony with the outside world, so that they are actually awake during the night and sleeping during the day. Their sleep and wake times continue to drift since their body clock is using a day that is 1 hour longer than the normal 24-hour day–night cycle. Thus, for every 25 days of real time, these sleep research subjects only experience 24 days of psychological time.

If our internal biological clock is set for about 25 hours, why do our internal and behavioral rhythms continue on a 24-hour cycle? Why doesn't our daily activity cycle drift out of agreement with local time?

The reason is that there is a mechanism that synchronizes our internal clock with local time. If there were no such local time synchronizing process, we would have the setup for a very oddly organized species. Consider some early human ancestor who was born on the east coast of North America. Suppose that his sleep–wakefulness cycle was appropriately set for the Atlantic coast. Now suppose that he, being a nomadic hunter, followed the game that provided him sustenance. In this hypothetical scenario we can set up a situation where the game becomes scarce in the east and our hunter gradually wanders west in pursuit of better hunting. Over a period of many months or even years he finally reaches the west coast of the continent. If there were no way to reset our internal times, our poor ancestor would now find himself in a strange situation. He would find that the sun was rising and falling 3 hours later than his physiology was set for. This means that he would awaken 3 hours earlier than people born on the Pacific shore. It would also mean that his California cousins would still be awake hours after he went to sleep. He would be out of step with all of the natural activities in his environment as well. Certainly, an intelligent deity, or evolution acting in an adaptive manner, would provide some means for us to adjust our internal clock so that it could meet the changes in the external environment that are encountered simply by our traveling in an eastern or western direction.

The example presented above shows that if we want to be in harmony with time in a given geographical location, we certainly want to have our internal cycles coordinated with the local rising and setting of the sun. Since it is necessary to have our internal time in synchrony with the external daily light-to-dark-cycle, evolution simply adopted a mechanism that uses light to reset our biological clock. Sleep researchers say that light is the primary *Zeitgeber* (which is a German word "time giver").

There are some easy ways to demonstrate that light is the Zeitgeber that resets our internal clock. The easiest way is to return to our cave or our sleep isolation chamber and to make one small change in the environment: instead of keeping the light on continuously, as we do in a free-running experiment, we will dim the light for 6 to 8 hours out of each 24-hour period, to simulate for our research participants the variation between day and night light levels. Even though they still have no clocks or other signals, our research subjects continue to have a regular 24-hour day length. Now they tend to sleep when the light dims and to awaken sometime after it brightens again. Their internal timer now seems to be in synchrony with the light in the environment, instead of reflecting the 25-hour day we get with no variation in light.

If light is needed to keep our internal clocks synchronized to local time, this raises an interesting question. What happens to blind people who can't see light? Can they reset their biological clock? Keeping in step with the environment is much more difficult for blind people. As a group, blind individuals have a very high rate of sleep complaints: about 76 percent report that they have difficulty falling asleep at their usual bedtime. They also have frequent nighttime awakenings and are often subject to bouts of sleepiness during the day. This is exactly what we would expect if a person's internal clock is out of adjustment with real time. The blind are often telling their body that it's time to go to sleep, when their internal clock is telling their body that it is time to be awake and moving around. Furthermore, most blind people report that these sleep problems are cyclical in nature, occurring in cycles around a month in length. This is exactly what we would expect if blind people have a free-running internal clock that is an hour or so longer than 24 hours.

Several studies have looked at individual blind people over a longer term and have confirmed the fact that their internal circadian timer is not resetting normally. For example, one study looked at the sleep–wake cycle of a completely blind person over an 80-day period.[1] Although this person was living under normal conditions for a Western society, his sleep and wake periods were just not consistent with the 24-hour day. His periods of sleep gradually drifted so that for a week he was sleeping during the night but 2 weeks later his maximum periods of sleepiness were during the day. This pattern of behavior is consistent with an individual whose internal clock is set at a day length of 24.9 hours. Thus, the absence of a normal light sense in the blind seems to hamper more than their ability to process visual information; it also leaves them with a sleep–wakefulness cycle that is out of step with the cycle of those with normal sight.

The daily cycle of sleep and wakefulness is only one of the aspects of our physiology that shows a circadian rhythm. We have already noticed that there is circadian cycle of temperature change in the body. There are many other daily rhythms as well, including cycles controlling urine release and the release of hormones and steroids (such as cortisol) into the blood. There is even a circadian cycle of cell growth and division. Under normal conditions these cycles all seem to be quite synchronized with each other. For example, our nightly sleep is usually preceded by a downward turn in body temperature. Under free-running conditions, where the internal clock does not reset, the various cycles sometimes break apart and lose their coordination with each other. Under these conditions it is possible for people to begin their long sleep for the day on a rising body temperature. It has been observed that in blind people, especially those whose blindness is of recent onset, there is sometimes a disruption in the usual synchronized nature of circadian cycles. One of the important functions of light as a *Zeitgeber*, then, is to lock all of these cycles together. Thus, light variations do not simply reset the circadian clock that governs sleep and wakefulness; they also reset all of the other circadian clocks in the body, allowing for harmonious and consistent cycling across the 24-hour day.

Where is the biological clock that gives the daily rhythm to our sleep and wake times? The first hint came in the 1960s, from Curt Richter, who was working with rats at Johns Hopkins University. He found that if he damaged the hypothalamus, which is a deep central brain structure, he eliminated any regular sleep-and-wakefulness cycle in the rat. The hypothalamus is an old part of the brain (in evolutionary terms) and can be found in many primitive animals, like fish and reptiles, that tend to have very little in the way of a complex cerebral cortex. This relatively small brain structure has many connections with other brain regions, and it has been shown to contain specific regions that control hunger, thirst, body temperature, and a variety of other vital functions needed for survival.

Richter's surgical procedures were fairly coarse. His work was followed up by Robert Y. Moore, then at the University of Chicago, who had the technology to destroy smaller, more precisely located regions of the hypothalamus. It is lucky that this precision was possible; the specific location that must be eliminated to wipe out circadian rhythms turns out to be very tiny, containing only a few thousand nerve cells. This brain site is called the *suprachiasmatic nucleus*. It gets its name from its exact location, which is directly above a region in the optical pathway that carries information from the eye to the brain. This region is called the *optic chiasm*. (The *chi* in *chiasm* comes from the name of the Greek letter χ. If we think of the optic nerves from the two eyes as being like highways, then the optic chiasm would be a major intersection.) Various optical fibers are sorted out here and sent on for further processing in the brain.

The suprachiasmatic nucleus gathers information from some of the nearby optical fibers so that it can monitor light levels that the eyes are exposed to. If we cut the optic nerves of rats before they reach the optic chiasm, we deprive the suprachiasmatic nucleus of its light information, and the animals lose their ability to keep their sleep and activity cycles in step with the 24-hour day. This is just like the blind people we discussed earlier. Suppose that we cut the optic tracts that are leaving the optic chiasm. In this case the animal is still quite functionally blind: it cannot see patterns or brightnesses since the information from the eyes never reaches the higher brain centers. However, since the surgical damage to the visual pathway occurs at a location beyond the area where the light information has been sent off to the suprachiasmatic nucleus, these animals, although quite blind, will still show sleep and waking cycles that follow the 24-hour day-to-night variations in light in the environment.

Remember, the suprachiasmatic nucleus is actually a 24-hour timer in its own right. Light simply resets it each day to keep it in agreement with the outside world. Shin Ichi Inoue and Charles Kawamura of the Mitsubishi Institute in Tokyo removed some brain tissue from animals that included the suprachiasmatic nucleus. This tissue was then kept alive in an organ culture, and electrical recordings were taken from it. Even though this group of cells was in isolation from the rest of the animal and any other brain activity, there were still systemic increases and decreases in its electrical activity. These followed the same circadian cycle observed in intact animals, that is, rising and falling with an approximate cycle length between 24 and 25 hours. It is possible that these are the signals that the suprachiasmatic nucleus uses to instruct other parts of the brain about the passage of time. In addition, this brain center is also known to contain certain very large long-chain proteins, or *peptides*, that might serve as chemical equivalents of clock chimes to tell the rest of the brain that it is time to sleep or wake.

The suprachiasmatic nucleus, however, does not work alone. There is a small region of the brain, known as the *pineal gland,* that also plays an important role in the circadian activity cycle. The pineal gland is interesting in terms of its evolution. It appears to be all that is left of what used to be a third eye. This eye would have been located quite high and in the middle of the head. Although it lacks the variable lens and other features associated with our eyes, the pineal gland is sensitive to changes in light levels. In many of the lower animals, such as some fish and reptiles, the pineal gland still serves as a light sensor. It is usually not visible from the outside since it is often covered with a thin membrane of skin that the light must pass through. It is probably sensitive enough, however, to warn an animal if a shadow falls on its back, which might indicate a predator trying to sneak up from behind. Its main function, however, seems to be to monitor general levels of light in the environment and to control various hormonal secretions.

In mammals, one of the important functions of the pineal gland still has to do with light levels. When darkness falls, the pineal gland secrets a hormone called *melatonin.* The direct effect of an increased amount of melatonin in the blood is to make us sleepy. In fact, there are a number of recent studies that have attempted to treat insomnia and disrupted sleep patterns in humans by administering measured doses of melatonin.[2] One of the advantages of using melatonin for this is that since it is a naturally occurring hormonal substance, it often assists in promoting sleep but lets patients wake up without the sleeping pill "hangover" that is common with drugs like barbiturates. Some research suggests that melatonin can act directly on the suprachiasmatic nucleus and, like the input of direct light, can keep a person's timing cycle in agreement with the 24-hour day.

There may be other factors that can also reset the biological clock. Some researchers have suggested that regular mealtimes can help; others have proposed that regular exercise periods can serve the same function. There are even some researchers who contend that social stimulation will also work. All of these *Zeitgebers,* though, are much weaker and less reliable than light itself. Our circadian biological clock was designed to keep our behaviors in step with day and night variations in light levels. Therefore, the tiny suprachiasmatic nucleus, which does the timing, seems to look mostly to variations in light levels in order to keep us in synchrony with our 24-hour world.

Since our internal timer is biological in nature, it would be reasonable to expect that this timer would speed up or slow down if we varied conditions that we know change the rate at which other physiological processes in the body proceed. One of the most obvious of these factors is body temperature. When body temperature increases, many normal physiological processes become faster.

A relationship between body temperature and body time was first demonstrated by Dr. Hudson Hoagland.[3] It all began during an influenza epidemic in the 1930s. His wife was ill and had very high fever, somewhere around 103°F (39°C). Hoagland needed to go to the drugstore for some medication for her. When he got home, his wife was quite upset with him for taking so long, claiming that he had been away for hours. In truth, his trip had only taken about 20 minutes. His wife's misperception interested Hoagland. Therefore, without telling her what he was thinking, he asked her to estimate the duration of a minute by counting to 60 at a rate of one number per second. By following her counting with a stopwatch he could get a reasonable idea of what was happening to his wife's time sense. It turned out that his wife's estimates of a minute were only 38 seconds long. What was happening was that her high body temperature was increasing the rate of various physiological activities, and this caused her biological clock to tick more rapidly than usual. In other words, any block of physical time will be perceived as "too long" when one's body temperature increases and makes bodily processes work faster. More recent studies on scuba divers whose body temperature was lowered by immersing them in cold water show that under such conditions the internal timer runs more slowly.

If simple factors, such as body temperature, can affect our internal timer and if people differ physiologically, it should not be much of a surprise to learn that our biological clocks do not run at the same speed. While everybody may start the day when the light resets their circadian clock, we do not all follow the same pace through the day.

Benjamin Franklin's famous maxim "Early to bed, early to rise makes a man healthy, wealthy, and wise" describes one particular circadian lifestyle. If Franklin had been a bird, he would have been a lark. These birds rise early in order to satisfy their thirst with the morning dew; when that is done, they often begin singing their beautiful morning song, which serves in the spring as their mating call. People who are like larks, or who show the psychological predisposition that some researchers call "morningness," are early risers. From the moment they get out of bed they seem awake, alert, and ready to begin daily activities. They work busily through the morning but start to fade as the afternoon comes on. They are usually quite ready to fall asleep early in the evening.

We can contrast these morning "larks" to other people for whom Franklin's advice is simply not a possibility. These people, if they were birds, would surely be owls, the bird most noted as a prowler of the evening and dark hours. People who are like owls display the predisposition called "eveningness." Getting up early is painful for them. They mope and stagger their way through the morning but begin to pick up speed as the day progresses. By evening they are moving quite well, and they can often be found working well into the late hours of the night.

"Larks" and "owls" both show a circadian rhythm, but their cycles differ, with the "owls'" cycles peaking about 2 hours later. This difference occurs in all the physical cycles, including the daily rise and fall of body temperature and the increase and decrease in various hormones. Psychologically, however, the differences in rhythms seem to be much greater. Larks do their best work in the early hours, owls do their best work in the later hours. Owls are just plain miserable in the morning whereas larks are buzzing around enjoying the morning light. At night, owls are feeling peppy and ready to play while larks are beginning to crash for the day.

If a couple living together consists of a lark and an owl, there is a much higher likelihood of tension and argument than if both are larks or both are owls. It is really difficult for the two types of people to understand each other. The lark will stand by the bed where the owl is still sleeping, poke at his or her partner and wonder how anyone can be so lazy. The owl simply does not understand how someone can get up so early in the morning, let alone be cheerful about it.

A classic example of the fact that larks and owls live in two different worlds, each scarcely recognizing the existence of the other, comes

TEST TO DETERMINE MORNING VERSUS EVENING PEOPLE

To see if you are a lark or an owl, answer the following questions by circling the answers that apply to you.

1. I am most alert during the   morning   evening

2. I feel that I have the most energy during the morning   evening

3. I feel that I remember material better if
   I read it or hear it in the   morning   evening

4. I am most productive during the   morning   evening

5. I come up with my best ideas during the   morning   evening

6. I feel that I am most intelligent during the morning   evening

7. I prefer recreation during the   morning   evening

8. Considering what makes me feel best,
   if I were completely free to plan my day,   before   after
   I would get up   8 A.M.   8 A.M.

9. Considering what makes me feel best,
   if I were completely free to plan my day,   before   after
   I would go to sleep   11 P.M.   11 P.M.

10. During the first hour after I wake up in the
    morning, I would judge my alertness and
    energy as   fairly good fairly low

To score this test, count the number of responses that you circled in the right-hand column. If you have seven or more circled, you are clearly an owl; if you have three or less circled, you are clearly a lark. If your responses are between four and six you are fairly average (with not very pronounced larkish or owlish tendencies).

from the life of Ferenc Molnár, the Hungarian dramatist and writer. Molnár's reputation was primarily based on his plays, the most successful being *Liliom* and, later, *The Red Mill*. Molnár was a classic owl, who virtually never emerged from his house before 1 P.M. While he was living in Budapest, there arose an occasion when he was required to testify as a witness in a lawsuit. The problem was that Molnár had to be at court at 9 A.M. It took the energetic and combined efforts of his servants to get him out of bed and dressed; then they personally escorted him out of the house at 8:30 A.M. Molnár found himself standing right in the middle of the rush hour crowd flowing past his downtown home. He simply looked from side to side at the people bustling along the street on their way to work, then turned to his servant, and asked, "Good God—are all of these people witnesses in this fool case?"

A number of simple tests have been designed to determine if individuals are high on the dimensions of morningness or eveningness. You might want to see if you are a morning lark or an evening owl by taking the test on the opposite page.[4]

There is a proverb that goes as follows: "In vain they rise early that used to rise late;" this reflects the idea that it is difficult to change owls into larks. This is generally true. In fact, asking owls to keep the schedule of a lark, or vice versa, generally leads to great dissatisfaction and lowered efficiency. That does not mean that there is never the possibility of any change. Several studies have now confirmed that as we grow older, we all develop a bit more of a tendency toward morningness. Owls, however, show the greatest changes, becoming much more larkish with age. So, for couples living in a lark-versus-owl mismatch, just hang in there. If you live long enough, things may get better.

Riding the Daily Seesaw of Sleepiness ⇄

We have just seen that there are regular cycles and changes in our body over the day. Since these circadian cycles can affect the impact that any sleep debt will have on us, it is important for us to know which times of the day we are most likely to be hit by bouts of sleepiness. Does sleepiness just follow the 24-hour cycle, or does it follow one of the other body cycles, perhaps rising and falling every 12 hours, 4 hours, or even 90 minutes? To determine this we have to find a way to track sleepiness over the day. Some people might believe that measuring sleepiness is a fairly trivial task. Couldn't you, for instance, simply count the number of times that a person yawns during any given hour or so?

In most people's minds, yawning—that slow, exaggerated mouth opening with the long, deep inhalation of air, followed by a briefer exhalation—is the most obvious sign of sleepiness. It is a common behavior shared by many animals, including our pet dogs and cats but also crocodiles, snakes, birds, and even some fish. It certainly is true that sleepy people tend to yawn more than wide-awake people. It is also true that people who say they are bored by what is happening at the moment will tend to yawn more frequently. However, whether yawning is a sign that you are getting ready to sleep or that you are successfully

94

fighting off sleep is not known. Simply stretching your body, as you might do if you have been sitting in the same position for a long period of time, will often trigger a yawn.

Unfortunately, yawns don't just indicate sleepiness. In some animals, yawning is a sign of stress. When a dog trainer sees a dog yawning in a dog obedience class, it is usually a sign that the animal is under a good deal of pressure. Perhaps the handler is pushing too hard or moving too fast for the dog to feel in control of the situation. A moment or two of play and then turning to another activity is usually enough to banish yawning for quite a while.

Yawning can also be a sign of stress in humans. Once, when observing airborne troops about to take their first parachute jump, I noticed that several of the soldiers were sitting in the plane and yawning. It was 10 A.M., just after a coffee break, and I doubted that they were tired; I knew for a fact that they were far too nervous to be bored. When I asked about this, the officer in charge laughed and said that it was really quite a common behavior, especially on the first jump. "Maybe they're trying to suck in extra air to make themselves lighter in case their chutes don't open," he playfully suggested.

There is also a social aspect to yawning. Psychologists have placed actors in crowded rooms and auditoriums and had them deliberately yawn. Within moments there is usually an increase in yawning by everybody else in the room. Similarly, people who watch films or videos of others yawning are more likely to yawn. If you pay attention to your own behavior, you may also be noticing, just about now, that even reading about yawning tends to stimulate people to yawn!

The truth of the matter is that we really don't know what purpose yawning serves. Scientists originally thought that the purpose of yawning was to increase the amount of oxygen in the blood or to release some accumulated carbon dioxide. We now know that this is not true, since increasing the concentration of carbon dioxide in the air seems not to make people more likely to yawn but to make them breathe faster to try to bring in more oxygen. On the other hand, breathing 100 percent pure oxygen does not seem to reduce the likelihood of yawning.

Part of the answer to the puzzle of yawning may actually have to do with stretching the face and mouth muscles. To see what I mean, try to inhale through your clenched teeth the next time you begin to yawn, or keep your mouth closed and inhale through your nose. In either case, the air passes quite easily in and out of your windpipe; although you are not interfering with the breathing process, yawning this way (without the big mouth stretch) seems very unsatisfactory. Many people report that yawning this way feels as if they have stalled or become stuck in mid-yawn. Somehow, the stretching of the jaws is a vital component of the process, whatever the real function of yawning may be.

Since yawning seems to be associated with a lot more than the need for sleep, we obviously have to find some other measure of sleepiness. Some researchers have simply tried to ask people how sleepy they feel at any time using some sort of self-rating scale. There are, however, problems with getting people to make these kinds of judgments. Sometimes people simply lie to researchers when asked about how sleepy they are. This occurs because in many areas of our society admitting that one is fatigued and sleepy is considered a sign of weakness or lack of ambition and drive. In other instances, people simply don't know how tired they are. For example, people may admit that they need four cups of coffee to make it through the morning, but it may never occur to them that this might be due to the fact that they are so sleepy that they need stimulation from caffeine to be able to do their required work. It never seems to occur to some people that the reason that it is so difficult to drag themselves out of bed in the morning is because their body is pleading with them for a few more hours of sleep to pay off some of their sleep debt and restore them to a normal level of functioning. For these reasons, many researchers have developed an alternate method to determine how sleepy a person is. It is based upon a simple definition of sleep need: The greater your sleep need, or the sleepier you are, the faster you will actually fall asleep if given an opportunity to do so.

In today's sleep labs the "gold standard" of sleepiness tests, in one or another of its forms, is the Multiple Sleep Latency Test. The test requires that individuals be wired so that their brain waves can be recorded. Their EEG patterns are used to tell researchers exactly when the brain enters the first stage of sleep. At intervals of about 2 hours the test subjects are asked to lie down on a comfortable bed in a dimly lit room and to simply relax and try to go to sleep. The time between the dimming of the lights and the moment when the first evidence of sleep appears in the EEG record is the person's *sleep latency.* The moment the brain waves indicate sleep, the person is immediately awakened, so that the actual test procedure might only add a minute or two of sleep to the test person's daily sleep total and will not affect any experimental procedure that involves depriving people of sleep or maintaining a particular sleep schedule. I have taken this sleep latency test, and it feels like you have just begun to relax and drift off when the experimenter comes in to awaken you.

Generally speaking, a normal individual living under today's usual sleep schedules will take about 10 to 15 minutes to fall asleep. (The longest an individual can stay awake in this test is 20 minutes since at that point the test is stopped.) Individuals who are fully rested usually do not fall asleep during the 20-minute interval, but those who are running a sleep debt will fall asleep in less than 10 minutes. If a person falls asleep in less than 5 minutes, he or she is considered to be very sleep-deprived, and such short sleep latencies in people who are not deliberately denying themselves sleep may indicate a medically significant sleep disorder. For individuals with certain sleep disorders, such as sleep apnea or narcolepsy, it is not unusual to see the person drop into sleep in 2 minutes or less.

One of the most interesting and reliable findings from sleep latency tests is that the pressure to fall asleep varies over the day, corresponding to some of the circadian rhythms we looked at earlier. Many studies have now shown that the greatest pressure to sleep comes in the early morning hours, with a peak perhaps sometime around 1 to 4 A.M. This is the slowest time for the body's metabolism; we are groggy with our sleep need, inefficient, a bit clumsy, and feeling dismal during this dark period of the morning. It is well documented that workers on night shifts are most susceptible to accidents at these times. This low point of the day is noticeable enough so that many people have commented on it. It is quite common to interpret this slowing as a general sense of apprehension and defensiveness during these wee hours of the morning. Thus, the novelist F. Scott Fitzgerald wrote, "In the real dark night of the soul it is always three o'clock in the morning." Similarly, in his thoroughly spooky book *Something Wicked This Way Comes,* Ray Bradbury uses the term "the soul's midnight" to refer to 3 A.M., which is right in the middle of this circadian depression.

The sinister and disquieting feelings associated with these early morning hours may well be justified. In a series of studies that have examined nearly a half million deaths, researchers find that there is a peak of vulnerability in the early morning hours. Perhaps, argue some scientists, any life-threatening physical occurrence, such as a heart instability or a breathing difficulty, simply cannot be met with enough vigor by the body when our circadian cycle is at its lowest ebb. If we are already weakened by illness, our debility is multiplied by the slower and weaker responsiveness of our body in the early morning hours.

The sleep latency test data, however, produced a bit of a surprise: while most readers are probably not surprised to learn that we are at our sleepiest around 1 to 4 A.M., many might not have predicted another point of maximum sleepiness 12 hours later. This second low occurs around 1 to 4 P.M., when the day is still bright and people are still actively moving around, working, doing chores, and, for all intents and purposes, seem quite wide-awake. Yet the sleep latency measures show that we are much more likely to fall asleep quickly at, say, 2 or 3 P.M. than we are at 10 A.M. or 6 P.M.

A moment's thought might help you remember that at times you yourself have occasionally experienced these waves of afternoon sleepiness. In many countries, predominantly those with warmer climates, this is the time of the siesta, where people take an afternoon nap for an hour or two. The siesta is a common practice in many Mediterranean countries, such as Spain and Italy. In Greece, for instance, most businesses close in the afternoon for the *messi medianos ipnos* ("sleep in the middle of the afternoon"). The siesta is also customary in many countries in South and Central America. A colleague of mine traveled through China and noted that the siesta is also common there:

> I was startled to see people just lying along the sides of roads, and in alleys and side streets even in some cities, in the middle of the afternoon. When I asked our translator about this, she said that this was called hsiuhsi. According to her, this afternoon sleep is actually officially condoned as an interpretation of a line in the constitution that reads something like "the working population has a right to rest." I presumed, however, that this custom was confined mainly to rural peasants and urban manual labourers, since I had never heard of it before. I was wrong. When we arrived at the government

offices in the small town that we were going to use as our base for the week,
it was in the early afternoon. We were stopped at the door by a guard. "It is still
hsiuhsi," our guide told us. "We should come back in an hour when they have
finished their rest." She later told us that in some businesses, especially where
there was active commerce with Western countries, the practice was becom-
ing less common. "Our businessmen are being told by people in your country
that sleeping in the afternoon is a sign of laziness. We are not lazy and do not
wish to appear that way, so most business people have given up hsiuhsi."

It has always been argued that the afternoon nap or siesta is a cultural invention of southern countries designed to allow people to escape the midday heat, which would make it impossible to work effectively, anyway. In warm climates, escaping to a cool, dark room for a
brief nap makes sense. It turns out, however, that midday heat is not
the cause of this siesta-time sleepiness. Consider the city of Edmonton,
in Canada. It is the home of the University of Alberta, where underground tunnels are provided to shield students from the bitter cold of
the northern winters as they go from building to building. Even on a
midwinter day with the external temperature at −40°C (by coinci-
dence, it's also −40°F), the sleep latency tests produce the same two
peak periods of sleepiness as at the equator. Midday heat is certainly
not the cause of afternoon sleepiness during winter in Edmonton.

Some people have an alternate explanation for our afternoon dozi-
ness: to explain why they feel themselves dropping off to sleep at their
desks, cash registers, or assembly line positions in the middle of the afternoon, they blame lunch. The suggestion is that a big sandwich or a
heavy main course is the cause of afternoon sleepiness. This is an old
theory that can be traced all the way back to Aristotle, whose notion
was that drowsiness is caused by vapors that are generated by the digestion of food and that move upward. The larger the meal, the greater
the quantity of vapors generated, and the sleepier one gets. Today we
just refer to this as the "postlunch dip."

This suggested cause for afternoon sleepiness, like the midday heat,
is also a myth. It probably came about simply because lunch is the
major event that usually precedes our bout of afternoon sleepiness. A
number of researchers have now tested what is technically called the
"postprandial sleepiness hypothesis" and have used a variety of differ-

ent techniques. Some have given research subjects equal-sized small meals spaced out over the course of the day whereas others have varied the size or the content of the meals or have even deprived people of meals. The results are always the same: sometime between 1 and 4 P.M., sleep latency tests show, people become very sleepy. This occurs even if they have no lunch at all that day. On the other hand, there is never any "postbreakfast dip" in alertness even if the size and content of breakfast make it the exact equivalent of lunch. Thus, it is obvious that our after-lunch sleepiness has more to do with our internal biological clock than with heavy eating at midday.

There is one little complication to all of these lunch studies. Suppose that you are already running a sleep debt. In other words, suppose that the sleep latency measures show that you are relatively sleep deprived. If we now give you a big lunch with lots of carbohydrates and starches, lunch does make a difference. It doesn't cause you to become sleepy, but it makes the usual afternoon bout of sleepiness deeper and more irresistible. Things are made even worse if lunch is accompanied by an alcoholic drink. In other words, if your circadian rhythm already has you at a low, running on too little sleep makes that low even lower and makes you more susceptible to factors that might slow or alter physical and psychological functioning, such as the diversion of energy to the process of digestion.

Recall the data that indicate that there is a circadian low point at 1 to 4 A.M. when people are more likely to die. These same data confirm that there is also a midafternoon dip in our bodily functioning, suggesting that maybe there is a second time during the day when we are especially susceptible to death. Although this increased risk is not quite as large as the nighttime rise, it is still quite noticeable. A review of around a half million death records reveals that there is a peak time in the afternoon when we are also very vulnerable to death—at around 1 to 4 P.M., exactly 12 hours after the nighttime peak.

The studies using sleep latency data have also revealed another oddity about our daily cycles of alertness: there are times in the morning and early evening when you will have difficulty falling asleep even if you are sleep deprived and want to fall asleep. These times are often referred to as the "forbidden zones" for sleep. The first of these times occurs in the midmorning hours and tends to reach a peak at about 9 to 11 A.M. Most people are feeling quite good at this time of day and often rate these hours as their most productive. The second peak occurs around 10 to 12 hours later, centered around 7 to 9 P.M., when we again seem to have a surge of alertness. People who bring work home with the idea of finishing it up in the evening often report that 8 P.M. (which would be in the middle of this period when sleep is least likely) is the time when they feel awake and alert enough to actually sit down and work on the material they had planned to complete. In many Latin American countries this is also the time of the evening meal.

These sleepless zones can actually mask the effects of massive sleep deprivation. Totally sleep-deprived people often claim during the early morning peak periods of this internal cycle that they are getting their "second wind" and are no longer really feeling much need for sleep. It is at this time that people engaged in sleepless marathons announce that they can tough it out for several days more. A similar rejuvenation occurs during the early evening sleepless zone. Performance of various tasks becomes easier, and you feel a lot better. These periods of feeling good may lure individuals into pushing harder and going without sleep even longer.

The larger the sleep debt a person has built up, the greater the effects the 12-hour cycle of alertness will have on them. We can see these 12-hour variations in sleepiness quite clearly in the sleep diaries of soldiers who were engaged in a series of experiments conducted by the U.S. Army. Since military operations often involve loss of sleep, knowledge about how people think and perform without sleep or with only minimal sleep is obviously important to the army. In this particular experiment the operation was simulating a radio relay and observation post. The soldiers who served as test subjects had a number of tasks. As in the case at a real observation post, there were things the soldiers had to continuously watch for and information they were always processing. The most important part of the task was the quick and accurate decoding of a series of incoming messages. Once a message was decoded, the soldier had to perform certain tasks based on the information in that message. In addition, there were other tasks and tests that showed how well and how quickly sleep-deprived soldiers could make decisions, do physical work, remember information, and so forth. Most interesting to us, however, is the fact that every 2 hours the research participants were required to type a brief entry into a diary kept on a computer. Although the entries were to be kept short, the soldiers were asked to say how they were feeling, how tired they were, how well they were performing, and whether they thought they would be able to successfully finish this operation (they had been told that the experiment might involve going completely without sleep for 72 hours). The excerpts from the diary reproduced below come from a 20-year-old infantry corporal. (I have added the times, since participants were not informed as to the actual clock time when entries were made.) The material in italics is my commentary on the soldier's entries. Although diary entries were made every 2 hours, I have only included those that are near the critical times in the sleep–alertness cycle. The experiment was 22 hours old when these excerpts begin. The young corporal had entered the laboratory and had started the experiment at 8 A.M. the previous day. This means that he had already gone a full night without sleep when he made the first entry and that by the last entry reproduced here he had been without sleep for 48 hours.

6 A.M. [*He is just coming out of the early morning low point.*]. Really tired. Wonder why I volunteered for this. Made a real mess of the decoding test. Could really use some sleep. I don't like this place.

8 A.M.: Feeling better. A couple of hours ago I felt pretty sleepy, but I think that eating something helped to perk me up. That test with all of the switching around went OK.

10 A.M. [*He is now entering the midmorning alertness peak.*]. I feel pretty good. I really cracked that decoding thing. I don't know why it gave me so much trouble before, but I got it knocked now. I'm feeling pretty good. I don't think that finishing this simulation will be any problem.

2 P.M. [*He is now entering the afternoon low point.*]. Still OK. I think that the meal made me a little tired, and it is catching up with me now. Don't think that there are any problems in the tests they gave me.

4 P.M. [*He has been going through the afternoon sleepiness peak.*]. Tired. Had a real slowdown about a half hour ago. Think that I missed or screwed up one of the messages. Just heard the last part. Missed the whole front end. Only boring stuff going on, anyway.

8 P.M. [*He is now at the evening peak of alertness.*]. "Going OK. Eating picked me up. I had been having problems with that list-making test, but I got the hang of it now. The decoding thing is really easy once you got the keys in your head. It's sort of interesting to see the answer come out. I didn't think that going without sleep would be so easy.

12 MIDNIGHT. Still at it. A little fatigued. Not much happening. Same tests over and over. I should make it OK.

2 A.M. [*He has now entered the nighttime sleepiness zone.*]. Pretty tired. I think that they are trying to make things harder by speeding up the messages. That is not fair. Same old boring junk, anyway. I'll finish this thing just to show them I can.

4 A.M. [*He has now gone through the lowest point of the cycle. This entry contained a number of spelling or typographical errors, which have been corrected.*]. "Need sleep bad. Eating did not help. Think I fell asleep during part of the message. Must have because the decoding didn't make any sense. Stupid system, anyway. No one can learn those keys. I wonder if I really can just get up and walk out of here. Tired and pissed enough to try it.

6 A.M. "Need some rest. Could sleep standing up. Few hours ago I felt like I was wearing gloves on my hands. Made working on the keyboard feel funny. OK now. Decoding is going slow. I asked W. [*the research technician*] to tell me what time it was. SOB wouldn't.

8 A.M. I am OK. Eating helped pick me up. I think I got the messages and decoding under control. Could use a nap, but think I will make it.

10 A.M. [*We're back to the beginning of the morning alertness high.*]. "I'm OK. Feeling stiff, fatigued, not sleepy. I can still go a couple days more like this. I told W. that I'm going to break the record when I decode the next message. Watch my time.

There are several things about these diary entries that are interesting. First of all, they seem to confirm that there are periods of maximum sleep pressure in the early morning and midafternoon. Notice, however, that in the midmorning and early evening there were periods of time when this totally sleep-deprived individual seemed to be showing few signs of sleepiness at all. Since he did not know that it was his body cycles that were determining his sleepiness at any time, this young corporal mistakenly credited most of his changes in alertness to the meals he ate. In his electronic diary, at times he claims that the meals are making him more alert; at other times he blames meals for making him sleepier. It is also interesting to notice that the corporal's mood shifts along with his sleep need. When he is sleepiest, things are "boring," and one can even pick up traces of anger and hostility in the diary entries. When he is at his alertness peaks, his mood is quite good, showing pride in his accomplishments and good-natured competitiveness, as in the last entry (after 48 hours without sleep), when he is trying to "break the record" for speed in decoding the incoming messages.

Let's consider the implications of all of the data. We already know that there are circadian cycles that our body follows. There is the basic 24-hour cycle that shows up physiologically as variations in our body temperature and metabolism. However, the sleep latency test data, which is really a measure of our overall sleepiness and fatigue during the day, has demonstrated that there is an important second cycle, one that reaches a peak and a trough every 12 hours. At the low points in the cycle, in the early morning and the middle afternoon, we act as though we are sleep deprived and sleepy even if our sleep debt is not very large. At the height of the cycle, in the middle morning and early evening, we act as if our sleep need is virtually nonexistent even if we have a large sleep debt. This cycle has some real consequences, since it shows up in vital data such as the times death is most likely to occur. As we will soon see, it also predicts the times we make the most mistakes and are most likely to have accidents.

Sleepy Children and Sleepy Parents

Sleep is not a constant phenomenon; rather, it changes over our life span. It was the British writer Walter Savage Landor who gave his summary of all of life's changes by saying, "In the morn of life we are alert, we are heated in its noon, and only in its decline do we repose." When it comes to sleep, however, he had it backwards. There is more repose in infancy than in old age. Each age seems to have its own characteristic sleep length and pattern. For example, a newborn infant sleeps between 16 and 20 hours a day, as opposed to the 8 hours a day for the young adult and the 6 or 7 hours a day normally attributed to the elderly.

Not only is the sleep of the young infant longer than the sleep of adults, but it differs from it in some important ways. Many parents have noted that infants are often very expressive and active even though they are obviously asleep. While they are sleeping, most young babies produce a surprising variety of facial expressions, including smiles, grimaces, looks of surprise, scowls of disdain, and so forth. They make noises, too: little cooing sounds, moans, and babbles. An infant's body does a lot of moving: tiny hands may stretch or clutch or form balled fists, and sometimes the whole body seems to react as if the infant has just been startled or gently stroked. When you see a baby going through such contortions, look at the eyes. You will probably be able to see them moving behind the closed lids, which is evidence that all of this activity is going on while the infant is dreaming.

Scientists who observed this pattern of infant behaviors were initially puzzled. In adults there is very little movement during dreams. To prevent us from acting out our dreams, most of the large muscles that move parts of our body are turned off or inhibited. Apparently, in young infants the processes that inhibit motor activities have not yet fully matured. This means that watching an infant sleep is the best way to appreciate the brain activation that takes place during the dream stage of sleep. It gives us an opportunity to imagine the sequences of body movements and motor activities that form the basis of our dream scenarios.

There is another puzzle associated with infant sleep: the amount of time infants spend dreaming. Dreams seem to occupy about half of an infant's total sleep time. From a psychodynamic viewpoint, like that of Sigmund Freud, this makes no sense at all. Psychologists of this ilk have always supposed that dreams were related to activities during the day. It has been argued that we use dreams to work out the emotional situations that we encountered during the day or, alternatively, that we use them as part of the processing necessary to store material permanently in our memory. Yet how could this apply to the newborn infant? It may have been awake only 4 hours that day. Most of that awake time involved simple feeding and elimination processes. The most exciting event of the day may have been a diaper change or a sponge bath. Certainly, 10 hours of rapid eye movement dreaming is not needed to work out the emotional and memory-related aspects of the events that occurred during that brief experience of wakefulness. More recent research by Dreyfus-Brisac and Monod in Paris has allowed us to learn about the sleep patterns that occur in the womb. It appears that while still in the womb, at around 25 weeks or so of age, the infant dreams virtually all of the time! From that age, the proportion of rapid eye movement sleep gradually diminishes until birth, when half of the sleep time is spent in this state. Why so much dreaming?

Three researchers, Howard Roffwarg, Joseph Muzio, and William Dement, all of whom were working at Columbia University in the mid-1960s, proposed an interesting theory. They suggested that dreams are not simply a replay of the day's activities but are actually necessary for development of the brain. Noting that muscles must be exercised to develop fully, they suggested that brain tissue, too, especially in the parts of the brain that control our senses and our thinking processes, must be stimulated to develop normally. Obviously, the womb does not provide a lot of stimulation from the environment. Therefore, dreams are supplied in order to stimulate and activate the various developing parts of the brain. We know that adults' dreams can involve all forms of sensory impressions, not just vision and hearing but touch, taste, smell, and even pain. For the infant in the womb, then, the dream state provides a form of theater, a relatively continuous flow of sensory stimulation, all generated internally. Once activated by dreams, the neural circuits that will be needed after birth have a chance to fine-tune themselves, to learn how to adjust to varying stimulus conditions, and to keep themselves in a state of readiness for later use.

Recently, one of these researchers, Dement, commented, "Our theory, which we proposed in 1966, is still viable 25 years later—partly because it has a compelling logic and partly because it is extraordinarily difficult to test." Actually, he is being modest, for there is some recent support for the idea. Roffwarg, who is now at the University of Texas, found some drugs and other techniques that selectively eliminate the rapid eye movement dream phase of sleep. Using newborn kittens as his test subjects, he has shown that a disruption of dreaming in the extremely young can lead to some specific disruptions in their developing brains.

If the primary purpose of dreams is to allow the infant's brain to develop normally, then dreams should not be needed in later life. Some researchers think this is one of the reasons the amount of time we spend dreaming decreases as we grow older. A cynic might point out that this is scientific evidence that as we grow older, we are robbed not only of our vigor, but also of our dreams. A more positive spin would be to note that we never do stop dreaming.

If the brain stimulation theory is correct, dreams are superfluous in old age and hence should not be there at all. The fact that we continue to dream throughout our lives is interesting. Perhaps dreams are needed to assist the infant in brain development but have another function in later life. What this function is, is still a matter of controversy. There is some recent research that suggests that dreams may actually help our memory processes. Some data suggest that dreaming may be an integral part of the method we use to establish long-term memories.

Not only dreaming but also deep sleep is different for young children. One must recognize that sleep, from an evolutionary point of view, has always involved a bit of a balancing act. Deep sleep seems to be the most restorative and physically necessary part of sleep. Unfortunately, in deep sleep an animal is also most vulnerable to predators and other dangers. Human beings, compared to other animals, have an extended childhood that requires the protection provided by parents. With parents around as guards, children can safely afford the luxury of long, deep slow-wave sleep. By adult standards, the deep sleep of young children is very deep indeed. During this phase of sleep they are very unresponsive to sounds, light, touch, and heat stimuli. This was graphically shown in one experiment in which children went to sleep wearing earphones.[1] When the children entered deep sleep, as shown by EEG recordings, a loud hissing sound (much like radio static) was played through the earphones. The children showed no sign of arousing or breaking out of deep sleep even when the sounds reached 123 decibels. This is an incredibly loud sound; it may be compared to the loudest human shout ever recorded, which was only 111 decibels. The researchers refrained from increasing the volume any further because it was reaching intensities that might have damaged the children's ears— despite its failure to awaken them!

Infants are not born with well-established circadian rhythms. In fact, the well defined day/active and night/quiet pattern is not established before about 4 months of age. Prior to that time, rhythmic variations in behavior can be seen, but these are the shorter *ultradian cycles*. The first of these to appear is a 90-minute basic rest–activity cycle that causes sleep periods that last between 1 and 2 hours and are followed by brief episodes of wakefulness. This pattern continues throughout the day. Between 2 and 8 weeks of age another cycle begins to show itself: a roughly 4-hour rhythm of sleep and activity. This cycle seems so strong in infants that early childrearing experts, such as Arnold Gesell of Yale University, recommended it as the pattern of timing for infant care. Hospitals soon adopted the 4-hour pattern of feeding and changing children, which continues to this day in most pediatric units and seems to correspond quite well to the needs of most children in this age range.

For most parents, the critical milestone in their child's sleep is the first time the infant actually sleeps through the night. For the vast majority of children, this will not occur until about 3 months of age. About 10 percent of parents are lucky enough to have an infant who sleeps through the night at 1 month of age; however, an equal number will be unlucky and have an infant who will not sleep through the night until 6 months of age. Moreover, these statistics merely refer to the *first* time the child sleeps through the night, not when sleeping through the night becomes the regular pattern.

Between 3 months and 1 year of age, the child's sleep patterns start to stabilize, and the night's sleep will last 6 to 8 hours. This is not necessarily continuous sleep, since at this age most children usually awake once during the night and may require a parent's attention. Some children will still have unstable circadian rhythms. About 12 percent of parents are faced with children who still have the 90-minute rest-activity cycle of the newborn superimposed on their developing 24-hour cycle. This means that the child may be awakened three or four times during the night and that the parents may be awakened as well. During this period of time the child will also have regular daytime sleep periods. These last usually from 1 to 2 hours. At first there will be a nap in the morning and one in midafternoon. After a while, however, the morning nap will disappear. The afternoon nap will remain as a fairly well-established behavior, usually occurring between the siesta hours of 1 and 4 P.M. Most young children go to bed for their long night sleep between 6 and 8 P.M., although about one-quarter of all children will not fall asleep until well after 8 P.M.

At around 2 years of age the afternoon nap will have disappeared for about 25 percent of children (although one out of three children may require this nap regularly up to age 4 or even 5). Most 2-year-olds will have established a regular circadian rhythm, and about one-third can comfortably stay awake to 8 P.M. or later before showing signs that they want to settle in for the night. It is at this age that many children make additional demands upon their parents before settling, and about 25 percent of children take more than half an hour before showing signs of dropping off to sleep. This additional settling time is quite wearing for many parents and is a constant source of complaints.

There are several techniques that seem to help settle children and facilitate their going to sleep without protest. The first involves establishing a predictable and regular ritual associated with settling in for the night. This ritual might involve a pre-bedtime glass of milk, a regular pattern of bathing and putting on pajamas, a brief bedtime story, and maybe a lullaby or soothing song or a spoken prayer before being tucked in for the night. Children appreciate a routine, and it is not unusual for them to ask that the same story be read or told for many nights in a row.

Another technique to help calm childhood fears and permit the child to relax into sleep is the simple use of a night-light. This should be a dim light, just bright enough to allow objects in the room to be identified but not sufficiently bright to disturb sleep or lure the child into other activities. Darkness is often equivalent in the child's mind to abandonment; not being able to see things around you means that you must be alone. In addition, darkness allows familiar objects to metamorphose into terrifying monsters when the child awakens in the middle of the night. Awakening to even a dim view of familiar furniture and favorite toys reassures children and provides a feeling of safety.

Another aid to reducing settling time and improving the continuity of sleep is to provide what psychologists call a transitional object. Usually, this is a stuffed toy or even a familiar blanket. You probably remember the character Linus from the cartoon strip "Peanuts"; his transitional object is his "security blanket," which he requires at all times in order to feel comfortable and safe. The purpose of the transitional object is to ease the way for the child to separate from parents and caretakers. Because the object is soft, it conveys a sense of physical warmth, closeness, and security. Research done on infant monkeys has shown that one of the most important things a mother provides is a soft and warm touching sensation to her young child. If an infant monkey is denied the opportunity to have such comforting touches, it does not develop normally and shows many symptoms of extreme stress. Not only does the transitional object—the stuffed animal, the blanket—provide the important soft contact feelings, but, because it is always available, it usually conveys a sense of permanence and stability.

These feelings are particularly important when children are falling asleep or when they awaken during the night.

Parents should not be surprised or distressed if the transitional object seems to develop a unique importance. As a rule, children develop the habit of taking the object with them wherever they go. The stuffed rabbit or bear is much more than a toy; its presence means familiarity and good feelings, and these are not to be let go of easily. I can still remember my daughter Rebecca sleeping with a plush toy dog she called Barfy. She dragged him around with her all the time, and he got pretty dirty. We once tried to sneak him away during her nightly sleep in order to wash him. She awakened to find him missing and became almost hysterical. Fortunately, Barfy was just finishing his last cycle in the clothes dryer, so we were able to snatch him out and give him back to her. After that, we made sure that she was awake whenever Barfy was washed. She would wait by the washing machine, comforted by a midcycle check that he was still inside. She would then sit patiently in front of the glass window of the dryer and watch Barfy tumbling around until the end of the cycle, when she would snatch him out and hug him while he was still warm.

Eventually, Barfy got so ragged and worn that he was in danger of falling apart. I wandered through a number of toy and department stores to try to find another stuffed dog that looked exactly like him; although some were similar, no duplicate could be found. I eventually hit upon a subterfuge that seemed to work: First I purchased the most similar toy dog that I could find. Then we made a big fuss about doing Rebecca's hair in a different way, using a mirror to show her how different she looked in her new hairstyle. Finally, we told her that we were going to do Barfy's hair in a new style but that it had to be a surprise to her. I then took the frayed toy dog into the next room, leaving the door slightly ajar. I made all the noises appropriate to the occurrence of a spectacular grooming event. I also provided occasional glimpses of the event—first of Barfy's worn head, then of just a paw, then of the paw of the new dog. Finally, I emerged with the new dog under a large bath towel. With great fanfare I revealed "Barfy" in his new hairstyle. Rebecca was ecstatic, hugging Barfy II with great joy and no suspicion at all. (The original Barfy, carefully hidden in a paper bag, was slipped quietly out the house and went to the great toy box in the sky.)

From a psychological point of view, the value of a transitional object goes beyond helping the child fall asleep. It is a companion and a testing ground for ideas and activities; it can even serve as a patient listener when parents are unavailable or appear to be uncaring (for example, by refusing to gratify some wish). As an aid to sleep, though, it is invaluable: it allows the child to learn to fall asleep without the parent's physical presence. In addition, when children awaken in the middle of the night and find their familiar companion right by their side, they learn that there is no need to call for the parent. In this way, the transition object provides both the parent and the child with a better chance for an uninterrupted night of sleep.

At age 2, especially if there is a transitional object present, children have far fewer night wakenings than before (or at least fewer wakenings that require the parent's attention). Only about half of the children will still require a parent to regularly attend to them at least once during the night. However, there are large individual differences, and about 1 in 20 children will continue to waken three or more times each night.

How much sleep is optimal for any given child? Unfortunately, scientists do not have the answer for this since children differ in their sleep needs. However, just as is the case with adults, some children who seem to be getting by with less sleep than their contemporaries might well function better if they were getting more sleep. Children differ from adults in that a developing sleep debt does not always appear in the form of increased daytime sleepiness. Some children who are getting an inadequate amount of sleep develop a very deceptive pattern of symptoms: instead of appearing sleepy, they may actually appear to be hyperactive, showing behaviors that are often described by caretakers as "manic" or "wired." More precisely, these children may show a degree of impulsiveness that, when combined with strong emotional swings, may lead to poor social relations with other children or with caretakers. Sometimes these children show irritability or aggressiveness. They are also often described as being inattentive, as if their minds are drifting or their attention is elsewhere when they are interacting with adults or attending shows or classes.

Most parents can't imagine how a child can develop a sleep debt. However, there are a number of reasons why this is possible. Some have to do with emotional or stress factors in the child, others with an environment that is not conducive to sleep, such as one with too much noise and activity in the vicinity of the child's bed. However, one of the major reasons children often get inadequate sleep is that parents frequently set the child's bedtime and morning wakening to fit in with their own sleep patterns. Children may be sent to bed only an hour or two before the parents go to bed and required to get up in the morning when their parents' alarm clock goes off, in order to join the family in morning activities. Thus, the child, whose sleep need might be 10 or even 12 hours a day, may be attempting to survive on the same 7 hours a night the parents sleep (or at best an hour or two more). Unfortunately, this is not a sufficient amount of sleep for a child.

Suppose that your child is showing either excessive daytime fatigue or the pattern of irritability that I described above. Is there any way that you can tell if this is due to inadequate sleep? There is a simple test that works for many people. The general rule is that children should get enough sleep so that they normally awaken in the morning without the necessity of any parental prodding. If you have to shake your child awake in the mornings—if he or she seems slow getting out of bed or tries to ignore your urgings to get moving in the morning— you may be looking at a child who needs more sleep. Further signs of inadequate sleep are sluggish moving in the mornings and arriving at the breakfast table still yawning, rubbing eyes, or mentally "out of it." If there is any question or possibility that your child is developing a sleep debt, the final test is to simply increase the child's sleep time. If your child has been running up a sleep debt, some improvement in his or her behavior should be seen within the first week or two.

Sometimes, extra sleep works to correct childhood behavior problems. For instance, children who have been diagnosed as hyperactive or as having an attention deficit disorder may show improved behaviors and better school work if their sleep time is extended. One study looked at a 10-year-old girl who had been sleeping just over 7 hours a night. She had been showing poor school performance, an inability to sit in one place to do her schoolwork for any length of time, and poor social interactions with her classmates. When her times for going to sleep and wakening were made more regular and her sleep time was increased by 2 hours, many of her symptoms disappeared. She seemed calmer, worked more efficiently, and had much better social relations with her classmates and teachers.[2] Many parents of "difficult children" are quite surprised at the positive effects a regular increase in sleep time can bring.

Perhaps one of the most important, but least discussed, aspects of childhood sleep patterns is the influence they have on the sleep of the child's parents. A child who hasn't yet developed a standard daily sleep–wakefulness cycle and whose sleep is fragmented may have problems, but he or she is not going to be required to operate dangerous equipment, to drive alertly in traffic, or to make logical and accurate decisions that may influence the future of the family or the success of a business; unfortunately, that child's parents do have to perform such functions even though their own sleep has been badly disturbed by the demands of the child.

Parents of newborns may have to interrupt their own sleep at 90-minute intervals throughout the night, and parents of slightly older children may still have their sleep interrupted several times every night. We have already pointed out that fragmenting sleep, that is, interrupting it at various times each night, reduces its restorative nature. When sleep is fragmented every night over a period of time, people can accumulate a very large sleep debt. Several studies have shown that up to one-third of all parents complain about their children having sleep problems. When carefully explored, the vast majority of these complaints turn out to be due to the disturbance that normal childhood sleep habits have caused in the parent's own sleep behaviors. Unfortunately, these problems do not stop at 3 or 4 months when the child first shows some evidence of being able to sleep through the night but continue on until the child reaches the age of 2 or sometimes 3 years.

Several studies have looked at the effects young children have on their parents' sleep behaviors. Typically, a new baby will result in 400 to 750 hours of sleep lost in the first year, usually averaging more than 2 hours lost each night until the baby is 4 or 5 months of age and then gradually dropping to about 1 hour lost each night from the age of 5 months to about 2 years. With whatever sleep they get being fragmented, some parents seem to sleepwalk their way through the first few months of their child's life. The general findings are that for the first month most of the mothers report a sleep pattern that is quite unconventional. Often, mothers start off actually matching their child's sleep habits by taking many short naps of an hour or two in duration. One mother described it this way to me:

I find that I am tired all of the time. The baby gets up every hour or two and needs some kind of care. I feed him or change him at those times. In between, at least during the day, I just try to sleep whenever I can. I put the baby down, then stretch out on the sofa for a nap. The naps aren't very refreshing. This may be because they are so short. Rickie [the baby] seldom sleeps more than 2 hours. At night Dennis [her husband] gets up and changes the baby if he's messed and brings him to me for feeding. That helps a little since I don't have to really wake up and be alert and I can doze while the baby is nursing. A friend visited yesterday and asked what I wanted as a baby gift. I told her that all that I wanted was a good night's sleep. She didn't believe me, but it's true. I feel like I'm in a half-doze all of the time.

This mother's actual total sleep time was about 7 hours, only one hour less than before the child was born. However, her sleep was clearly fragmented and was probably neither deep nor efficient. It is the sleep fragmentation that is probably the greater culprit here; 7 hours of fragmented sleep may be only equivalent to 5½ hours of continuous sleep in the ability to restore mental efficiency.

One mother, Robin Abcarian, wrote of her experiences in a humorous vein:[3]

My once-large circle of friends has dwindled to a few people who became parents around the same time I did. We have devolved from interesting, articulate, involved, and curious people into sleep-deprived, nap-craving parents of small children. . . . Our every conversation begins on the same sad note: how little sleep we got the night before.

It's a complete perversion of the keeping-up-with-the-Joneses mentality we laugh at in other people: "You got up with the baby at 4? Ours woke us up at 2, 3, and 4! Top that, you pathetically well-rested fool!"

Husbands often don't fare much better. They are often asked to assist with the night wakenings but still have to keep to their work schedules; this means that they can't make up their sleep debt with day naps. For example, one new father told me:

I think that Alice decided not to breast-feed Katie so that I could get up and take care of her at night. This first month has been hell. I'm up every hour and a half. It then takes me a half hour to feed and change her, and then I head back to bed. I think that I pass out as soon as my head touches the pillow. Anyhow, I'm really tired. Today I sat down for lunch with the guys at work, and I just fell asleep. They woke me in time to get back to the job. I'm afraid that I may have fallen asleep at work last Wednesday. Charlie said that the foreman was looking for me. He told him he thought that I was on the toilet, and then he came to get me. He said I was sitting at the back workbench with my head leaning on the side wall and my eyes closed when he found me. What keeps me from getting really stressed out is knowing that this will only last for a couple of months.

Unfortunately, the presumption that the child's sleep patterns will approximate those of an adult in a few months, hence letting the parents sleep normally again, is really not true. Most parents continue to have fragmented sleep because children awaken during the night and demand attention well into the second year of life. Intermittent awakenings can continue up to the age of 5. Compared to childless couples of the same age, parents of 2-year-olds still report more daytime fatigue, reduced motivation, bouts of depression, and concerns about their work efficiency, as well as a higher accident rate. All of these are symptoms associated with a sleep debt. Perhaps the situation was best summed up by the poet and essayist Ralph Waldo Emerson, who noted in 1836, "There was never a child so lovely but his mother was glad to get him asleep."

TWELVE TIPS FOR SLEEPY PARENTS
AND SLEEPLESS CHILDREN

Here are a few things parents can do to help establish regular, all-night sleep patterns in their children:

For infants

1. Never wake a sleeping baby—not even for a scheduled feeding. The child will set his or her own sleep and wakefulness schedule. If you interfere you will make the pattern more inconsistent and slow progress toward a regular 24-hour cycle.

2. Make sure your baby has a full feeding at the end of the day.

3. Keep these nighttime feedings very quiet and low-key. Dim the lights and keep talking, singing, cooing, and eye contact to a minimum.

4. Make daytime feedings exciting: Interact, talk, sing, play. Turn the lights up bright or, better still, feed your baby near a window where daylight comes in.

5. Sometime between 9 and 12 months, eliminate the nighttime feeding. Simply let the baby cry until he or she falls asleep, which usually takes only 10 to 20 minutes. After three or four nights, most babies will sleep through the night.

For both young children and infants

6. Provide a transitional object, for example, a stuffed animal or a doll. It should be small enough that a 1-year-old can drag it around but large enough to be easily found in bed at night.

7. Use the bed or crib only for sleep, and do not keep toys (except the transitional object) in it. Use a playpen or safe part of a room for waking activities like play.

8. Avoid cocoa and cola or other soft drinks before bed. Milk is acceptable.

continued

9. Develop predictable bedtime activities. Always put the child to bed at the same time. Use the same sequence of behaviors, such as having a bit of milk, washing, putting on pajamas, saying good night to the family pet, and so forth.

10. Keep a nightlight in the child's room.

11. For some children, a low-level sound such as a softly playing radio or, even better, white noise (see page 161), will help.

12. Do not make yourself too available to your child during the night. When the child fusses or cries, wait a few minutes before entering the room. If it stops, don't go in. If it continues, go in and soothe (don't pamper) the child. Rub the child's back or chest lightly once or twice. Make sure she or he is comfortable (and dry), but avoid picking the child up. For older children, add verbal reassurances by saying something brief like "Everything is OK. Mommy and Daddy are right next door. Go to sleep." Then leave.

Sleepy Teenagers

In *The Winter's Tale*, Shakespeare has one of his characters comment, "I would there were no age between ten and three-and-twenty, or that youth would sleep out the rest; for there is nothing in the between but getting wenches with child, wronging the ancientry, stealing and fighting." Obviously, adolescents do not "sleep out" this period of their lives. In fact, current evidence suggests that adolescents may be an extremely sleep-deprived group. Some researchers even suggest that some of the impulsive, irresponsible, and unthinking behaviors often seen at this age may be a consequence of this lack of sleep.

Between the ages of 6 and puberty (let's call it 12), the total amount of sleep children get shows a steady decline. While the 6-year-old may be getting 10 or 11 hours of sleep, the 12-year-old, about to enter adolescence, is typically getting 8½ hours of sleep a night. Children shorten their sleep time by extending their activities into the night. Some of these activities might be related to school, such as homework or studying; however, many are social or recreational in nature. Children tend to fill their evenings with television, listening to music, game playing, and socializing with friends (either in person or over the telephone). In other words, these children are doing exactly what their parents do. They are allowed to push back their bedtimes but are still committed to getting up early. After all, their schedule is locked into the beginning of the schoolday in the same way that their parents' wakening is fixed

119

by the start of their workday. As the American writer James A. Baldwin put it, "Children have never been very good at listening to their elders, but they have never failed to imitate them."

Unfortunately, adopting the shortened sleep length that adults have is not a good idea for teenagers, either physically or psychologically. We find many individuals in later childhood showing patterns of thinking and acting, as well as variations in mood, that are common for people who are carrying a sleep debt. Laboratory research by Drs. Mary A. Carskadon and William Dement suggests that 10 hours of sleep are needed to fulfill the sleep needs of 12-year-olds. In fact, 10 hours of sleep may also be a fair estimate of the requirements of older adolescents as well.[1]

It is in adolescence that we begin to see real evidence of sleep debt in children. From age 10 to 18 we see a steady pushing back of the time at which young people go to bed. It is not unusual for a 10-year-old to go to bed at 9 P.M. while the 18-year-old delays this until 1:30 A.M. on a weekday night. Some of this delay is due to the increasing demands from schoolwork and extracurricular activities on the adolescent's time, but some comes from the fact that additional time is often spent in working at a part-time job, either for luxury items and entertainment or for more vital purposes such as tuition and school expenses. There is evidence that teenagers who work more than 20 hours a week have very high levels of daytime sleepiness because of the inevitable lack of sleep.

There is a social factor that leads to sleep debt in teenagers as well. While most adults sleep longer on weekends in order to try to make up their sleep loss, many teenagers actually sleep less. Teenagers will often use the weekends for long nights of social activity. Although they might sleep late the morning after a night out, the actual amount of time spent asleep may be less than they get during the school week. This means that on Monday morning, when the alarm goes off, a teenager's sleep debt may actually be larger than it was on Friday. With this pattern of behavior the average teenager can build up a sizable sleep debt over the school year.

Sleep debt is more than a minor problem for teenagers. There have now been several large surveys of sleep habits for this age group, and one consistent finding is that more than half the teenagers studied wish that they had more time for sleep. There is evidence that during vacation periods, especially when away from home and in settings where social pressures for late night activities are reduced, teenagers revert to a sleep pattern in which they commonly sleep between 10 and 11 hours each day. This sleep duration seems to be much more consistent with estimates of their actual sleep requirements. On their usual sleep diet at home during the school year, most teenagers report bouts of sleepiness during the day. Teenagers also show periodic reductions in their alertness and their performance levels in tasks that require focused attention, precise movements, memory, problem solving, and other cognitive skills. These problems are frequently associated with times when the adolescent reaches a level of sleepiness in which he or she begins to have brief, unpredictable microsleeps, such as the afternoon low point in the daily circadian cycle. During these microsleeps the person simply slips, without any warning, into a sleep state for periods of a few seconds up to several minutes. An example of this comes from Alonzo, a 17-year-old high school junior:

I was sitting in my history class, with my notebook open and my pencil out, the way that I always do. This class is always hard 'cause it starts right after lunch and I'm tired then. That day Mr. G. was talking about taxes or something during the time when America was still an English colony. He was saying something about whisky and Pennsylvania, which wasn't too clear to me. The next thing I know, everybody is standing up. It took me a minute to figure out that class was over. I didn't hardly remember it starting. I looked at my notes for the class. I had written only two words: "Whisky Revolution." It freaked me a little. I knew I was tired and all that, but this was like just being unconscious.

One of the major signs of a teenager's sleep debt is the difficulty the parents have in waking him or her. While preadolescent children tend to wake up spontaneously in the morning and seem eager to start the day, adolescents and college students often need several reminders and prodding. The following solution to the problem of awakening is typical of college students:

Especially when I have a test in the morning, I really need more than one alarm clock. I set the clock-radio alarm next to the bed and make it loud.

Then I set this world-class loud wind-up alarm on the dresser all the way across the room. I set it for 15 minutes later. I sleep through the clock-radio alarm a lot, but I have to get out of bed to turn the other alarm off or it will wake everybody in the house. That usually wakes me.

One story from a parent's viewpoint comes from the father of a college student:

Jeff had slept through one of his chemistry lab quizzes and was worried about doing it again. So he says to me, "Dad, you got to make sure I'm awake tomorrow because we've got another lab quiz. Just give me a good shake, and if I'm not awake kick me out of bed." So the next morning I go in, and he's like dead to the world. So I shake him, but he just makes noises. Finally, I got frustrated, so I grabbed his mattress by these little handles sewn on the sides and I flipped him right out of bed and onto the floor. "You up?" I asked him. "Yeah, Dad, I'm up," he says. So then I go off to work. When I get home that night, he's really angry at me. "Why didn't you stop and make sure I was up?" he asks. "I slept through the damn quiz again." So I say to him, "I rolled you onto the floor and you said you were awake." And he says to me, "You should have stayed and made sure I was awake. I always lie when I'm asleep!"

The common difficulty noted by parents in rousing their teenage off-spring is one clear sign that they are not getting enough sleep. It may also be a sign that teenagers are suffering from a shift in their internal clocks. Dr. Mary A. Carskadon of Brown University has data that suggests that teenagers may have a *phase advance*, meaning that their circadian clock wants them to get up later and go to sleep later than most adults. A child's clock pattern seems to make a sharp change at around the time of puberty, and then it continues through to the 20s. In effect, teenagers become more like owls—happiest in the evening hours. One solution to the circadian shift in adolescence would be to shift the hours of high school so that the school day starts later and ends later.

Making changes in educational schedules to accommodate the internal timers of adolescents makes sense educationally. However, it is difficult to fit such changes into an already complex schedule of athletic and other after-school activities. Such changes would also conflict with the life rhythms of the adult world. In addition, some people feel that making such changes would be equivalent to "coddling" teenagers rather than forcing them to meet their responsibilities, which obviously include complying with educational schedules.

Some college administrators have now become aware of the problems associated with this pattern of teenage behavior. One of them reported that many classes that are held early in the mornings have absenteeism rates as high as 40 percent, even when the classes are taught by popular instructors. One university department head told me the following:

> *For a while we recommended that required first- and second-year courses not be held in the first two or three hours of the day but should be pushed off until the afternoon. At least then we know that most students are prone to be awake and on campus. Unfortunately, this led to a space crisis. We didn't have enough lecture halls for the large first-year classes that were all trying to squeeze into the afternoon. When a committee came up with a suggestion that we build more lecture theaters for this purpose, the Provost exploded: "If they [the students] can't get the hell out of bed in time to attend classes, then that is their problem. The next thing I expect is that the committee will be asking that we install cots in the lecture halls for the comfort of students who like to sleep in class!"*

Perhaps one of the aspects of adolescent sleep that is most important for later life is the fact that teenagers are developing the adult attitude toward sleep, that is, the attitude that whenever anything interesting or important comes up that requires more time, the way you find that time is by cheating on sleep. This kind of behavior in college students is reflected in expressions like "burning the midnight oil" or "pulling an all-nighter." These terms are usually applied to studying deep into the night before an exam or in order to finish a paper or other required project. Since school in adolescence is equivalent to employment in adulthood, the patterns of behavior teenagers develop toward work, leisure time, and sleep are usually carried over into their adult lives.

All-nighters are mostly the result of instances in which the student has simply put off doing required work or studying because there were more interesting or pressing activities to pursue. As the deadline grows closer, time must be stolen from somewhere to make up for the earlier procrastination. This usually means sacrificing sleep for an all-night work or study session. Students are rewarded for this effort in two ways: First, they are rewarded socially by friends and even by parents, who seem to admire such heroic efforts and often view the sleep loss involved as evidence that the student is committed, ambitious, energetic, or at least tough enough to take the stress. This reflects the attitude of society as a whole. The person who sleeps in is viewed as lazy while the person who goes without sleep is strong and to be admired. The second way in which the student is rewarded is by the actual results. At least for material that requires rote memorization (such as language courses, some aspects of history courses, and aspects of science courses that require learning labels for species, body parts, geological formations, and so forth), cramming all of the material into one extended night of study works—sort of. This kind of material can be held in memory despite the sleep loss, at least for a short while. Often it is retained for long enough to make it through the exam. Unfortunately, this material is soon lost from memory. In the absence of adequate sleep the memories do not "consolidate" (which is the technical term for being entered into our long-term memory storage). Long-term memory is virtually unlimited in capacity and relatively indestructible. Studies have shown that foreign words learned in a high school course but never again used can be remembered 50 years later if they made it into long-term memory when they were originally learned. Conversely, items that do not make it into long-term memory begin to fade and are quickly lost.

All-nighters are also not very effective in learning material that requires the student to solve complex logical problems or use "divergent thinking." Divergent thinking is important when we are trying to come up with creative solutions or when problem solving requires us to be flexible and try new approaches. There is a good deal of research that shows that it is these aspects of thinking that are lost most quickly following sleep loss. Thus, all-nighters might work for a course where students "spit back" memorized material, but when this material must be used to solve problems or discuss complicated issues or points of view, they are not very effective. This also means that if the student is going without sleep in order to finish a term paper and if this term paper is going to be graded on the basis of the quality and originality of thought, the all-nighter is really counterproductive. Papers produced during all-nighters often seem flat and uninspired and frequently show obvious gaps in logic and organization.

Despite evidence that losing sleep in order to study is not a productive strategy, it still seems to be admired and demanded by segments of our society. In fact, in some cultures the process has become quite institutionalized. In Japan, for example, students are under a lot of pressure to do well in the national college entrance exams. As part of what is viewed as "diligent studying," many students attend special schools known as *juku* after the regular schoolday is finished. These schools attempt to cram as much material into the students as possible. Following *juku*, the students are expected to go home and continue studying. It is not unusual for them to continue their study deep into the night. Students are often actually encouraged to reduce the amount of sleep they take nightly in order to study. A common expression many Japanese students have adopted as their motto is "Pass with four, fail with five"; the numbers refer to the number of hours of sleep the students take each night. If, as research shows, this process is not very useful as a strategy to produce good long-term retention of the learned material and if this sleep loss is actually reducing the quality of creative and original thinking in these students, why is it encouraged? Some cultural researchers have suggested that the Japanese system serves as a sort of initiation rite: by doing well on the exams, especially under these conditions, students prove to colleges and also to future employers that they have the stamina, ambition, and personal fortitude to take the pressure and still succeed.

Sleep Thieves in the Kitchen 🍴

One way to add to your sleep debt involves a simple trip to the kitchen. Throughout human history we have used various foods, drinks, potions, and concoctions to induce changes in our mental states. Although some changes in mental state may be extremely subtle, basically there are two kinds of changes that dominate all others. There are things we eat or drink to make us more alert (stimulants) and things we eat or drink that make us calmer and sleepier (depressants). It is quite amazing to find that people often have great misconceptions about which substances perform which of these functions. This means that when trying to improve our sleep we often make the situation worse.

Many foods, even those that seem very comforting and safe, may contain hidden stimulants that can disrupt our sleep for hours. The most common hidden stimulant is caffeine, which is one of a group of organic compounds that occurs naturally in more than 60 species of plants. Most of us know that caffeine is apt to be found in coffee and tea; however, it is much more pervasive than that and is found in soft drinks, some baked goods (where it is used for flavoring), and many over-the-counter drugs.

Caffeine produces such a vigorous stimulant effect on the body that it is medically classified as a drug. One of the striking facts about caffeine is that it operates so quickly. It blasts its way into the bloodstream

126

within minutes and begins to produce neurological effects immediately. Caffeine's effects peak within 30 minutes to 1 hour, which is about the time its concentration in the blood is greatest. It may then take up to 6 hours for the drug to effectively clear from the system. Virtually every culture around the world has developed some form of caffeine-containing drink.

The source of caffeine that has the greatest antiquity is probably tea. There are suggestions that nearly 5,000 years ago aboriginal tribesmen in Asia were preparing tea by boiling green leaves of wild tea trees in kettles over campfires. A medical diary dated 2737 B.C. and attributed to the legendary Chinese emperor Shen Nung declares, "It quenches thirst. It lessens the desire to sleep. It gladdens and cheers the heart."

In the 6th century tea spread to Japan, where it was first used by Zen monks. They needed the caffeine stimulation in order to stay awake during the long sessions of meditation. Tea drinking eventually became a part of Zen rituals and ultimately led to the formal Japanese tea ceremony *chado* ("the way of tea").

Tea was introduced into Europe in the mid-1500s by Jesuit missionaries returning from Asia. Some historians say that the importance of tea as a drink and an opportunity for afternoon socializing in England was confirmed when Catherine of Braganza, who was destined to be the wife of King Charles II, brought chests of tea leaves with her as part of her dowry. As the popularity of the beverage spread to the whole population, tea was already singled out for criticism by those who were major proponents of the industrial revolution: one important English economist of the middle 1800s lambasted tea, blaming it for paralyzing the English economy, his argument being that time previously used for work was now being spent in the unproductive activity of tea drinking.

Tea comes from the buds, leaves, and stems of one species of plant, namely, *Camellia sinensis*. Technically, then, herbal teas are not really tea. Tea is classified into three broad groups on the basis of the way it is prepared. Black teas have been fermented in the enzyme released when withered tea leaves are crushed. This method produces the sweetest of the teas, which have a rich amber color. The fermentation of tea can be stopped by steaming or roasting the tea leaves. Green teas are unfermented and produce a mild, slightly bitter, pale greenish-yellow brew. Partially fermented teas include the oolong varieties; these produce a pale brown-green tea with a distinct smoky flavor.

Regardless of how tea is prepared, about 4 percent of the solid matter in tea leaves is caffeine. Depending on the heat of the water, the steeping time, and the amount of tea actually used, an 8-ounce cup of tea will contain between 40 and 90 milligrams of caffeine. This is enough to noticeably increase alertness in most people. Tea can be decaffeinated by rinsing it with methylene chloride, a solvent that dissolves the caffeine out of the leaves.

Although there is a popular belief that tea can be a calming bedtime drink (especially if certain additions, such as milk and honey, are included), this is false. Experiments show that tea drinking increases the time it takes to fall asleep, reduces the amount of slow-wave deep sleep, and makes the night's sleep more restless.

Everybody knows that coffee also contains caffeine. The amount of coffee consumed in the world today is greater than that of any other beverage except water, with the United States having the highest per capita consumption rate. Current estimates are that every day in the United States 550 million cups of coffee are consumed.

Many legends describe the discovery of coffee. One of the most popular is of an Arab goatherder named Kaldi who lived in the middle of the 9th century. Kaldi noticed that when his goats ate the red berries from one particular bush, they acted oddly; they seemed more frisky and frolicsome. He then took a chance and chewed some of the berries himself. When the result was a feeling of friskiness in himself, he took the news of the wonders of the coffee berries to his fellow tribesmen. Over the next 400 years people consumed coffee just as Kaldi had: Arabs simply chewed the coffee berries in order to get the stimulating effect.

In the 13th century Arabs began to brew a beverage from roasted coffee berry seeds. This drink became so popular that coffee plants were exported throughout southern Arabia. The Muslim population of this region developed an enthusiasm for caffeine that verged on an addiction to it. It was prized because of its ability to energize people. It was believed that the invigorating effects improved a man's fighting ability and sexual prowess. In fact, the effects were so widely touted that a religious problem arose: One orthodox Islamic priest declared that coffee was an intoxicant and, since all intoxicants are banned by the Koran, the holy book of Islam, coffee also must be banned. The ever-clever Arabs managed to find a way out of this quandary by pointing out that the stimulating effects of coffee allowed its users to engage in longer and more vigorous religious devotions and also kept them awake and alert into the night so that they could be more vigilant against the enemies of Islam. As a compromise, however, for many years in some Arabic regions women were forbidden to have coffee (it was feared that their "frail minds" might not be able to withstand the exhilarating effects of this beverage).

There are two popular sources for coffee. The original Ethiopian plant is *Coffea arabica;* a related African plant is *Coffea robusta.* Both varieties produce fragrant white jasminelike flowers that produce the berries that contain the coffee bean (actually a seed), which is dried and roasted. Coffee differs from tea in that the way in which it is initially prepared has a major effect on the amount of caffeine in the final product. Longer roasting makes the coffee beans darker and raises their caffeine content.

The sleep-inhibiting component of coffee is, of course, the caffeine. Dry coffee grounds from beans taken from C. *arabica* contain about 1.2 percent of caffeine by weight. Coffee from C. *robusta* has nearly twice the caffeine content, averaging around 2.3 percent caffeine by weight. A typical cup of coffee, then, using one of the blends common in the United States (which are mostly made up of C. *arabica* beans) contains 80 to 120 milligrams of caffeine. A cup of coffee made from pure C. *robusta* has nearly twice this level of caffeine, with a range from 160 to 220 milligrams. Instant coffee contains significantly less caffeine, averaging around 65 milligrams per cup.

The first decaffeinated coffee can be credited to Dr. Ludwig Roselius, the head of a large European coffee-marketing business—and to luck. In 1903 a ship load of coffee consigned to Roselius was deluged with sea water during a storm. Since the coffee was now considered to be unfit for commercial sale, Roselius turned it over to a group of chemists in Montreal to see if anything could be salvaged. When the chemists examined the coffee, they found that most of the caffeine had been leached out of the beans by the immersion in the sea water. With appropriate washing, the salts could be removed, leaving a coffee that tasted much like the original but had up to 97 percent of the caffeine removed, typically leaving less than 3 milligrams per 8-ounce serving. Roselius named the new product Sanka, which is simply a contraction of the French phrase *sans caffeine*, meaning "without caffeine."

An average cup of coffee contains enough caffeine to disrupt sleep quite significantly. Although the caffeine works very quickly, it is often slow to clear from the body. It is metabolized by the liver in a process that typically takes 3 to 6 hours in adults. In older individuals the clearing time is considerably longer and may take up to 24 hours. A single cup of coffee taken 2 hours before going to bed has been shown to more than double the amount of time it takes an average adult to fall asleep. In addition, it halves the amount of deep slow-wave sleep that night and may quadruple the number of nighttime awakenings that the person will suffer.

Many people are completely unaware that chocolate contains caffeine, along with some other stimulants. Chocolate is a product of the New World. Its flavor is derived from cocoa beans from a tree found in South and Central America called *Theobroma*, which literally translates to "food of the gods."

Chocolate came to Europe via the Spanish conquistadors who had come to appreciate the mild exhilaration that the stimulants in it produce. The beverage, eventually called cocoa, was made by dissolving chocolate in hot water and adding generous amounts of sugar and small amounts of ground vanilla and cinnamon. The drink became such a sensation in the Spanish royal court that King Ferdinand declared that the recipe was a national secret. No one was to disclose any information about this new drink, under penalty of death. This clearly put a scare into those who knew how cocoa was made, and the process remained a secret for a full century. It was the Spanish princess Maria Theresa who literally "spilled the beans." When she married King Louis XIV of France, in 1660, she arrived with several cases of cocoa as part of her dowry. The French royal court went wild over this new drink, and it was soon being spread throughout Europe.

Chocolate also was beginning to take some different forms. The process of making cocoa butter was developed in the Netherlands in the early 1800s. In 1847 the English company Fry and Sons created the first "solid eating chocolate" by mixing finely ground sugar with the cocoa butter, which produced a very dark, sweet confection. Daniel

Peter of Switzerland is credited with the process of making milk chocolate, which initially involved adding milk powder to the mix. The Swiss immediately fell in love with this new sweet, and even today Switzerland has the highest per capita consumption of chocolate in the world. The Swiss eat an average of 20 pounds of chocolate per person each year. Americans also eat a lot of chocolate, but they average only about 11 pounds per year.

Chocolate is a stimulant because it contains not only caffeine but also another stimulant, theobromine. Work done in the 1980s suggested that chocolate contained a number of other compounds that are chemically similar to some components in amphetamines. This means that when we focus on only the caffeine content of chocolate, we are actually underestimating its stimulant value. Because of the nature of the chemistry involved, it appears that the amounts of the other stimulants in chocolate are related to the amount of caffeine in it. That is, an increase in the amount of caffeine is associated with an increase in the amounts of the other stimulants. One researcher has suggested that the actual stimulant effect of a chocolate product is about double the amount of caffeine in it. Generally speaking, the darker the chocolate the more caffeine there is in it. A 1½ ounce serving of dark chocolate will have 32 milligrams of caffeine; the same serving size of milk chocolate will contain only 9 milligrams of caffeine. White chocolate is not even officially chocolate—it contains too little of the material extracted from the cocoa bean; thus, in the United States white chocolate must be called something else, like "confectionary coating" or "Swiss snow candy."

Many people drink hot cocoa to relax before going to sleep. A typical cup of hot chocolate contains around 15 milligrams of caffeine plus the other stimulants; together, these ingredients give an arousing effect equal to that from approximately 30 milligrams of caffeine. This is less than a cup of coffee or tea but may still be enough to disturb sleep in some people. Some food producers have now produced caffeine-reduced hot chocolate drink mixes to address this problem.

Most people are quite surprised to find that apparently innocent soda pop, such as Pepsi-Cola, Dr. Pepper, Mountain Dew, or Sunkist Orange, actually contain significant amounts of stimulants, usually in the form of caffeine. The original carbonated sodas contained neither caffeine nor flavorants of any sort. They were simply attempts to duplicate the effervescence of water from mineral springs, which was extremely popular during the late 1700s and continues to be so even today. These waters were considered to be pure and pleasant to drink, and were also believed to provide various health benefits. Carbonated water was first marketed around 1800 and was labeled "imitation mineral waters." Shortly thereafter, people began to flavor the soda water, and within 80 years a number of familiar brand names began to appear.

Probably the best-known soft drink in the world is Coca-Cola. It was originally created by John S. Pemberton, who had been a Confederate cavalry officer and was also a graduate pharmacist (hence, he was known around Atlanta, Georgia, as both "Major" and "Doctor"). Pemberton was looking for a stimulant product (the 1880s equivalent of No-Doz or Vivarin) and ended up using two powerful stimulants. He turned first to the cocoa plant but not for the chocolate: he wanted the cocaine that is extracted from the leaves. In low doses cocaine has a simple stimulating effect, equivalent to ten times its weight in caffeine. Next Pemberton added an extract of the African "hell seed," which we know as the kola nut. The kola nut extract contains highly concentrated caffeine and was prized for its stimulant effect when incorporated into various medicinal potions. The problem with the extracts of both the cocoa leaf and the kola nut is that they are quite bitter and unpleasant to taste. To mask this taste, Pemberton then added large amounts of sugar and flavoring. The major components of this flavoring were citrus, cinnamon, and vanilla, blended so that no one individual flavor dominates. The result of this combination of sugar, flavoring and the two active ingredients was a syrup, which was named Coca-Cola by Pemberton's business partner, Frank M. Robinson. (The second half of the name is *cola*, not *kola*, simply because he thought the two capital Cs looked better in the Spencerian writing script he had chosen for the logo.)

During its early years Coca-Cola was sold in pharmacies in its syrup form, and it was meant to be taken straight or mixed into water. After Pemberton died, the rights to the formula were bought by Asa G. Candler, another pharmacist from Atlanta. He began to promote it as not just a stimulant but a general health tonic and beverage. The taste became popular, and Coca-Cola was commonly sold as a soda fountain drink created by mixing the syrup with carbonated water. The specific formula for Coca-Cola remains one of the company's most guarded secrets. It is claimed that only two people know the full formula and that company policy forbids them to ever travel in the same airplane. Despite this, we do know some important facts about the formula. To begin with, after 1903 cocaine was no longer included in the recipe. We also know that chemically pure caffeine is still being added to the drink to give it stimulant properties. Every 12-ounce serving of Coca-Cola still contains around 35 milligrams of caffeine.

Given the popularity of Coca-Cola, it is not surprising that a number of other cola drinks have appeared as competitors. Virtually all of these also have healthy doses of caffeine in them. A 12-ounce serving of Pepsi-Cola contains 37 milligrams of caffeine, and Tab contains 44 milligrams. Many noncola drinks also contain caffeine. Some citrus-flavored soda drinks (like Mountain Dew, with 52 milligrams, or Sunkist Orange, with 42 milligrams) have doses of caffeine that approximate the caffeine content of a cup of tea. The non-caffeine-containing soft drinks, such as 7-Up, Fresca, and Hires Root Beer, have managed to keep a good share of the market, but, in general, soft drinks with caffeine have continued to outsell those without.

While most adults are not particularly fond of drinking carbonated soft drinks shortly before bed, it is quite common for many modern parents to allow their young children to drink these beverages with dinner (or sometimes as a bribe to go to bed peacefully). Since the caffeine concentration in the blood will peak within 30 to 60 minutes, this is obviously not a good choice for a bedtime inducement. Furthermore, given the child's metabolism, it may take 5 to 7 hours for the caffeine to be effectively cleared from the child's system. Thus, the cola drink with dinner at 6 P.M. may well be the reason the child is still restless and sleepless at midnight.

There is one truly hidden and insidious way in which caffeine can disrupt sleep. Caffeine may pass from a nursing mother's blood and accumulate in the breast milk. Mothers of young infants are typically quite sleep deprived, as we have already seen. Such a mother may drink a lot of coffee because the caffeine helps to keep her awake enough to do her daily work. However, to the extent that she is passing some of her own caffeine on to her child, the child will be more restless and will have a more fitful sleep. Thus, we end up with a vicious cycle in which the child sleeps poorly because it is ingesting caffeine through its mother's milk and the mother, awake most of the day, must take in more caffeine to function, which in turn, raises the dose of caffeine in the child's milk, and so forth.

In some respects, the effectiveness and popularity of caffeine may well be another indication of the sleep-deprived state of society. Caffeine increases our alertness and can make us function better both mentally and physically, especially when we are doing tasks that require a lot of sustained attention, like monitoring a radar screen or doing continuous quality checks on a production line. Similarly, people who are deprived of sleep can often maintain their normal levels of performance with doses of caffeine. The odd fact is that several studies have shown that if we begin with well-rested and alert people, who have no evidence of any sleep debt, their performance is *not* improved by giving them caffeine. What this suggests is that caffeine doesn't simply perk us up and increase our arousal state; rather, it offsets or erases some of the symptoms of fatigue that we have developed through inadequate sleep. If our performance has not been degraded by insufficient sleep, then there is no benefit conveyed by caffeine. This may well help explain why more coffee and tea is being consumed in highly industrialized societies, where time pressure is greatest.

While caffeine is the most widely used psychoactive drug in the world, the second most widely used legal drug is also a stimulant. When tobacco is smoked, nicotine, the major active ingredient of tobacco is released. Despite health warnings and restrictions placed on smoking in public in many places, in the United States about 32 percent of adult men and 27 percent of adult women still smoke, which averages out to a consumption of about 2,800 cigarettes a year per adult in the United States. Smoking is even more common in many other countries. In Italy, France, and Japan, there is some evidence that tobacco smoking may actually be on the increase. Tobacco was first introduced into Europe by Christopher Columbus. When he discovered the Americas, he found native Indians using it much the same way we do today. These Indians attributed various medicinal properties to tobacco, and it was for this reason that Columbus brought it home with him. It was, however, the stimulating and addictive qualities of nicotine that ensured its popularity.

When you smoke tobacco, the nicotine in it is readily absorbed by the mucous membranes lining your mouth. The rate at which you absorb nicotine from smoke drawn into the lungs is almost as efficient as if it were administered intravenously with a needle. The nicotine in tobacco smoke reaches the brain in about 8 seconds after you inhale the smoke. The surge of arousal this causes is described as being very pleasurable and satisfying. The main effects of nicotine are increased alertness and reduced sleepiness; there is some suggestion that it may actually facilitate some thinking processes by improving memory. Nicotine acts both directly and indirectly. The indirect action includes the release of epinephrine (commonly known as adrenaline) and the related hormone norepinephrine (noradrenaline), both of which are powerful stimulants that increase heart rate and blood pressure.

The amount of nicotine in tobacco varies with the species of tobacco and the manner in which it is cured and prepared. Dark air-cured and fire-cured tobaccos contain around 4.5 percent nicotine, while flue-cured tobaccos contain only around 3 percent. The popular Burly tobacco contains around 4 percent nicotine, while the Maryland and Turkish tobaccos, which make up much of cigarette fillers, contain about 2 percent. Fermenting the tobacco, which is common in the preparation of cigars and many types of pipe tobacco, reduces the nicotine content and hence also reduces the overall effects of nicotine on the body.

Nicotine is quite addictive. Within an hour after smoking a cigarette, when the nicotine concentration in the blood has been reduced by about half, the craving for another cigarette will typically begin. It is quite difficult to stop smoking once addicted to it, and some estimates suggest that only about 20 percent of people are able to do this for longer than 2 years.

What is important to us here is that the use of nicotine has been shown to have negative effects on sleep. Several studies have shown that smokers who consume about one pack a day typically have difficulty falling asleep. Their brain wave pattern shows that they do not sleep as deeply, and this is supported by the fact that when they stop smoking, there is a sort of rebound effect in which the smoker seems to be getting much more slow-wave deep sleep, apparently to make up the sleep that has been lost previously. When smokers do manage to stop, they may initially complain of sleepiness and fatigue, although their brain wave recordings indicate an improvement in sleep. This fatigue is not due to poor sleep but, rather, to the fact that the smoker is no longer taking in many doses of the stimulant nicotine during the day.

Another way in which nicotine affects sleep is through its effect on the smoker's respiratory system. Smoking tends to increase congestion in the nose and throat. It also causes swelling of the mucous membranes lining the throat and the upper air passages. These factors tend to increase snoring and to make the symptoms of some sleep disturbances, like sleep apnea, worse. Smoking also reduces the ability of the lungs to take in oxygen from the air. Thus, with more constricted air passages and reduced oxygen uptake, the smoker is more apt to briefly awaken many times a night gasping for air. These awakenings may go unnoticed by the smoker, except for daytime fatigue and sleepiness, although they are often quite noticeable to bed partners and family.

As in the case of caffeine, nicotine passes to the breast milk of mothers who smoke. Some studies have shown that infants whose mothers smoke are more than twice as likely to have difficulty sleeping as infants of nonsmokers. The guess is that this is because the infant has now, in effect, become a second-hand smoker and suffers all the consequent sleep disruptions from nicotine intake.

We have been dealing with stimulants so far. There are, however, some common foods and beverages that have been used to actually induce or trigger the onset of sleep. I will not be dealing with prescription controlled sleeping pills, such as the barbiturates, since these are not apt to be unknowingly self-administered in the course of preparing a snack from your refrigerator.

In passing, it might be worthwhile to say something about nonprescription sleep medications. Virtually all of these are antihistamines, similar to the compound you take to relieve a runny nose. Early in the development of antihistamines it was found that many of them had the side effect of making people drowsy. Some drug manufacturers have capitalized on this side effect and now market these antihistamines solely for their sedative effects. Experts are not very enthusiastic about these drugs. They have a very mild effect generally, are usually slow in their initial effects, and are slow clearing from the body. The slow clearing often means that people are actually suffering from daytime sleepiness and fatigue because of the medication they took the night before to help induce sleep.

If you are looking for an over-the-counter drug that might help you, you might look at the most used medication in the world today, namely, aspirin. People in the United States, for example, take 80 million aspirin tablets a year, which would amount to about 16,000 tons. Throughout the Middle Ages it was known that tea made from willow bark is good for curing fevers and pains and also seems to produce more restful sleep. In 1874 the first aspirin factory was built in Dresden, Germany, and it used the formula that we use today, namely, acetylsalicylic acid, which is a compound made of salicylic acid (the active component of willow bark), and acetic acid (commonly found in vinegar). The pharmaceutical firm belonged to Friedrich Bayer, and he patented the product and sold it under the name of "aspirin." I am told that the name comes from St. Asprinius, the patron saint of headaches.

Many people have claimed that taking aspirin does help them to sleep. Peter Hauri of the Mayo Clinic in Rochester, Minnesota, showed that for many insomniacs this is true. The aspirin, however, works mostly in the second half of the night, increasing the total amount of time people remain asleep and decreasing the number of nighttime awakenings. The dose is two tablets at bedtime, which should be taken with a large glass of water. The water is critical, since an aspirin tablet lying relatively dry on the stomach wall while you sleep through the night can cause a serious stomach ulcer by morning.

The most commonly self-prescribed drug to induce sleep is ethyl alcohol from whisky, beer, wine, or liqueurs. Virtually everyone who has used alcohol has observed the relaxing feeling associated with it. After just a few drinks one often begins to feel noticeably drowsy. This side effect is often sought out by people who are having trouble sleeping.

The effects of alcohol depend upon many different factors. The rate that we absorb it depends, first of all, on its concentration. The more concentrated the alcohol, the faster the rate of absorption; thus, alcohol from whisky at 40 to 45 percent will be absorbed more quickly than that from beer, which is only 3 to 7 percent alcohol. If there is some food or other fluid already in the stomach, this has the same effect of diluting the concentration of the alcohol. The physical fitness of the person also affects the way in which alcohol is absorbed. Since alcohol is distributed through the water content of your tissues, a more muscular person ends up with a lower dose of blood alcohol than a fat person who drinks the same amount.

One interesting thing about alcohol is that its rate of elimination from the body through metabolism is very regular and orderly. It does not depend at all on the actual dose of alcohol that the person has taken. We metabolize about 10 to 15 milliliters of absolute alcohol per hour. This is roughly the equivalent of the amount of alcohol you would get from one ounce of 80 proof whisky, 12 ounces of beer, or 4 ounces of wine. The rule of thumb, then, is that we clear our bodies of the effect of one drink per hour.

The research on the effects of alcohol on sleep has produced a remarkably clear and reliable pattern. Taking alcohol makes you feel sleepy and reduces the amount of time it takes for you to fall asleep. Its beneficial effects, however, only last for the first half of the night. During the early part of the night you have a lot of slow-wave deep sleep, but your rapid eye movement dreaming periods are greatly reduced in length or eliminated. In the second half of the night, people who take alcohol actually have poorer sleep and are far more restless.

Just how sleepy a dose of alcohol will make you depends upon the sleep debt you are carrying. Alcohol hits you harder if you are sleepy to begin with.[1] In one study researchers had participants build up a sleep debt by allowing them to spend only 5 hours a night in bed for 5 consecutive days. The ability of alcohol to cloud these individuals' minds and make them sleepy and less efficient was increased by this sleep debt to the point where three drinks' worth of alcohol was actually having the same effect on their performance that 6 drinks had when they were rested. The reverse is also true: extending one's sleep time reduces the ability of alcohol to disrupt thinking and also reduces its sedative effects. In one study, participants spent 10 hours in bed each night for 6 nights. When they were later given a dose of alcohol equivalent to four drinks, which had been enough to make them sleepy and inefficient when they had only their usual 8 hours of nightly sleep, the alcohol had virtually no measurable effects on them.

The effects of alcohol seem to depend upon the sleepiness state of the individual regardless of how the sleepiness came about. We have seen that there are peaks of alertness and sleepiness associated with our normal circadian cycle. These arousal cycles also predict the effects of alcohol. Thus, a dose of alcohol given in the early evening when we are most alert has little effect on us. This same dose, given a bit after midday, when we are entering our afternoon sleepiness peak, has a much greater ability to interfere with our thinking and reasoning and to make us even more drowsy.

What about warm milk, that good old standby? The answer to this is somewhat complex and requires that we step back just a little and look at a bit of sleep chemistry. There is a substance in the brain called serotonin, which is a neurotransmitter. Neurotransmitters are chemicals that carry messages between nerve cells. Serotonin seems to be intimately related to the parts of the brain that are responsible for our feelings of sleepiness. When serotonin levels in these areas of the brain are high, such as is usually the case in the late evening, we tend to be considerably sleepier. When serotonin levels are low, as in the midmorning, we are usually more alert. When we deliberately deprive individuals of sleep, we notice that their serotonin level builds up, and this buildup is directly related to their craving for sleep. Research on both animals and humans have shown that if we administer drugs that block the action of serotonin or that deplete the level of serotonin in the brain, this disrupts sleep, causing agitation and insomnia. On the other hand, drugs that raise the level of serotonin seem to relax people and make them sleepy.

Now let's turn to our warm glass of milk. Neurotransmitters, like serotonin, are composed of chemicals called amino acids. One of these, called tryptophan (technically, L-tryptophan), is the major building block out of which serotonin is made. Tryptophan is found in many sources of protein that we eat, and milk is a particularly good source of it. (So are cottage cheese, yogurt, ice cream, chicken, turkey, cashews, soy beans, and tuna.) Some research at MIT has shown that eating something rich in tryptophan can increase the level of this substance in the blood and brain and also increase the concentration of serotonin.

There is also a sort of backdoor way to increase the level of serotonin in the brain. This involves releasing tryptophan that was already in the body. Tryptophan is unique among the 20 amino acids in that it sticks to many large protein molecules that are a normal part of the blood plasma, much like lint sticks to a fuzzy woolen sweater. What this means is that under normal circumstances only about 5 percent of tryptophan actually in the blood is freely available. When we eat a lot of carbohydrates, our blood sugar rises, which in turn causes the pancreas to release some insulin to keep the sugar under control. With the release of insulin, some of the tryptophan is freed from the proteins that it usually rides on. If vitamin B_6 and some other enzymes are around, the tryptophan can then be rapidly converted to serotonin. Actually, there is some evidence that drowsiness may be increased by simply taking vitamin B_6 in the late evening, perhaps because it allows more efficient conversion of tryptophan to serotonin.

It should be obvious, however, from this discussion that the average pantry is filled with more things that may rob us of sleep rather than assist us. The best bet for kitchen treatment of sleeping difficulties may well be a glass of warm milk used to wash down a couple of aspirins. Just about everything else found in the average kitchen will keep you awake rather than put you to sleep.

Ondine's Curse 🦅

$\mathcal{S}$ome of our daytime sleepiness is simply due to sleep loss, and some to where we are in the circadian cycle. There are, however, certain medical and lifestyle problems that can also rob us of sleep.

There is a myth about the water nymph Ondine. Like all her sisters, she was magically beautiful. Free and independent, Ondine was very wary of men, since they are the only threat to a nymph's immortality. If a nymph ever falls in love with a mortal and bears his child, she loses her gift of everlasting life; she will start to age and will die after the span of a normal life. Despite all this, when Ondine saw the handsome young knight Sir Lawrence near her pond, she was impressed by him. When Lawrence saw her, he was, as they used to say, smitten by her beauty. He longed to know her better and came back many times to try to see her again. Ondine soon found herself looking forward to the knight's visits. In time they met, they spoke, and they fell in love. As happens in most fairy tales, these two attractive and special beings married. When they exchanged vows, Sir Lawrence said, "My every waking breath shall be my pledge of love and faithfulness to you." Ondine in turn promised, "As long as our love is true, my magic will serve as your shield and will never be turned against you." Unfortunately, however, this tale is not one in which the couple lives happily ever after.

141

A year after their marriage Ondine gave birth to Lawrence's son. From that moment on she began to age. Her body became susceptible to the weathering effects of sun, wind, and time, and her spectacular beauty began to slowly fade. Sir Lawrence, it turns out, seems to have been driven more by passion than by love. As Ondine's physical attractiveness diminished, he began to develop a wandering eye, with particular interest in some of the younger, prettier women living nearby.

One afternoon Ondine was walking near the stables when she heard the familiar and distinctive snoring of her husband. Amused by the fact that he had apparently fallen asleep in the middle of the day in this odd place, she decided to wake him up and take him home to finish his nap. When she entered the stable, however, she saw Sir Lawrence lying on a pile of hay in the arms of some woman. Items of clothing strewn around the stable told the story. Ondine's sacrifice of her immortality for this man, who had now betrayed her, demanded retribution. Still retaining enough magic to achieve her vengeance, Ondine kicked her husband awake, pointed her finger at him, and uttered her curse: "You swore faithfulness to me with every waking breath, and I accepted your oath. So be it. As long as you are awake, you shall have your breath, but should you ever fall asleep, then that breath will be taken from you and you will die!" The tale ends with the favorite line of many old story tellers: "And so it was."

There are some interesting aspects of this version of the story of Ondine, because there is a condition in which people actually do stop breathing when they go to sleep. Such individuals suffer from a condition known as *sleep apnea*. Technically, an apnea is a cessation of the usual breathing process for a defined period of time. One of the revolutions in sleep medicine over the past 20 years has been the recognition not only that breathing processes can be disrupted during sleep but that this condition is much more common than we had believed. Some estimates suggest that about 10 percent of all men and about 4 percent of all women will suffer from some form of sleep apnea as they grow older. This makes this problem one of the most common chronic disorders suffered by humans. Sleep apnea is not a benign condition. People with this condition are much more likely to suffer from coronary problems and high blood pressure. They have a higher susceptibility to strokes and an elevated risk of various central nervous system problems. They often show excessive daytime fatigue and sleepiness, as well as loss of motivation, inability to concentrate, poor stamina, inefficient problem-solving abilities, depression, and a higher risk of accidental injuries. Notice that most of these problems are associated with a large sleep debt, which is to be expected since sleep apnea is a major disrupter of normal sleep. It not only steals our sleep but also steals our health and vitality.

If you recall, Ondine's unfaithful Sir Lawrence was partly undone by the fact that he snored. Snoring is intimately associated with sleep apnea. The snoring sound is caused by the vibration of the soft parts of the mouth and throat area. It is usually loudest when the individual is inhaling. Specifically, the noise is caused as the air passages are rhythmically blocked and unblocked, causing a sound that is sometimes described as rumbling, clicking, flapping, or sputtering. Snoring is really much more common than most people believe: it is found in about 1 out of every 4 men and about 1 out of every 7 women. It is more common in overweight individuals and in older people.

One scientist actually speculated that snoring may have had a useful function back in the dim past of the human species. One must remember that our ancestors would have been most vulnerable to predators when they were asleep. The speculation is that snoring provides a loud sound that mimics the growling or roaring of a large predator. To a hunting animal passing by our sleeping ancestor's cave, this sound announced: "There are other big, dangerous beasts around—stay away or there will be trouble!"

For many years snoring was simply viewed as an annoying sound. Snorers have found themselves the butt of many jokes, such as in the old saying "Laugh and the world laughs with you; snore and you sleep alone." Numerous cartoon characters, such as Dagwood Bumstead, Beetle Bailey, and Garfield the Cat, have been shown in humorous situations involving, or triggered by, snoring.

Snoring is unpleasant to those who must live with a snorer. Marriages have been strained, or even terminated, because one partner snored too loudly. One striking example of how annoying snoring can be comes from the life of John Wesley Hardin. Born in 1853, Hardin grew up in the lawless frontier that was then Texas. He became well known as a gambler and a gunfighter. In the early 1870s Hardin was sleeping one night in a typical ramshackle western hotel. In the middle of the night he was awakened by the loud snoring of a man in the room next door. Hardin shouted for the man to be quiet and kicked the wall several times to get his noisy neighbor's attention. When that had no effect, Hardin picked up his heavy .45 caliber revolver and fired several shots through the wall. One bullet hit the reverberant sleeper, who then limped off to get medical help, leaving Hardin with enough quiet to allow him to return to sleep. Hardin's neighbor was more fortunate than the husband of a California woman: She called the police to say that her husband was dead, shot five times. She explained to the investigating officer, "I told him to do something to stop that God-awful snoring and to get rid of that stupid, dangerous pistol he kept next to the bed. He did neither, so I solved the problem."

From a medical point of view, snoring is important because the sound is evidence that there is restriction or blockage of the air passages. This is an early sign that there is a predisposition toward developing sleep apnea. Let's consider the case of Gordon:

Gordon was a 44-year-old who was overweight at around 210 pounds (95 kilograms) and a height of 5 feet 10 inches (178 centimeters). He was the owner of a moderate-sized souvenir shop (located in a tourist area of a large city) and employed four people in addition to his wife. Gordon was pressured by his wife to go to the sleep lab to see if anything could be done about his snoring. The noise was disturbing her sleep, and she would sometimes go into another room to get away from the sound. She was threatening to permanently sleep in a separate room if he didn't seek help.

Gordon admitted that he had been snoring since he was a child, and he remembered that his father had also been a loud snorer. Gordon had tried several different methods to stop snoring, including a special pillow his wife had bought for him and, when that didn't work, a special antisnoring collar. When the collar proved ineffective, Gordon's wife got him plastic clips that were supposed to be attached to his nose. They didn't work, either.

Gordon felt that he was a reasonably deep sleeper and claimed that he typically awakened only once each night when he felt pressure to go to the bathroom to urinate. He did complain that he perspired heavily during the night and that his pajamas and pillow case were often so wet that he would change the pajama top and turn the pillow over to the drier side before returning to sleep. He admitted that although he seemed to sleep deeply, he often found it difficult to awaken and felt rather unrefreshed or "foggy" upon doing so. He also often complained about diffuse headaches in the mornings. When Gordon was asked about his daytime level of alertness, he responded that he felt that it was "about average." However, as the interview continued, it became quite clear that sleepiness was a real problem for him. He admitted that he drank a lot of coffee and that if he didn't he would get very sleepy. His wife and his employees often found him dozing off at his desk in the back of the store at various times during the day.

Gordon's wife provided some additional information: "When he is out in the front of the store, he always paces around. If he sits down on the stool near the cash register, his eyes tend to droop and he looks as if he needs a nap. Unfortunately, he complains that naps aren't very refreshing for him. He always had a terrific sense of humor and a lot of interests, but lately nothing seems to interest him. He used to watch movies on television a lot with me in the evenings. Now when I put a videotape on, he just goes to sleep on the sofa. He complains that the films that I choose are boring. He says if they weren't boring, he wouldn't fall asleep. He is starting to act more depressed than he used to and seems to be losing his motivation. We had always talked about expanding the store; when the little shop next door became vacant, it seemed like a good opportunity to buy it and enlarge the store. When I suggested this, he just waved it off as being too much trouble for too little gain. He is also starting to ignore important details having to do with the business."

Watching Gordon's night in the sleep lab was both fascinating and distressing. He was quite hopeful that something would come of the tests so that his wife would no longer "have to sleep next to this outboard motor." He was wired with the standard sleep-monitoring EEG electrodes but was also equipped with some additional devices, including a tiny box-shaped monitor that was taped to the top of his shoulder and that recorded his sleeping positions (whether he was resting on his back, front, or side) plus all of the movements he made during the night. A microphone was suspended above the bed to measure the actual snoring sounds. In addition, three important things were done to measure Gordon's breathing: First, a pressure-sensitive strap was placed around his chest to measure the lung expansions and contractions that accompany breathing. A device that looks like a tiny microphone on a head-mounted support was used to measure the temperature of the air going into and out of Gordon's mouth. Air that is exhaled has been warmed by the body, so it has a higher temperature than inhaled air. Finally, the amount of oxygen in Gordon's blood was continuously tracked. This was done using something called an *ear oximeter,* a gadget that clips onto the earlobe and contains both a light source, which is pressed against one side of the earlobe, and a sensor, which is on the other side of the lobe. The sensor is really measuring the amount of light passing through the earlobe. When blood has high oxygen content it becomes very red, as opposed to the blue tint associated with blood having little oxygen; the redder the blood, the greater the amount of red light from the other side of the earlobe reaching the sensor. Thus, simply by measuring the variations in the light passing through the ear, one actually ends up with direct measures of the oxygen content of the blood—with no needles and no punctured veins.

Despite all of these monitoring instruments, Gordon fell asleep virtually instantaneously. According to his EEG, he was asleep only 143 seconds after the lights were turned out. However, his sleep was not to last very long. After only 59 seconds of sleep, Gordon issued a sputtering snoring sound; then, as the EEG showed him coming out of the normal sleep pattern, he produced a noticeable gasp and seemed to gulp at the air. For the remainder of the night, this cycle continued. Gordon would drop into the lighter stages of sleep, and then, following some intermittent snoring sounds, his EEG pattern would indicate that he had momentarily awakened. Between snoring episodes the breathing measures showed that no air at all was entering or leaving his lungs. Thus, the only time he got air was when the snoring sounds were present. Gordon was in bed for a total of 456 minutes (just over 7½ hours). He awakened 426 times during the night, which means that he was awakening 56 times an hour. The average length of time for each sleep episode, then, was only around 63 seconds.

Perhaps the most frightening aspect of all of this comes from the measure of blood oxygen. If we call the maximum amount of oxygen that blood can carry 100 percent, then a normal person's blood oxygen levels during sleep will be in the 96-to-99-percent range. Many researchers think that if the blood oxygen drops below 90 percent, there is a real danger that cells may die, particularly in the brain and nervous systems. After each breath Gordon took, the oxygen levels rose, but then they systematically began to fall as he lay there without breathing. The blood oxygen levels would usually drop to a low value between 80 and 85 percent before breathing would start again. At one point I was amazed to see that the oxygen level actually dropped below 60 percent! If we look at the total amount of time across the night that Gordon had blood oxygen levels below the critical 90 percent value, we find that it amounts to 112 minutes, which means that approximately one quarter of the night was spent without enough oxygen in the blood to maintain normal tissue health.

How did Gordon feel in the morning? He felt that it was a typical night's sleep. He thought that he might have awakened a few more times than usual because of the strange surroundings, wires, and so forth, and estimated that he awoke around six times during the night, which is 420 times less than he actually awakened. He admitted that he was still feeling a little fatigued and felt that he could use some more sleep. He also had a bit of a headache and took some aspirin along with his first cup of coffee for the day. Unfortunately, Gordon is not an unusual case of sleep apnea.

Recently, scientists have been able to learn a good deal about the processes associated with sleep apnea by looking at the English bulldog, which has this same problem. Its rounded face and short nose are much more similar to a human being's than is true for most other dogs. This shape leads to both snoring and sleep apnea. From human and animal research we have learned that there are two main processes that can produce sleep apnea. The first involves the level of brain activation, specifically, the brain's ability to monitor things going on in and around the body. Obviously, as we fall asleep, the brain becomes less vigilant and our bodily functions all begin to switch over to some neurological equivalent of an "automatic pilot." One major form of sleep apnea involves the failure of this automatic pilot to monitor the levels of oxygen in the blood. When a person with sleep apnea goes to sleep, so does the automatic pilot that controls breathing; that is, the neurological automatic pilot, which is located in the brain stem, doesn't monitor the oxygen levels well enough in sleep apnea. When people with sleep apnea fall asleep, they simply stop breathing. It is not until the oxygen levels drop far enough or the carbon dioxide levels build up to too high a level that the stimulation becomes intense enough to awaken the brain momentarily. There is a sputtering gasping for breath to restore the oxygen balance as the barely conscious brain triggers a snorting but really voluntarily controlled sucking of air. The brain then resets its faulty automatic controls and returns to sleep until the next physical crisis triggered by lack of oxygen awaken it again, somewhere between 30 seconds and 10 minutes after the apneic sleeper enters the sleep state again.

This kind of sleep apnea is called *central sleep apnea*. When it was first discovered in the 1950s, it was called *Ondine's curse*, in honor of the myth of the unfaithful Sir Lawrence, who was doomed to have his breath taken from him and to die should he ever fall asleep. This evocative label seems to have died on the altar of language sensitivity, where labeling people as suffering from some form of curse is seen as being insensitive rather than colorful.

The second kind of sleep apnea involves simple mechanical blockage of the air passages used in breathing. As we fall asleep, we have a general relaxation of muscles throughout our body. This includes the muscles of the tongue, the back of the mouth, the throat, and the airway itself (technically, the *pharynx*). In normal sleepers the airway slowly collapses enough to cause the body to adopt the deep, slow-breathing pattern we have all come to recognize as peculiar to sleep. The most common victim of sleep apnea is an overweight middle-aged male. Age is a factor in sleep apnea since muscle tone tends to decrease with age; weight is a problem since fat tends to gather in the neck and face, providing additional pressure on the airway and encouraging it to collapse. Once there is the slightest closure, attempts to breathe may actually close more of the airway. To see how this works, take a soft drinking straw and pinch one end. Now, if you suck on the straw (which is a model of the airway) the entire straw flattens and closes. You must actually reverse the direction of the airflow to first reopen the straw before anything further can be sucked in. This is what happens in the human airway. The sputtering, snorting, and snoring as the air is momentarily inhaled, then exhaled, then inhaled again is an attempt to open up the air passage. This form of sleep apnea is called *obstructive sleep apnea,* and it is the most common form of this malady.

Is there some way to tell whether you have sleep apnea without actually going to a sleep lab? You can get a reasonable idea for yourself by answering the items in the sleep apnea inventory presented here. It is not as sensitive as some of the more complex inventories and a full physical screening, of course, but it is accurate enough to catch most cases in which the symptoms are clear.

SLEEP APNEA QUESTIONNAIRE

To determine the likelihood that you have sleep apnea, read the questions below, circling *Yes* or *No* as your answer to each.

1. Have you ever been told that you snore loudly?   Yes   No

2. Have you been told that your snoring is worse when you are lying on your back?   Yes   No

3. Have you been told that you are more likely to snore, or that your snoring is louder, when you have gone to sleep right after drinking alcohol?   Yes   No

4. Do you sweat a great deal at night?   Yes   No

5. Have you ever been told that you stop breathing or seem to hold your breath when you are sleeping?   Yes   No

6. Have you ever been told that you have high blood pressure?   Yes   No

7. Have you sometimes awakened at night feeling that you are either gasping for breath or having difficulty breathing?   Yes   No

8. Does your nose have a tendency to block up when you are trying to sleep?   Yes   No

9. When you are in bed at night, do you have more difficulty breathing when you are lying on your back?   Yes   No

---

continued

10. Do you have more difficulty breathing at
    night if you have been drinking alcohol?   Yes   No

11. Have you (now or at some time in your past)
    ever been a regular tobacco smoker for a
    period longer than 1 year?   Yes   No

12. Do you usually wake up in the morning
    feeling still tired and not fully refreshed?   Yes   No

13. Do you sometimes wake up in the morning
    with a headache or awaken during the night
    with a headache?   Yes   No

14. Are you 35 years of age or older?   Yes   No

15. During the day, do you often find that
    there are times when you feel extremely
    sleepy or fatigued?   Yes   No

16. Have you been told that you are a restless
    sleeper or that you turn, twitch, or move
    a lot when you sleep?   Yes   No

17. This last question has to do with your body mass. To
    answer it you have to look at Table 2. Find your
    approximate weight on the left, then look at the
    height figures on the right. If your height is *less than*
    the height listed there, circle the *Yes* response for
    this item; if you are *as tall as* or *taller than* that value,
    circle *No*.   Yes   No

To score this questionnaire, total up the number of times you answered
yes to any question. If your score is 9 or more, you are showing a number
of symptoms common to people with sleep apnea. If this is the case, you
might want to look into this matter with your doctor or a sleep clinic. If
your score is 12 or more, the chances that you have sleep apnea are very
high, and for your own safety and well-being I would urge you to have a
professional examination.

Suppose that you have been diagnosed with, or suspect that you have, sleep apnea. This disorder is associated with increased risks of heart disease, high blood pressure, accidents, daytime fatigue, and other problems. It may drastically shorten an individual's life through suffocation if the blockage becomes too severe and the waking reflex is delayed for any reason. (This has often been observed in English bulldogs: after

TABLE 2

Table Required for Answering Question 17

Your Approximate Body Weight		If your height is *less than* the value listed here, circle *Yes* for Question 17.	
Pounds	Kilograms	Feet and Inches	Centimeters
Less than 105	Less than 48	Circle *No* regardless of height	
110	50	4'6"	139
120	54	4'9"	144
130	59	4'11"	151
140	64	5'2"	157
150	68	5'4"	162
160	73	5'6"	168
170	77	5'8"	172
180	82	5'10"	178
190	86	6'0"	182
200	91	6'2"	187
210	95	6'3"	191
220	100	6'5"	196
230	104	6'7"	200
240	109	6'9"	205
250	113	6'10"	208
Greater than 255	Greater than 116	Circle *Yes* regardless of height	

the age of 5 years, members of this breed may die as a direct result of their sleep apnea unless it is treated.) Clearly, then, if you have sleep apnea, some attempts should be made to reduce or eliminate it.

What can be done for sleep apnea? If the condition is severe enough, it may require involved medical treatment. One of the currently popular medical treatments involves wearing over the nose and mouth a mask that is attached to a small air pump that provides constant pressure to keep the air passages open. Several surgical procedures are available to help relieve the airway obstruction. (Surgery works on the bulldog, too.)

If your condition is not too severe, there are some simple procedures you can try in order to reduce the symptoms of sleep apnea:

- *Lose weight:* Since it is the case that nearly all people with sleep apnea are overweight, losing weight can, by itself, often stop the problem. This works by reducing the amount of fatty tissue around the base of the tongue, which tends to obstruct the air flow, and also by providing more room and less pressure on the airway itself.
- *Avoid nightcaps or sedatives:* Alcohol depresses the central nervous system in a manner that serves to reduce muscle tone during sleep even further than usual. Some research has shown that the number of episodes of sleep apnea can double if you drink before going to bed. Sedatives have the same relaxing effect on muscles.
- *Avoid allergens:* Anything that increases your nasal congestion will increase the likelihood of sleep apnea attacks. Avoid foods that you are allergic to, and use room air filters if you have dust allergies or hay fever.
- *Don't smoke:* Tobacco smoke irritates the upper airways, causing them to become more congested.
- *Clear your nose:* A nasal decongestant spray or an over-the-counter nasal decongestant pill will often help. Be careful to get a decongestant pill and not an antihistamine; antihistamines have the same muscle-relaxing effects that alcohol and sedatives do.
- *Use a firm pillow and mattress:* Anything that puts a kink in your neck can increase the likelihood of apnea attacks. Getting rid of your pillow helps to straighten your airway. A firm mattress may also help.

- *Play ball a new way:* Sleep apnea attacks are more likely if you are lying on your back. Lying either on your side or stomach seems to reduce the pressure on the airway. Unfortunately, you can't monitor your sleeping position while you are asleep. One clever solution to this problem involves sewing a pocket on the back of your pajamas and inserting a tennis ball into the pocket. Now when you roll over onto your back at night, the ball will be an uncomfortable lump to lie on. It will cause an automatic or unconscious adjustment of your body position, and you will end up lying on your belly or side.
- *Remember Ondine:* There is one last recommendation. It has no scientific support. I add it merely for completeness so that you may know yet another means of reducing the likelihood that you will succumb to sleep apnea. If you marry a nymph or other magical person and pledge fidelity, don't get caught fooling around with someone else!

Sleepless Nights 🐉

W.C. Fields once said, "The best cure for insomnia is to get a lot of sleep." For people who have difficulty sleeping, the most likely diagnosis they will hear is that they are suffering from a case of "simple insomnia." Unfortunately, the problem with insomnia is that it is not simple. Insomnia is generally defined as difficulty falling asleep, difficulty staying asleep (which includes awakening too early in the morning and being unable to return to sleep as well as frequent night wakenings), and generally poor quality of sleep. However, insomnia is not a specific problem; rather, it is a symptom, something like a fever. No responsible physician would refer to a fever as "simple," since it can be caused by a variety of different problems. While you can treat the fever symptom directly—with aspirin, say, and maybe with cold compresses on the head—this does not solve the underlying problem. The same thing holds true in the case of insomnia. It is possible to treat the symptom directly with some form of sleeping medication; however, this does not deal with the underlying problems that caused the insomnia symptom in the first place. These underlying problems may be quite complex, or they may be laughably simple.

The number of people who complain about occasional insomnia is about 35 percent of the population, with about 17 percent of the population complaining about frequent and disruptive insomnia. Sadly, much of the treatment to date has been symptomatic. There are over

13 million people in the United States alone who are taking some kind of prescribed medication to improve their sleep. This makes sleep-inducing drugs the second most commonly prescribed single class of medication in the world today, trailing behind only birth control pills.

Most patients get their prescription for sleeping medication solely on the basis of their own description of their symptoms. That is to say, the patient tells the physician that he or she sleeps very little at night, or sleeps restlessly, and the drug is prescribed on the basis of this testimony. Very few patients are actually observed during a night's sleep in a sleep laboratory. This makes insomnia one of the few medical problems physicians treat for whose existence in a given patient there is no objective clinical evidence. This is particularly unfortunate since your subjective impression that your sleep is poor can be extremely inaccurate. For example, when we compare personal reports of the quality of sleep with more objective measures taken in a sleep laboratory, we find that in four out of five individuals the subjective complaints of insomnia cannot be confirmed by any of the current scientific measuring devices we have today. Often, on the basis of the sleep records alone there is no way to tell the difference between the supposed insomniac and the supposedly normal individual. Most people who are observed in the sleep lab because they have major complaints about their sleep actually sleep anywhere between a half to a full hour longer than they think they do. They also tend to fall asleep about 30 minutes faster than they think they do.

This is not to deny that insomnia exists. It is just that even when a true problem does exist, we often feel that the situation is worse than it actually is. For a person to be characterized as having a clinically significant case of insomnia, one of the following statements should be true:

- It takes *more than* 30 minutes to fall asleep.
- There are five or more awakenings at night.
- The total amount of sleep time lost during awakenings should be more than 30 minutes, and the total amount of nightly sleep should be 6½ hours or less.
- If there are early morning awakenings and the person can't get back to sleep, the total amount of sleep for the night should be less than 6½ hours.

- The nightly total of deep slow-wave sleep, as measured by the EEG, is less than 15 minutes.

Just occasionally fulfilling one or more of these conditions does not automatically make you an insomniac. After all, everybody has a bad night of sleep now and then. If you truly have insomnia, these symptoms should be relatively persistent; that is to say, they should occur in runs of at least 3 weeks at a time. In addition, there ought to be some effects that are noticeable during your waking life. Usually, this means complaints about being fatigued, washed out, and very sleepy at various times during the day.

Many people feel that they are insomniacs simply because they are not getting 8 hours of sleep a night or because their sleep is sporadically disrupted or delayed. I had one colleague who came to me for some advice about his insomnia. He complained that it took him nearly a half hour to fall asleep and that he was awakening three or four times each night. When I pointed out to him that neither of these conditions was really any different from what we expect of a normal sleeper, he looked puzzled. A few weeks later, however, he told me that he was sleeping much better since we had our conversation. His sleep problem, apparently, was not insomnia but, rather, anxiety caused by the fear that he might have insomnia.

When I later thought of my interaction with this colleague, it dawned upon me that if he had gone to a physician simply to complain about his poor sleep, he would probably have been prescribed some sort of sleeping medication. The end result of taking this medication might have been real insomnia. There is an irony in the fact that one of the most important causes of insomnia seems to be the use of sleeping medication. It comes about this way: Since insomnia is a symptom and not a disease, treating the symptom does nothing to alleviate the underlying problem. If the problem that caused the insomnia, whether it is psychological or physical, is not treated, then the use of the sleeping medication will have to be continued. Patients who use sleeping medication for any length of time tend to develop a tolerance to the drug. That is, the drug loses its effectiveness, which means that the patient has to request larger doses from the physician. If the patient tries to sleep without his or her now accustomed medication—or even if the patient tries to reduce the amount to a smaller dose—problems arise. There is a withdrawal effect that comes in the form of a "rebound." This means that sleep is severely disrupted and difficult to obtain. The poor patient is now faced with worse symptoms than before and quickly becomes convinced that his or her condition has worsened. The result of this is obvious: most patients return to the medication and take even higher doses than before.

This pattern is so common that it now has been given the official name of *drug dependency insomnia*. A number of studies have shown that using some sleeping medications for as little as 3 days in a row and then stopping their use can produce a noticeable backlash, with insomnia and sleep disturbance for several nights afterward. What is particularly disturbing about all of this is that, according to the U.S. Institute of Medicine, when insomniacs take the usually prescribed dose of sleeping medication, the effects on their sleep are really quite slight in the first place. The time to fall asleep is usually reduced by about 15 minutes, and the average increase in total sleep length is only about 30 minutes a night. Given the unfavorable drug side effects, this seems like a small benefit indeed. It probably suggests that use of sleeping medication should be limited to only a few days at a time, and then just as a bridging treatment while the underlying cause of the problem is being attended to.

It is certainly the case that insomnia can result from illnesses that cause pain and discomfort and from various neurological diseases, especially those that lead to bodily twitches and shakes. Since the time of Hippocrates (around 4 B.C.), it has been suggested that certain psychological problems, such as anxiety disorders or stress (or, as Hippocrates called it, "the throes of life"), can disrupt sleep patterns. Depression, for example, causes a characteristic early-awakening pattern, with fatigue and lethargy that last throughout the day. One of the most obvious, and predictable, causes of insomnia seems to be age, since, as we noted earlier, our sleep patterns become less consistent as we grow older.

There is one form of insomnia that is basically medical in nature but is easily cured by a slight change in the sleeping environment. About 11 percent of the population report that they are occasionally awakened or kept from falling asleep by heartburn, which is a burning, biting, or smarting sensation that seems to locate itself in the middle of the chest. Despite its name, heartburn really has nothing to do with the heart. The discomfort actually results when the highly acidic contents of the stomach back up (the technical term used is *reflux*), causing the lower part of the esophagus, which is the tube that connects the mouth to the top of the stomach, to be exposed to this caustic material. Although the stomach has a special lining that protects it from the effects of strong acids, the esophagus does not. Thus, as the contents of the stomach leak past the valve that separates the stomach from the esophagus, the esophageal tissue becomes damaged and one feels the effect as a burning in the chest. Sometimes this is accompanied by a taste of bile or a sour taste in the mouth, depending upon the nature of the reflux. In extreme cases this may cause coughing fits, especially if the vocal cords are exposed to this acid bath. If the reflux is persistent, the acid may actually cause blood to be coughed up at this time.

Heartburn and acid reflux most often occur when a person is lying down. The reason for this is simple: in this position the force of gravity cannot help move the food from the stomach and down into the small intestine to finish the process of digestion. Obviously, since we usually sleep in a horizontal position, reflux will be more common at night, when we are trying to sleep.

The solution to this problem is really quite simple. In addition to avoiding eating heavy meals within 3 hours of bedtime, the safest remedy to curb acid reflux is to raise the head of the bed. This allows gravity to help the stomach contents flow along their natural path, which will take them down into the small intestine rather than bubbling back up on a reverse course into the esophagus. To elevate the bed, blocks may be placed beneath the legs of the headboard. You should start with only a little bit of lift because, in some instances, only 2 to 4 inches of elevation is enough to keep the stomach contents where they belong and to keep you free of sleep-disturbing heartburn. I have tried using several pillows as a means of elevating my upper body, but this just didn't seem to work very well since I kept rolling off the pillows as I slept, thus ending up back in a horizontal position. Tilting the bed is the surest way, or, if you can afford it, you might consider an electrically adjustable bed. Both provide reasonably sure and safe remedies for this medical source of insomnia.

There is one warning here: you should not raise the bed too much. One universal feature of all beds and mattresses is that they are always designed so that we may stretch out in a horizontal position. It is certainly true that people can fall asleep in a sitting position (many teachers and university professors believe that most of their students are restfully sleeping through their lectures while sitting at their desks). From an environmental and architectural design standpoint, places to sleep where the person is in a sitting position seem to make good sense (an armchair, for instance, takes a lot less floor space than a bed). More people could be packed into smaller living quarters if only sleeping accommodations did not require the sleeper to stretch out flat. Why, then, don't we use sleeping chairs rather than beds?

The rejection of chairs as sleeping units actually seems to be based on considerations of good health and sleep quality. Many of you have probably had the experience of taking a late night flight in order to be at your destination early in the morning. The reasoning that accompanies such a decision usually goes like this: "If my flight leaves at 10 P.M. and gets in by 6 A.M. current time, then I can still get close to 8 hours of sleep by tilting back that airline seat, wrapping myself in a blanket, and placing a pillow under my head. In this way I'll arrive fresh for that 8 A.M. meeting." The reality, of course, is quite different. Despite the fact that you fell asleep immediately (even before the stewardess finished her safety instructions to the passengers), you probably found that when you were awakened 7 hours later, you were still unrefreshed (and perhaps felt like you really hadn't rested at all). Still worse, you had to face that important morning meeting in that condition!

Actually, your poor sleep had nothing to do with the noise, the vibration, or the unfamiliar environment of being in an airplane. The poor quality of your sleep seems directly due to the fact that you were in a sitting position. EEG recordings of people sleeping in comfortable armchairs, or in chairs that have been pushed up in front of a table, show that sleep quality is very poor compared to what you get when you are stretched out horizontally. The amount of slow-wave deep sleep you get under the former conditions is reduced to virtually nil. In general, it is the amount of this deep sleep that best predicts how invigorated and revitalized you feel after your night's sleep. People in a sitting position seem to hover through the night in the two lightest stages of sleep.

Why can't we successfully sleep while sitting? The answer to this may be quite simplistic and silly. Obviously, it would not do for you to fall asleep while standing up; if you drift into any form of sleep where your body becomes very relaxed and limp, you would simply fall down. If you fall wrong, perhaps hitting a hard surface or the sharp edge of a piece of furniture on your way down, you could easily cause yourself grave bodily harm. It is not impossible for people to fall asleep while standing; however, the sleep states that are reached are very light, so that if the body begins to sway or fall, the person can quickly awaken in time to pull back up before actually toppling over. It may well be the case that the sitting position, with the torso mostly upright, is interpreted by the brain as being more like standing than lying down. For this reason, we are unable to fall deeply asleep while in a sitting position; the body monitors its position, allowing only a light sleep to occur. In theory, there may be a sitting position at some critical angle of inclination that the brain would interpret as sufficiently horizontal to allow deep sleep. However, researchers have not yet found it. In any event, since it is clear that the sitting position, no matter how comfortable the chair, does not provide adequate rest, all beds are functionally flat. In the context of a cure for acid reflux, then, the bed should have only a slight tilt, one that is nowhere near the inclination you would have even in a reclining chair.

There are also insomnias that are caused by lifestyle factors that induce negative physical conditions. Exercising in the evening often increases arousal levels and makes it harder to fall asleep. Eating a heavy meal, especially with spicy foods and high fat content, within a couple of hours before retiring can inhibit sleep. Alcohol, nicotine, or caffeine use also reduces the likelihood of sleep or tends to fragment and disrupt it.

Some of the causes of insomnia are so simple to eliminate that one wonders why people did not address them long ago. It has been estimated that around one-third of all cases of insomnia are the direct result of a poor sleeping environment. Some obvious factors have to do with the bed itself, or the pillows. A mattress that is too soft will restrict normal nighttime movements of the body, often making it difficult to get comfortable in a new position and causing the person to awaken feeling stiff. For some people, especially thin individuals who lack the cushioning layer of fat that their plumper friends have, a mattress that is too hard will cause painful pressure on the hips, arms, or shoulders. Comfortable sleeping apparel is also important, since pajamas that bind will awaken you in the night as surely as a loud noise will.

It is really quite surprising to see how many bedrooms have light problems. When it comes to sleep, a light problem is generally in the form of too much light. Light, as we have seen, is important in helping to maintain our daily sleep–activity cycle. For this reason, if street light enters the room, shades or curtains should be hung, and these should be opaque enough to block out the light. Another simple and inexpensive solution is a set of eye shades for sleeping. (These are available in virtually any drug store.) If you use a night-light, make sure that it is dim enough that you can't sense it through your closed eyes. If you often use the bathroom at night, a night-light is quite useful, since exposing yourself to a bright light in the middle of the night may trigger the sequence of neural responses associated with morning, thus increasing the time it takes for you to fall back to sleep.

Sound in the bedroom is another potential environmental problem that may result in insomnia. Research on people who live near airports has shown that some noises, such as those from jets passing overhead, may jog their sleep into a lighter stage (even if it does not awaken them), thus making it less restful. Street noises have similar effects. Closing windows helps some, but it is usually impossible to completely eliminate all sounds. The solution to this problem is to actually generate some noise. The noise that is wanted is called "white noise," a sort of whooshing sound. Air conditioners and ventilation systems produce a white noise sound. You can also put at the head of your bed a small white noise generator (these start at prices of around $50) or use continuous tapes with good approximations of white noise, often advertised as "surf sounds," "wind sounds," or "falling rain." The sound of a fan works well, too, and it will also keep you cool in the summer. It works, in part, by simply drowning out unpredictable noises in the environment. The white noise itself, being monotonous and unchanging, doesn't cause awakenings as a TV or radio might. It keeps our ears busy and focused on these continuous, unarousing, but complex sounds. There is quite a bit of evidence that indicates that low levels of white noise do seem to have a calming effect, and there is even evidence that this works on newborn children who are having trouble sleeping.

Another important environmental factor affecting sleep is temperature. Humans and other warm-blooded animals seem to sleep best when the surrounding temperature is around their "thermal comfort zone." This is a range of temperatures in which the air is not so cool that the animal has to increase its metabolic rate (or expend additional energy shivering in order to stay warm) and not so warm that the animal needs to pant or expend body fluids sweating. Most humans prefer something around 77°F (25°C). However, there are large individual variations, and the preference range may go from 70°F to 85°F (21°C to 30°C). (My wife, for example, seems to be descended from a race of penguins and is always too hot, whereas I seem to have Sahara Desert camel in my bloodline and am always too cold.) In general, if the temperature drops below a sleeper's comfort zone, there is an increase in the number and length of waking periods. If the temperature is too high, people tend to move around in bed much more, which may cause fragmented sleep or wakefulness. It is interesting to note that rapid eye movement, dream-related, sleep is much more sensitive to temperature variations than is slow-wave deep sleep.

Variations in temperature can be used to induce sleep onset. As you fall asleep, your body temperature gradually drops. Setting up a situation where the body is warm and then gradually cools is often enough to induce sleep. The most common way to do this is to simply take a hot bath immediately before going to bed. You should take a bath, not a shower, since the noise and stimulating impact of the shower may actually raise your arousal level and make it harder for you to sleep. At the end of the bath, towel gently (vigorous toweling stimulates) and go to bed. A drier alternative is to turn your electric blanket up to its maximum for around 15 minutes to a half hour before you go to sleep. When you get into bed, turn the blanket down to your desired sleeping temperature. In both cases (bath and blanket) you start with a warm body that cools gradually, which tends to bring on sleep by simulating the gradual cooling normally associated with dozing off.

Whom you sleep with is also a factor in environmentally induced insomnia. There is experimental evidence that shows that when we sleep with someone, their movements affect the soundness of our sleep.

Thus, sleeping with an insomniac can make you one, too, since your partner's tossing and turning can keep you awake. A snoring partner can also rob you of sleep.

While most people are unwilling to eject their spouses or lovers from their beds simply because they are restless, there are others who sleep with us who can be equally disruptive and whose removal from the bed might be less difficult. I am referring, of course, to our pet dogs and cats. In many households, pets not only sleep in the bedroom but actually claim the right to sleep on the bed as well. Since pets move around at night, just as people do, a slightly restless pet can produce badly fragmented sleep. Some pets have other sleep habits that can reduce the quality of our sleep. For instance, there are the snugglers, pets that burrow next to you or lean on some part of your body with their head or paw. When that pressure becomes uncomfortable, you move over; your pet follows you and starts leaning again. If this goes on several times during the night, you end up hanging off the side of the bed—with your pet in splendid comfort in the center. Next we have the snorers. Pets with pushed-in faces, like bulldogs or pugs, tend to snore. The noise can be quite loud and can cause sleep disturbance. Then there is the playful pet, the one that drops its favorite toy on your pillow and starts to paw at you if you don't respond. There's also the hungry pet, the one used to eating breakfast at 7 A.M. that suddenly gets hungry and decides that perhaps you could be induced to go to the kitchen to feed it at 4 A.M. Then, there's . . . but I think you get the idea.

The solutions to pet-induced insomnia are really quite simple. The easiest is to close your bedroom door, leaving Rover and Tabby on the outside. Alternatively, teach your pet to sleep beside the bed on a pillow, rug, or its own bed. You can provide a sleeping space for a dog in a portable kennel, whose door you can close and latch if the dog refuses to stay off your bed. Feeding your pet only at night will also reduce the likelihood that it will awaken you in the early morning hours for a meal. (Or, as a last resort, you can ask my wife to describe her devastating "puppy-ejection kick," a foot maneuver that has trained my dogs that it is safer to stay well away from her side of the bed.)

What if I told you that some insomniacs have problems because they have learned *not* to fall asleep? If you recognize that sleep is a behavior as well as a physical state, this becomes clearer. For normal sleepers, the sight of the bedroom lit with artificial light, the feel of nightclothes, and all the related sights and sounds of sleep time become cues or triggers to the mind that indicate that sleep is approaching. Most of us follow a particular presleep ritual—wandering around the house, closing the lights, letting the cat in or out, checking that the door is locked, maybe drinking a glass of milk, brushing our teeth or hair, undressing, setting the alarm clock, and so forth. Whenever we successfully fall asleep, it is almost always after this ritual. Because of this, the mind becomes conditioned to begin to unwind and prepare for sleep when we start this sequence of activities. In this way we actually learn to fall asleep.

An example of how we learn the cues that put us to sleep can be illustrated with a story once told to me by the Hungarian-American mathematician and author George Polya. The story is about another mathematician, David Hilbert, a professor of mathematics at the University of Göttingen who was responsible for many fundamental advances in algebraic and analytic geometry. One night, according to Polya, there was a party to be held at Hilbert's house. Just as the first guests were arriving, Hilbert's wife noticed that her husband's shirt was soiled; she quickly sent him off to put on a clean one. In response to her request, Hilbert went upstairs. After 20 minutes or more had passed, he still had not returned. The guests were milling about waiting for him. Somewhat concerned, Mrs. Hilbert went up to the bedroom. There she found the great mathematician peacefully tucked into his bed, fast asleep. "You see," explained Polya, "it was a natural sequence of things. He took off his coat, then his tie, then his shirt, and so on, and went to sleep." Most of us are not so susceptible to the cues that signal our bedtime, but we do become conditioned to the natural sequence of our own routine and it does assist us in falling asleep.

For some individuals, the sight of the bedroom becomes associated with other activities. These activities may actually inhibit our ability to sleep. People often read in bed, watch television, eat, play cards, talk on the telephone, or do crossword puzzles. Children often invent games played only in bed; for example, they use it for a trampoline or build a tent out of the blanket. Some people use their bed for mental activities: they try to plan events for the next day or worry about tasks they left undone, and some have even become conditioned to worry about falling asleep. Using the bed for all these non-sleep-related activities results in a mental confusion of sorts. The mind doesn't know whether it is time to sleep, to watch TV, to read, or whatever. So when the time that you actually want to sleep approaches, you must then go through all of the winding down from your awake state, that is, without the benefits provided by cues for sleep.

There are several ways to tell if you have conditioned yourself not to sleep in your bedroom. One telltale sign is that although you have insomnia in your own bed when you try to sleep, you nonetheless find that you often can fall asleep when you are not trying to sleep and are not in your own bed. This will probably happen most frequently when you are reading, watching TV, or riding in a bus or plane. Another way to tell if you have conditioned yourself to stay awake in your own bed is to see how you sleep in a new place. People who have conditioned themselves not to sleep in their own room will often find it easier to sleep in an unfamiliar bedroom (such as a hotel room). One of my students, who had been complaining of difficulty falling asleep at home, told me that the best sleep she had in months came when she was out on a camping trip and had to sleep in her sleeping bag on the hard ground.

The best way to avoid conditioned or learned insomnia is to limit your activities in bed to only sleep. The single exception to the sleep-only rule involves sex. In Western countries sex is usually a presleep activity, but in some cultures sexual activity is most frequently reported to be an early morning activity that occurs at the time of awakening. Normally, sexual activity continues until orgasm, and for the majority of people orgasm is associated with a deep feeling of relaxation and well-being. It is this observation that has led people to assume that sexual activity promotes better sleep. But sexual activity itself involves an increase in arousal. The increased physical activity can have the same effect that any other vigorous exercise right before sleeping can have, and thus it may actually interfere with sleep. Psychological stressors associated with a bad sexual encounter, such as performance anxiety, failure to reach orgasm, or difficulties with erection, provoke tension and frustration that may well make it more difficult to fall asleep.

Several studies have tried to resolve the issue of whether sex aids sleep or interferes with it. In general, the results seem to indicate that having sex makes no difference at all. EEG recordings show that the time to fall asleep after normal sexual activity is the same as the time to fall asleep on nights when there is no sex; nor is there a difference in the duration of or soundness of sleep. One study even looked at a group of normal, healthy heterosexual men who had been deprived of sex for 10 days and who then had presleep intercourse; there was virtually no difference in any aspect of their sleep behavior on the night they had intercourse as compared to the previous night. This means that you can safely use your bed for sex as well as sleep without fear that it will keep you awake. It also means that trying to convince a hesitant partner to engage in sex because it will make you sleep better is an argument not supported by scientific data.

Some people actually induce insomnia in themselves by simply trying too hard to fall asleep. Most of us have been raised in a culture where we were told that we could accomplish just about anything if we worked hard enough at it: "If you want to win, give 110 percent"; "If at first you don't succeed, try, try again"; and "Never say die." Unfortunately, sleep is not like most other activities in your life. Concentrating on trying to sleep or attempting to force your body to rest simply won't work. Trying harder, relying on sheer force of will, may be the surest path to success in your waking activities, but it is the surest path to failure if you want to go to sleep. Trying harder raises your arousal level and energizes you, which is not what you want. The easiest way to achieve sleep is to relax. This can be done by emptying your mind of work or tension-related thoughts. My maternal grandmother knew that trick. When I was around 5 years of age, my father was still in Europe fighting World War II and my mother and I were living with her parents. One evening when my mother was at work as a department store clerk, I was having trouble falling asleep. I was obviously restless and ill at ease. My grandmother came into the room and studied the situation for a moment.

"Why are you so restless tonight?" she asked rhetorically. "It's probably just the dybbuks having fun with you."

"What are dybbuks?" I asked.

"They are little devils that like to pester people and keep them from sleeping. Now I'll tell you what to do. Whenever you can't fall asleep, you just get out of bed and turn your shoes over. That's where the dybbuks hide at night, you know. If they don't have a place to hide when they are teasing you, they'll go away and bother someone else."

This little trick certainly removed the diffuse tension that was keeping me awake that night, and I must admit to having used it a few dozen times, with great success, during my primary school years.

Most adults are not worrying about dybbuks, however. Instead, they have other anxieties, worries, and cares, any one of which, if focused upon, can easily lead to increased tension and arousal. The adult trick is to think about pleasant things. Let your imagination wander. Don't think about work (remember, you'll work better and be smarter if you get a good night's sleep), and certainly don't think about sleep. Some people find that performing some relaxation or deep-breathing exercises helps. Others find that thinking of songs or poetry, recalling pleasant events from the past, or fantasizing about pleasant evens in the future all help. Presleep thoughts should be personal thoughts; they don't have to make sense to anyone but you, and you need never tell anyone what they are.

I have outgrown the inverted shoe remedy for sleeplessness. Today, my favorite aid to sleep comes from trying to recall poems from various sources, such as *Alice in Wonderland* or the writings of Carl Sandburg or even old nursery rhymes. I know the beginnings of most of them, but somehow I seldom make it through them far enough to determine if I know the whole poem. I simply start wandering though one of those poems and begin to doze off. A typical one to put me to sleep might be that famous child's poem by Eugene Field. Now how did that go?

> Wynken, Blynken and Nod one night
> >   Set sail in a wooden shoe
> Sailed on a river of crystal light
> >   Into a sea of dew . . .
>
> >   . . .
> >   . . .

Sleep and Health

The intimate relationship between sleep and health is easy to observe on an everyday level. We all know of cases where a college student goes for two nights without sleep in order to cram for exams and then on the evening of the third day comes down with the symptoms of a cold. We have heard of cases where a businessman has his sleep disrupted for several nights because of tension over a lucrative contract that he is bidding on and on the morning of the big meeting finds that he has developed a sore throat and laryngitis. Then there is the case of the surgery patient in the hospital who is awakened four or five times a night for tests and medication but still shows a low-level infection and who, when discharged and sent home, is "miraculously" cured of the persistent infection after only one or two nights of continuous sleep. What is actually going on here?

Every day of our lives we are part of a war; on one side is our body, on the other a multitude of potentially infectious microbes. To the many species of bacteria, viruses, and fungi in the world, the human body represents a warm haven where food and fluids are plentiful. To win their battles, these microbes must breach several lines of defense, the most significant of these being our immune system. Of all of the troops mustered by the immune system, the most active and well known are the white blood cells, or *leucocytes*. There are several different kinds: *Scavenger cells* function by surrounding and absorbing bacteria and other microscopic particles that are present at sites of infection or injury. *Lymphocytes* are present throughout the bloodstream but tend to congregate in the spleen, where they filter microbes from the blood; they also gather in the lymph nodes, where they filter microbes from the lymph, a clear fluid that drains from body tissues and ultimately returns to the blood stream. If there is an infection, the number of lymphocytes in the lymph nodes increases, which causes the nodes to swell and sometimes results in pain in the area of the lymph nodes (for example, the neck, arm pits, or groin). The neck swelling associated with mumps is an example of this. The activity of the lymphocytes is coordinated by the release of members of a family of specialized molecules called *cytokines*, of which the most important are the *interleukins*. Although the main purpose of the interleukins is to rally the infection-fighting lymphocytes, they also interact with the central nervous system to cause other changes that will help the body fight the infection.

It is common knowledge that when we develop a sickness or infection, we become very sleepy. It is not unusual for sleep length to double when a person is ill. Work done by Dr. James Krueger, a physiologist at the University of Tennessee in Memphis, and his associates seems to explain why this is the case. Krueger was particularly interested in the interleukins, which become more plentiful when the immune system is activated. He took samples of these and injected them into various locations around the brain of animals. Two things happened: First, the animal's body temperature increased, and it began to run a fever. Fevers are actually defensive reactions that may fight infections and, as long as they do not rise too high, serve important healing functions. When the body temperature is a bit higher than usual, most internal processes actually run faster. This means that organs work more quickly, antibodies are synthesized more rapidly, and so forth. There is now evidence suggesting that even antibiotics are taken up more quickly and have a stronger effect if the body temperature is a bit higher than normal (say around 100°F—38°C). In addition, some microbes are quite intolerant of high temperatures, and many are weakened or even killed by the increased heat level. Diseases often run their courses more quickly if there is a moderate fever. This means that taking something like aspirin to lower a moderate fever may actually offset activities of the immune system and may lengthen the course of a disease.

The second effect of injecting interleukins into the brain is that it induces sleepiness. If enough is injected, a test animal can go into slow-wave deep sleep within minutes. The obvious effect of sleep is that the sleeper's metabolism slows down, conserving energy and resources. These resources may then be used to fight the invading microbes. It is strongly believed that sleep is part of the body's defense strategy.

Immune system activity can thus cause us to sleep more, but the converse is also true. The immune system becomes more active when we sleep. While we sleep there are regular waves of immune system activity, some of which seem to also be synchronized with the working of our digestive system. This was probably designed for routine housekeeping functions such as protecting the body from possible attacks from microbes that might have entered with our food. Although the colon is designed to deal with a certain level of "toxic waste," the small intestine has to be kept relatively sterile, and the body has to be protected from toxins that might find their way out of the intestinal system. Increased activity in the immune system during our periods of deep sleep can defend the body from any microbes that might have survived the acid bath of the stomach. At the same time, these lymphocytes, antibodies, and interleukins are also available for fighting off the infectious effects of other bacteria, viruses, or any of a variety of nasty microscopic beasts that may have entered our bodies through cuts in the skin or through the membranes of our air passages. Thus, the routine increase in immune system activity during sleep gives us a healthy bowel, and if we sleep enough it will also give us a healthy body as well.

To see the link between the immune system and sleep a little better, let's go back to a mystery that we left unsolved earlier. You probably recall that I described a series of studies by Dr. Allan Rechtschaffen in which rats were prevented from sleeping and began to lose weight after a few weeks of this treatment. Next, they lost their ability to regulate their body temperature; they then simply died. When Rechtschaffen's research team looked for the reasons for these deaths, they could find nothing obviously wrong in the organs, blood, or urine of these rats. What had killed them?

A possible answer to this mystery was provided by Dr. Carol Everson, a senior staff fellow at the National Institute of Mental Health at

Bethesda, Maryland. Everson had been a student of Rechtschaffen's and noticed that the rats that died of sleep deprivation looked very much like cancer patients whose bodies had been weakened either by chemotherapy or some form of wasting away caused by the disease itself. When cancer patients enter the final stages of the disease, they are often hit with many secondary infections simply because their overtaxed immune system is now failing and they can no longer fight off potential invaders. Thus, it is not unusual for the final cause of death in a cancer patient to be some infection rather than the cancer itself. This led Everson to the hypothesis that perhaps the sleep-deprived rats were actually infected with something. When Everson did a new series of tests, she found that the sleep-deprived rats had died from bacterial infections of the blood. Perhaps the most interesting part of these findings is that the fatal bacteria were strains that rats come into contact with every day. These common microbes usually do not cause disease because the immune system usually is quite aggressive in cleaning up and eliminating them when they assault the body. What seems to have happened in the sleep-deprived rats is a complete crashing of their immune system. Because their resistance was down, their body became prey to infectious microorganisms that normally don't stand a chance of passing its defenses.

Researchers are now gathering a lot of evidence that confirms the idea that sleep is a vital factor in staving off disease and fighting disease organisms that have already started their attack. Some of the most convincing evidence comes from research by Krueger and his associate Dr. L. A. Toth. They have conducted several studies using rabbits as their experimental subjects. In one study, animals were infected with bacteria called staphylococci. The rabbits that showed the greatest amount of deep sleep in response to the introduction of the infectious material also turned out to be the animals most likely to survive. A second study, which used different infectious agents, including a strain of *E. coli,* produced similar results, with the rabbits having the least amount of slow-wave deep sleep being the animals most likely to die of the infections.

Numerous examples of how sleep debt weakens the body have now begun to emerge from research laboratories. One study showed that if you deprive rats of sleep for only 8 hours and then challenge the body with a foreign substance, the antibody response is weak. Moreover, the defensive response is still below normal 3 days later. Mice deprived of sleep show decreased immunity to influenza virus infection in the lungs; they also show a reduced ability to reproduce interferon and other vital infection-fighting substances. Recent studies in humans have also shown that loss of just a few hours of sleep can disrupt the normal pattern of the immune system response.

This link between the immune system response and the individual's sleep patterns can explain a number of diverse observations: For example, first-year medical interns (who, as you will see later, are often severely sleep deprived) are also often plagued with flu, colds, and infections. Many people who lose sleep caring for family members with progressive and deteriorating diseases, such as Alzheimer's disease, seem to have more health problems themselves. Widows and widowers whose sleep is disrupted due to the depression and stress following the spouse's death often get sick and die within the year. Apparently, any situation that results in shortened sleep time may also result in a weaker immune system, which increases the likelihood of infection. Direct measures of the blood of individuals in the aforementioned groups have shown reduced numbers of lymphocytes, and their immune system seems to be weaker in many other ways as well.

The link between the immune response and sleep deprivation may also explain some other medical findings. Some varieties of cancer are quite painful and disrupt normal sleep. It has been noted that many of the victims of such cancers develop the same kinds of bacterial infections that sleep-deprived rats do. Perhaps this is another example of sleep loss weakening the immune system. These results also suggest the possibility that the practice of taking temperatures and blood samples of hospital patients many times during the night might actually be doing more harm than good. The resulting sleep disruption may actually be slowing recovery.

Many other studies have looked at sleep patterns and health in the general population. A hint of the health risk associated with too little sleep appeared in a study conducted by the American Cancer Society. Over one million volunteers who completed health questionnaires were monitored by the researchers for 6 years. Obviously, over this time period some of the participants in the study died. It is this death rate that gives us some indication of how sleep affects health. When these data were first looked at by researchers, it looked as if people who sleep between 7 and 8 hours are healthier than those who sleep either more or less than this amount. Since that time, several other research teams have reanalyzed the data. They did so to make sure that the original health status of the volunteer subjects was taken into account (remember, if you are already sick, you will be sleeping more than you did when you were well). Statistically, certain variables, like the age of the subject, the number of people in each category, the incidence of smoking and alcohol use, and so forth, had to be taken into account. When these were considered, the researchers still found, as we might have expected, that the people at greatest risk of dying early were those who slept the fewest hours each night.

A similar study was conducted in Finland with 10,778 adult subjects. A mailed questionnaire was used, and people were followed for 6 years. In this study, men who were poor sleepers were more than 2½ times as likely to die during the test period than were men who were good sleepers. No effect of sleep length on mortality rate was found for women, however. This was a bit of a surprise, but the questions used to determine sleep quality were not very sensitive. For this reason, several years later another group of Finnish researchers decided to do a more precise study. They began with a sample of 1,600 adults, aged 36 to 50, all of whom lived in Tampere, Finland. The researchers used several precise measures to determine the length and quality of their subjects' sleep. They then determined the health status of each participant in the study. The results are really quite striking. For the men, those who were poor sleepers were 6½ times as likely to report having poor health than those who were good sleepers. In this study, the effects also held for the women: poor sleepers were 3½ times as likely as good sleepers to report being in poor health.

We have observed a similar phenomenon in our laboratory. In one series of studies we were working with university students, mostly between 18 and 25 years of age. This is, generally speaking, a pretty healthy group of people. The data being collected included information on how much sleep these students got each night and on their medical status (for example, the number of visits made to their physician in the past year, a measure that serves as some indication of how healthy a person is overall). At the time we analyzed the data there were 2,103 participants. We first divided the group into short sleepers, who averaged less than 7 hours of sleep a night, and average sleepers, who regularly got 7 or more hours of sleep each night. We wanted to also look at long sleepers, those who habitually sleep 8½ hours a night, but in this group of university students there simply weren't enough of these people to make the analysis meaningful. When we looked at the average number of doctor's visits for the previous year for the average sleepers, it was, as expected, quite low: the average value was 1.6 visits. For the short sleepers, however, the value was much higher. Even when we eliminated from consideration any visits to the doctor where the complaint was fatigue or insomnia, the short sleepers still averaged 3.7 visits in the previous year, more than twice the rate for average sleepers.

We looked at one other measure in this study that is also of interest to us here. As a crude measure of just how well the immune system was working in these students, we tried to determine the number of infections the students had experienced. The measure consisted of two parts. The first involved a checklist of common infections that young people frequently come down with, including viral infections (such as colds and influenza), fungal infections (such as athlete's foot or yeast infections), and bacterial infections (including boils). These kinds of problems are often self-treated and wouldn't necessarily require the intervention of a doctor. In addition, we asked how many times in the last year each student had some condition that required the prescription of antibiotics. Such instances would clearly be a measure of how many times a physician felt a student's immune system had been challenged and needed the assistance of drugs. From these data we created an index indicating the number of infections a student had in the previous year, the idea being that a greater number of infections meant a weaker immune system. The results were very similar to the results based on visits to the doctor: compared to the group of average sleepers, the group of short sleepers averaged just over twice the number of infectious incidents. This strongly suggests that the short sleepers had immune systems that were simply not as efficient as those of the average sleepers.

The British writer Aldous Huxley noted, "That we are not much sicker and much madder than we are is due exclusively to that most blessed and blessing of all natural graces, sleep." It seems that every day new research proves him to be more and more correct.

Asleep at the Wheel ≈

$\mathcal{U}$p to now we have been dealing with the broad general implications of running up a sleep debt. Now let's see how it affects real people in real situations.

It is afternoon and I am sitting in the passenger seat of a huge Kenworth truck. The size of one of these vehicles is overwhelming to people like me, who feel they are driving something really big when they get behind the wheel of a minivan. The big man beside me is Joe. He has just taken me for a short ride to show me what is involved in driving and maneuvering a tractor-trailer rig like this. "There are eighteen wheels and eighteen gears on this combo," he tells me.

It had never occurred to me that city driving in one of these trucks is hard physical work. Simply starting the truck after a stop for a traffic light can involve three gear changes before the truck clears the intersection. That big steering wheel, with a diameter of 30 inches (75 centimeters) or more, is not there for show. Its large size is there to provide leverage to amplify the turning force of the driver, who is often trying to maneuver a trailer that is 40 feet (12 meters) long around corners designed for cars less than half that length. My reason for talking to Joe, however, was not about driving skill but about the sleep—or, more accurately, sleepless—factor in driving. Joe settles back in his seat, pours a cup of coffee from a thermos for both of us, and explains:

176

Before I got this here short-haul driving job for the construction company,
I used to do long-distance driving—all the way across the country sometimes.
It was pretty grueling work. Two, maybe three, weeks on the road, 900 miles
[1,500 km] per day. Some of the shippers have time requirements, where you
got to get the stuff there really fast. If you do, some of them give you a bonus;
if you don't, some of them give you a penalty. In some respects it don't matter
anyhow, because you're always pushing yourself. If you're a private trucker,
the more loads you haul the more money you earn, so you get this frame of
mind that keeps telling you to haul fast, drop this load, and then get another.

The U.S. government got pretty worried about the fact that a lot of us
long-distance truckers were pushing the edge when it came to sleep. So they
passed a bunch of regulations, like having to keep log books on our driving
time and only allowing a certain amount of time driving before you got to
rest. Now—and I ain't casting blame on you personally because I know it
wasn't you, but they did get themselves some kind of psychologist to set things
up. Whoever this guy was, he didn't know nothing about trucking and
couldn't even figure out how long a day is. On his recommendation they pass
this rule that says that you got to rest for 8 hours after you been driving for
10 hours. You add that up and you got an 18-hour day. With the extra 6
hours you just go back to driving. So that means that you're really driving 16
hours a day. What's worse is you're really not sleeping very good, either. That
18-hour day thing means that if you try to keep to the regulations, you are
sometimes sleeping in the morning, sometimes in the afternoon, and only
sometimes at night. Now I tried to keep to the rules. I had one of those sleep-
ers with a bunk bed in the back of the cab, and I would crawl in there after
driving 10 hours. Hell, there just wasn't any way to get to sleep at nine in the
morning, no matter how tired you were. So most of us log the time filling up
with fuel and the time we use to eat a hot meal in a restaurant as rest time,
and most of us felt that it was sort of rest, even if it wasn't sleep. Some other
guys just keep two or three different log books and just keep right on driving
no matter what.

Now what used to happen on long hauls or circle hauls is that you started
pretty fresh, but after a week or so of this kind of schedule you were tired all
of the time. It got to the point where I could fall asleep sitting on the john in
the men's room in a gas station. But then, somehow, in the morning, even
without any sleep, you felt okay again, at least for a few hours.

The fatigue thing would get pretty bad toward the end of a haul. It would get really bad when there was nothing going on—like crossing through Kansas, where there is nothing but flat farms all growing wheat or corn. Nothing to see but the road and the fields. My truck has a CB radio, and talking to the other guys helps some. I also have the radio and a built-in tape recorder. I used to take these "books on tape" out of the library—that's where some guy reads a book for you—and listening to the stories helped keep me awake some. But even with all that, I still had some pretty close misses that started to scare me.

Probably the weirdest was when I was doing this cross-country job. I was heading west or maybe southwest and getting pretty near to Salt Lake City. Coming on in that direction you go down this highway that crosses through the salt flats, and I'll tell you calling them flats is a good description. In the summer it looks like a big flat empty parking lot out there. It was, maybe, around 3 or 4 A.M. and I was really tired and I'd been tired for days on that run. At night out there, there are no lights, and all you've got is what you see in your headlights. Damn little other traffic, either. I would sort of line myself up on the white line down the middle of the road. Since there was no other traffic, it didn't matter much, and it gave me something to look at. Anyway, I'm tooling along at the speed limit, watching the road, and the next thing I know, the road is feeling sort of bumpy and sounding noisy, like I was going over gravel or an uneven road surface. I look at the road, and there's no white line in sight. I figure to myself, "They're repairing the road," so I go on for another couple of minutes but nothing changes. So I go to pull off to the side of the road, but there are no shoulders. I got really spooked. I stop the truck and put on my flashers in case someone comes down the highway, and I get out of the cab. I'm looking around and I'm seeing nothing. No road, no lights, no signs, just nothing. It's like I'm parked on this big flat airfield.

Now I'm not superstitious or nothing, but I started to think of one of the Twilight Zone spook shows, where this guy finds himself in the middle of nowhere and it turns out that he has landed in hell. Well, that's what it felt like. So I said to myself, "I'll just leave the lights flashing and rest until morning when it will be light enough to see." I crawl back into the cab, get into the bunk, and just fall asleep. Next thing I know, there is this pounding on the side of the truck. When I get out its daylight, and there is the highway patrol cop standing there. "What the hell you doing out here?" he asks. "Out where?" I asked, feeling pretty stupid. "Look it, you're nearly 10 miles off the highway in the middle of the flats. The patrol plane spotted your lights flash-ing," he says.

The only thing that I can figure is that I fell asleep, drove off of the road, and just kept on driving. It made me real scared to think that if I had been somewhere where there was traffic or houses or things on the side of the road, I could have killed someone and myself, too. I mean, there I was, 10 miles in the middle of nowhere. If the cops hadn't spotted me with that road patrol plane, I could have just got up in the morning, not known where I was, and driven off in the wrong direction. You sure couldn't see any road from where I was, and every direction looked just the same. If I got stuck out there, with-out fuel, I hate to think about it. Lots of people have died out in deserts like that, and I figure that no one would ever bother looking for an eighteen-wheeler out in the middle of the salt flats even if someone ever did report me missing.

Joe's case is not unusual. There are a number of reports of drivers who fall asleep but continue operating their vehicle on the highway, sometimes for periods of many minutes. There is a frightening example that comes from an experiment conducted in Germany by researchers who were interested in studying night driving.[1] They used a set of spe-cial mobile recording devices that could record the brain waves of the driver in addition to such basic data as the number of times he blinked. The subject of this experiment was then sent out for a drive in the mid-dle of the night. The drive lasted for just under 4 hours, and about 2 hours of that time was spent driving on a long stretch of multilane highway. The conditions were similar to those experienced by Joe. The highway was not well lit, there was not much traffic, and the view from the vehicle was monotonous, offering little to catch the driver's atten-tion. When the researchers later looked at the data, all of which had been stored on tape for later analysis, they found something incredible: for a period of about 20 minutes, while the car whizzed down the auto-bahn at around 70 miles an hour (115 kilometers an hour), the driver did not register any eye blinks! We normally blink every few seconds, even though we are not normally aware of this. The data record in this case indicated that for around 20 minutes the driver's eyes were either completely closed or open and staring. The only time we don't regularly blink is when we are asleep. It is possible to sleep with our eyes partially open, although this is regularly accomplished by only 1 in about 200 people. To find out what was going on, the researchers consulted the driver's EEG recordings. In fact, these recordings showed that for most of that 20-minute segment of time this driver's brain was actually asleep. Although the roadway that he was traveling was generally fairly straight, there were some turns that had to be negotiated. Obviously, although he was technically asleep, some of the information was getting through to him. It was almost as if there was a built-in autopilot that provided enough navigation information to prevent the vehicle from running off the road or hitting another vehicle. With this German study in mind, perhaps Joe's 10-mile excursion out onto the salt flats while sleeping seems less surprising.

Joe's story is one of many that truck drivers tell about their close calls. Many, however, are not so lucky, and their sleep debt is paid in their own blood or that of others. A typical case was described to me by Walter, a truck driver in his middle to late 50s:

I think that a lot of the problems that we have nowadays in trucking comes from the way the merchandisers are running their operations. You see, a lot of companies just don't want to keep a big inventory in their warehouses. It costs up-front money and raises their insurance rates and all that. So what they do is to wait until they're running low in a line of goods and then arrange for a "just in time" delivery. Because the companies don't want to lose any sales, they go to one of the trucking outfits and arrange for a delivery from the manufacturer on what they call a guaranteed contract. One of those contracts says that the stuff has to get there on a certain day (sometimes even before a certain time of day) or the trucker doesn't get paid for shipping. The trucking line then turns around to us drivers and says, "If you don't get it there on time, that means you don't get paid for hauling the load." That kind of thing puts a lot of pressure on the drivers to get the load there in time.

Even without that kind of gimmick, in most cases the time is tight. It's tight, but if you push a little you can get it done. The problem comes if the manufacturer is slow in loading or if the weather gets bad or if there is some kind of accident or other slowup on the road or if your truck gets a mechanical problem—that sort of thing. Then, on a long haul the only way you can make up the time is to go without sleeping. You either push the limit of the law or keep a phony log book or just plain lie about how long you've been driving. I'll tell you, you don't want to miss that paycheck after all that work.

Now, out there on the highway most of us have got CB radios, and we talk a lot with each other. It's really useful because you find out about traffic problems up ahead and things like where they've hid the speed traps. If your truck breaks down, you can always call for help, too, and that makes you feel a lot safer. Most of all, though, I think that it's the company that's important. You get to talk to other drivers, you learn some things, have some fun and all. After you've made the run a lot of times, you get to know the handles of the regulars on the route. [Handles are the call names or nicknames drivers use on the radio. Walter's handle is Silver Cat.] *The whole feeling gets to be sort of like family, and you look out for each other when you can.*

Anyhow, one night I'm on a long haul and it's around 3 A.M. or so, and I'm looking for someone to talk to. So I get on the radio and am doing the usual thing, calling, "Hello out there. This is the Silver Cat. Is there anybody up and moving tonight?" This night the first answer I get is from Turkey Buzzard, who is a livestock hauler that I know from some runs along this stretch of highway. Then this new voice comes on the radio: "Hi, out there. This is Blue Beaver, carrying a load of sticks [finished lumber] *south to T_____."* *The three of us chat for a few minutes but Blue Beaver is talking really slow and he sounds like his mouth is stuffed with cotton. He's also missing chunks of the conversation, and a couple of times he's said the same thing that he said just a minute ago. All of this is the kind of thing that tells you that this guy is asleep at the wheel. We hear it a lot on the road, especially on those night runs. When you hear that kind of thing, you feel that you've got to do something. Like I said, the CB makes you feel that all of the other truckers out there are family and have some responsibility for each other.*

Now Turkey Buzzard, I think, noticed it first. He's a smooth talker and says something like, "Well, Beaver buddy, you sound like you got a bad case of sandman fever. Seems to me that if you don't ease off the road for a lay down, you're just going to fall asleep in the fast lane." The Beaver comes back and says, "I'm tired, but I ain't sleeping," and he still sounds like he is chewing on a sock while he's talking. So I get on the speaker and ask him where he's at. He gives me a route junction and it's not far from where I am. So I make a stab at trying to get him off the road by telling him something like, "Listen up, Blue Beaver, you really sound weary. I'm only about 8, 9 miles from you. There's a place just a few miles up from you. Got a big green sign with a red star on top. They make coffee strong enough to wake the dead. Why don't you pull off there, and I'll meet you in a few minutes and buy you a jug of it?" I sort of thought that if I could get him stopped, then maybe he would listen to reason and take a nap. And if he didn't, well, at least the coffee might help to keep him awake until it got light again.

You know, I've done this a bunch of times. Lots of time you get lucky and they stop, but sometimes, if they're really spent, it's like their mind ain't working. The Beaver was one like that. He gets back and tells me, "No thanks, Cat. I'm just a little tired, that's all. I got a guarantee load that's got to be there by 7 A.M. or I'm out of the money. Lookee, this road is so straight I could put a brick on the pedal and sleep my way into town. Honest, I'm good for another two, three hours, and that's all I need. I've done this with less sleep before." I remember those words; I got a real chill because he said them so slow and slurred. Well, old Turkey Buzzard gets back on the air and tries to talk some sense into him as well. I mean, we were just about begging him to get off the road. Finally, the Beaver says, 'Thanks, good buddies, but I'll be okay. I just need to concentrate a little harder on the road, so this is Blue Beaver signing off.' "

Turkey and I tried to raise him again on the CB but just didn't get any answer. We were both right concerned. Well, I kept on driving down the road. When I came to the little restaurant with the green sign, I stopped to see if he had come to his senses and stopped. There were four or five truckers in there. So while the waitress was filling my thermos with coffee, I called out to see if anyone there had the handle Blue Beaver, but none of them did.

That part of the world is really flat and the roads really do run straight for a long ways. As you near the city, though, the highway takes a few turns because of these rolling foothills, I think. As I was coming up to one of those turns, I could see a bunch of flashing lights, like from cop cars and ambulances. I pulled my rig off to the side to see what had happened and if I could help. When I crossed the road, I saw what had gone down. A big cab hauling a load of lumber had missed the turn. It had kept going straight and had hit one of the cabins of some little motel that was there. The truck had flattened it so that it looked like a pile of scrap wood and mashed the station wagon that was parked in front of it; then the tractor had flipped on its side. "Anybody hurt?" I asked the cop. He looked really shook and told me: "There was *an old couple sleeping in there, and the paramedics say they are both gone. They just took the driver away. They don't know if he'll make it. They think he may have messed up his spine, and he was bleeding a lot. You know, there were no skid marks. Nothing to show that he tried to turn or to hit the brake. He must have been fast asleep and rolling at the speed limit."*

I looked at the cab of the truck. There was blood smeared on the dashboard and the windshield. On the top of the driver's door was painted this cartoon animal with big teeth, and there was this label that said BLUE BEAVER. *I felt sick and went back to my rig to try to raise Turkey Buzzard to tell him what had happened. I really needed someone to talk to.*

The tragedy of Blue Beaver is not an isolated one. In 1988 the state of Arizona conducted a large general survey; according to the analysis by the Department of Public Safety, between 42 and 49 percent of the commercial vehicle accidents in that state are due to drivers who are sleepy. The sleepy driver is inattentive and will often, like Blue Beaver, just doze off at the wheel. Obviously, individuals with sleep disorders are also likely to have problems driving. The Stanford Sleep Disorders Clinic has published data suggesting that up to 45 percent of all patients with sleep apnea, 30 percent of patients with narcolepsy, and 8 percent of patients with simple insomnia report that they have had at least one vehicle accident that they believe was related to their being sleepy while driving. These rates may, in fact, be low. One study reported that 93 percent of patients with sleep apnea have had vehicle accidents in which being fatigued, sleepy, or inattentive was a likely contributor to the problem.

Our daily sleep–wakefulness cycles also play a role in determining whether we are likely to have an accident while driving. Recall that we have a major low point in our alertness in the early morning hours, between around 1 and 4 A.M., during which we have an almost irresistible urge to fall asleep. It is noteworthy that the reports from both Joe and Walter refer to incidents that occurred during that low point. In addition, we also have another period of sleepiness in the afternoon hours—between 1 and 4 P.M. During these periods of time even if we are normally rested and have no sleep debt, our alertness flags and we feel fatigued and sleepy. The extent of our sleepiness at these two times will depend upon the sleep debt we are carrying. The urge to sleep is also greater if the activity that we are engaged in is not very stimulating. Under these conditions we let our attention wander, and we may drop into microsleeps. A microsleep is a short period of time, perhaps only a few seconds or a minute in length, in which the brain actually goes to sleep regardless of what you may be doing at the time. Given the fact that there are many people who are running up some kind of sleep debt and that driving is often not a very stimulating activity, there should be a lot of sleepy drivers out on the road in the few hours after midnight and in the few hours after noon. On the basis of this we can predict that there will be two peak accident periods during each day, periods corresponding to the two stretches of maximum sleepiness.

One has to be careful when looking at any statistic that involves vehicle accidents, since the likelihood of an accident depends upon many factors. One important factor is the number of other vehicles on the road. The more moving vehicles you have to contend with, the more likely it is that you will have an accident. This simple statistical consideration would place the peak accident times at rush hours, which in Western countries would be between 7 and 9 A.M. and between 4:30 and 6:30 P.M. To avoid the complications caused by variations in the number of other cars on the road, several studies have looked at a particular kind of accident, one that seems to be a pretty good indicator of fatigue-related problems. Specifically, these studies considered only single-vehicle accidents, that is, accidents in which the only moving vehicle is the one driven by the person having the accident. Typically, these accidents include running off the road or hitting a stationary object such as a tree or a parked car. Single-vehicle accidents are almost always caused by the driver not paying attention to the road and road conditions. Some of these gaps in attention are often due to sleepiness and include those instances when drivers are momentarily unaware of their surroundings because they have entered a microsleep period for a few seconds. Obviously, sleeping drivers, whether they have nodded off for a long nap or have momentarily blanked out due to a microsleep, are not apt to swerve to avoid another vehicle parked on the road ahead, nor will they correct for the fact that the car is veering off the road and into a telephone pole.

Researchers have analyzed more than 6,000 of these single-vehicle accidents and have confirmed what we expected: there are two daily peak times for these accidents. The major peak is between 1 and 4 A.M., which covers the period where our circadian cycle is at its low point and we are suffering from our strongest pressure to sleep. This peak in the accident rate occurs even though there are very few vehicles on the road at this time of day. In addition, there is a second, smaller, peak that occurs between 1 and 4 P.M., which is the midafternoon low point in our alertness cycle. Peretz Lavie, of the Technion-Israel Institute of Technology in Haifa, Israel, looked at the times of all the sleep-related traffic accidents that occurred over a 6-year period.[2] Over the years 1984 to 1989 the traffic accidents in Israel showed two pronounced peaks, which you can easily see in Figure 1.

If we are already running up a sleep debt, the daily low points of our sleep–wakefulness cycle become times when the urge to sleep, at least for a few moments at a time, becomes irresistible. Even at the modest

FIGURE 1

Times of occurrence of all sleep-related traffic accidents in Israel for 6 consecutive years (1984 to 1989). The two peak periods correspond to the peak periods of fatigue in our daily sleep–wakefulness cycle.

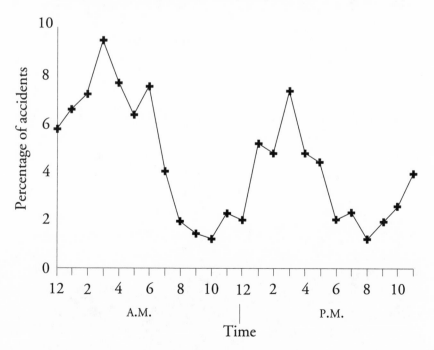

speed of only 30 miles an hour (50 km/h), a 10-second microsleep results in a car moving 440 feet (134 m), which can easily take you across several lanes of traffic and off the road for a distance longer than the length of a football field. Thus, in the open countryside you could drive off a cliff or embankment or straight into a tree; in the city you could drive into a wall or into parked vehicles. A small microsleep may have caused the problem, but the result is a large uncontrolled movement of the vehicle—even though you may be driving at a slow speed.

How common is the tendency to fall asleep behind the wheel? French researcher Damien Leger prepared a report for the National Commission on Sleep Disorders Research, which was released in 1994. Using data from the United States, he analyzed a full year's statistics on motor vehicle accidents. His most conservative estimates suggest that in 1988 sleepiness accounted for 41.6 percent of the total traffic accidents recorded. The numbers are staggering: they include 769,184 disabling injuries and 17,689 deaths due to sleepy drivers. The total cost of this to the economy of the United States alone, in terms of health care costs and lost income, comes to $37.9 billion. This dollar sum is larger than the national debt of many smaller countries in the world.

Asleep at the Operating Table ☠

There is another group of people who have even longer hours and more intense work schedules than truckers do. Like truckers, however, any errors they make because of their sleep debt can cost lives.

I was lying on a gurney in a hospital emergency room. The pain-killing drug I had been injected with some minutes before was starting to work, and I was feeling a bit better. Mainly because I knew two of the nurses, my anxiety level was probably a bit lower than it normally would have been. The younger one, who had set up my intravenous drip, had actually been a student of mine (she told me that she loved my course, learned a lot, and thought I was a terrific lecturer and said all those other nice things that are music to a professor's ears). The older nurse was someone I had met outside the university. (She was the wife of a man I knew through my activities with dogs. She often came to dog shows, and we had chatted pleasantly a number of times.) While I found it somewhat embarrassing to have these women helping me in intimate ways, such as undressing, this was offset by the feeling that someone who actually had a personal concern for me was around.

I looked across the room. The older nurse and a doctor were approaching. The doctor was young but looked rather worn. He walked over to the end of my bed with a listless shuffle and lifted the clipboard

187

that contained my records. He looked at the top sheet of paper blankly for a moment and then pointed to something written there.

"*Can you read this, nurse?*" he asked.

The nurse looked at him and asked, "*End of shift?*"

"*Yes.*"

"*Rough one?*"

"*Almost over.*"

She looked at her watch and said, "*Dr. M_____ will be starting in fifteen minutes. I think that this patient can hold till then, and that way there will be someone around to follow through on the tests.*"

"*Okay,*" he sighed in a dismissive way and began shuffling back across the ward.

The nurse walked over and checked my intravenous setup.

"*Was that a resident?*" I asked.

"*Yes,*" she said quietly. "*He's been on duty for around 24 hours, I think. He's got what some nurses call end-of-shift eyes. That's where the house staff can't even focus their eyes well enough to read the chart. They try to hide it by asking us to read it for them or getting us to tell them what the problem is. The good ones ask us to double-check medications and doses, that sort of thing. Dr. M_____ will be here in a few minutes. He's just starting his call, so you shouldn't worry.*"

She smiled and patted my hand as she left, but I did worry. What I found myself thinking about was the consequences of having emergency doctors make life-and-death decisions about their patients when they are suffering from massive sleep debt. There was a landmark case in New York State that dealt with this issue. In March 1984 an 18-year-old woman named Libby Zion was brought to the emergency room at New York Hospital. She was running a fever of 106°F (41°C). She was admitted to the hospital for treatment at 2 A.M., and by 6:30 A.M. she was dead. This case might have been viewed as just another situation where a patient was too ill to be saved or had just taken an unlucky turn that proved to be fatal. However, Ms. Zion's father was Sidney Zion, a well-known lawyer who also was a writer for the *New York Times*. He learned that the medical resident and intern who attended to his daughter had both been on duty for 18 hours when they admitted her and started treatment. Mr. Zion used his influence to convince the district attorney to start a grand jury investigation into his daughter's death. Although in the end the grand jury did not recommend criminal charges, they did find that this woman's death was due to medical errors, such as prescribing treatment with drugs that are known to produce adverse and harmful effects if used in combination. The grand jury concluded that these errors were due, in part, to the fact that the doctors involved simply did not have enough sleep to make sound and accurate judgments and diagnoses. Ms. Zion was admitted at 2 A.M. and had a medical crisis at 4:30 A.M. that resulted in the drug administration that ultimately proved fatal. This means that the effects of any sleep debt these doctors had was compounded and amplified because these events were taking place at the lowest point in their daily sleep–wakefulness cycle.

At about the same time the grand jury report was issued, New York City Council President Andrew Stein released another damning report. Stein had established himself politically as a sort of consumer advocate for health care in New York City. It is also the case that he was not a completely disinterested third party in this instance, since he had at one time employed Libby Zion as a student intern in his office. His report focused on a health department study that concluded that the Zion case was not unique and that many hospital deaths were due to sleep-deprived doctors making mistakes in treatment and diagnoses.

To understand the medical situation, one must know that at that time it was not unusual for staff doctors (residents and interns) to work 100 hours a week, presuming that the week included two nights on call. This schedule, although somewhat rarer today, is still common in many hospitals. Let's see how much a workweek like this leaves for other needed functions, such as sleeping: Suppose that the staff doctor lives between 30 minutes and 1 hour traveling time from the hospital. This means that between 5 and 10 hours are spent each week simply getting to and from work. On the five mornings that the individual sleeps at home, suppose that he or she can dress, wash, and eat breakfast in 1 hour, which would take another 5 hours. On nights at home, suppose that the staff doctor spends a half hour preparing dinner, an hour eating, and a half hour preparing for bed, which totals about 10 hours. Now suppose that we allow only 10 hours over the entire week to divide between doing chores (such as food shopping, laundry, house cleaning, maintenance, and so on) and socializing with family or friends. This leaves us with around 33 hours left to sleep for the week. This will probably be distributed as a 2-hour nap after each night's call, with the remainder being divided equally among the nights spent at home. This would mean that the longest expected sleep in such a week would be 5 hours and 48 minutes. A person who sleeps an average of 8 hours a week tallies up 56 hours of sleep over the course of a week. The house doctor develops his sleep debt by sleeping 23 hours less than this (for an average nightly sleep of 4 hours and 42 minutes per night). Clearly, as the grand jury in the Zion case and New York Department of Health recognized, this is not a tolerable situation.

New Yorkers were so distressed by the kind of information that was coming out about their doctors' sleep and work schedules that a special committee was convened to come up with regulations to ensure that the doctors got more rest. These were introduced in July 1989. What are these new regulations? In most medical settings, shifts were shortened to 16 hours of continuous work per day with at least one 24-hour day off per week. This means that a resident or intern can still work six 16-hour days per week (for a total of 96 work hours in the week) and still be within the legal guidelines. Those people working in emergency rooms are limited to 12 hours of continuous work, which must be followed by a minimum of 8 hours of time off. It does not take a mathematical genius to notice that 12 hours on plus 8 hours off adds up to only 20 hours. This means that if the emergency room resident starts his or her next shift immediately after the 8-hour rest, he or she will really be working 16 hours out of every 24-hour period. This is the same number of hours per day that residents in other specialties work; it's just that these 16 hours are not continuous.

Obviously, if the regulations had stopped at this point, virtually nothing would have been gained. However, recognizing that they had to provide hospital staff doctors with more than just a few hours of additional time, the drafters of the new regulations limited the workweek to 80 hours a week. This would represent a potential gain of 20 hours a week and would increase sleep time an average of 2 hours and 5 minutes a day. Unfortunately, the regulations say that residents should "average 80 hours per week over a 4-week period." The key word is *average.* A resident who follows a schedule of 16 hours a day for six days, then one day off, followed by 10½ hours a day for the next six days, then another day off, then back to six more days at 16 hours a day, and so forth, will actually be working 96-hour weeks alternating with 63-hour weeks. The average over a 4-week period is 79½ hours per week, clearly within the guidelines. Nonetheless, the doctor that you get during a 96-hour week is still getting only around 5 hours of sleep a night and may be deciding whether you live or die by looking through the haze of his mounting sleep debt. Remember, sleep deprivation effects add up over days. So by the beginning of the sixth day of work, residents who are depriving themselves of 3 hours sleep per day (which is what happens in the 96-hour week where average sleep length is about 5 hours) are really carrying a sleep debt of 15 hours or the equivalent of going two consecutive nights without any sleep at all!

"Certainly," you say, "no hospital is going to force their residents and interns into such a schedule, which might jeopardize the psychological well-being of their house doctors and the physical well-being of their patients." First, you must remember that in New York many residents and interns were working horrendously long hours before the change in regulations—and in other places they still are. A member of the administrative staff of a hospital in New York had this to say about the situation:

Many people think that interns and residents are putting in time chiefly to meet their educational requirements. In my administrative capacity that is of no concern. I have to look at these people as resources—resources that we use to deliver services at a reasonable cost. I'll tell you truthfully, in my book they are just cheap labor. With no effective union to back them, the fiscally wise procedure is for us to have them work as many hours as possible.

This new state regulation is a disaster. Looking at the situation statewide, I have seen estimates that claim that the hospitals are going to have to hire 5,358 full-time equivalent personnel to make up for the time lost because of this 80-hour workweek cap. Do you know what that will cost? It's in excess of 358 million dollars every year! And who is going to pay that? Your health insurance is going to have to cover those costs, and that means you. And for what? Do you know that there is no evidence whatsoever that residents ever get too sleepy to perform their duties. The Zion case was a fluke, and everybody overreacted. Those residents probably just didn't know what they were doing and probably would have made the same mistakes if they had had plenty of sleep.

Was the Zion case a fluke? If it was a fluke, it was only one in the sense that it was reported so widely and that the investigation was so public. There are numerous similar incidents that seldom get national coverage. For example, in April 1995 the *Denver Post* reported a case in which an anesthesiologist was charged with manslaughter. According to the prosecutor, Diane Balkin, Dr. Joseph Verbrugge, Jr., caused the death of an 8-year-old child by falling asleep during a routine ear operation. When the Colorado Board of Medical Examiners looked into the case, they concluded that because Verbrugge was asleep during surgery, he failed to monitor the vital signs of the child and thus did not detect the child's deteriorating condition until it was too late for the child to be saved. Testimony suggested that the doctor fell asleep for short periods of time, when his head would bob from side to side and then he would remain motionless and apparently unaware of activity around him. One witness suggested that during this operation he may have actually been asleep for as long as 20 minutes straight.

One of the surprises about the Verbrugge investigation was that this tragic incident was not the first time that the doctor had apparently fallen asleep during an operation. The assistant attorney general alleged that Verbrugge had fallen asleep at least six other times in the preceding 2½ years. These cases, apparently, never resulted in any direct action because none of the other patients died as a result of this anesthesiologist's dozing off. These other cases simply went to the hospital's peer review board, which has the practice of never releasing their deliberations or actions to the public. Apparently, such incidents are not widely publicized. I only learned of the Verbrugge case because I was alerted to it by a correspondent. It does not seem to have made the wire services or national TV news. I have now collected accounts of several similar incidents of fatalities due to doctors falling asleep, none of which received the broad coverage of the Zion case. As one hospital administrator told me:

We do not like the public to hear too much about such cases. It would tend to undermine their confidence in their physicians. For that reason, all staff members are informed that they should not speak to reporters and should refer questions to the hospital's public relations officer. Our public relations of-

ficer has the ability to make such stories sound dreadfully complicated and technical and not really exciting enough to report.

There is still one source of information that has not been fully choked off, namely, the house staff itself, those individuals who are still completing their internships and residencies. Many of these young doctors are still willing to talk about their experiences (if they are assured of confidentiality). I was allowed to visit a group of such young doctors just as they finished their shift. Four of them were willing to stay and talk because I had brought a large container of fine coffee and a collection of breads, cheeses, and sweet rolls. We sat at a table in a staff room and talked about the situation. One blonde, square-faced doctor had a bad case of end-of-shift eyes. Several times when he was speaking, he would simply stop in the middle of a sentence and then forget what he had been talking about until the original question was asked again. He had had the least sleep in the group, having just completed 36 hours of continuous work. (A hospital administrator might disagree with my estimate of the time on duty, since it was officially listed as a 12-hour day shift, followed by 12 hours that night on call and then another 12-hour day shift.) He began by speaking to me about being on call.

They tell us that call is not continuous duty and that we should catch a nap whenever we can. There are two daybeds back there [motioning toward a curtained area in the rear of the room], but we usually just grab a bed from whatever room is closest and empty. I'm not going to come all the way up here to use these beds and then get called back to the ER [emergency room] and then have to drag all the way down to the ground floor again. That can take 5 minutes or more each way, which I could have spent sleeping in the back of the ER. Sometimes I can get four or five naps of 10 to 15 minutes that way. Some call nights, if I'm lucky, maybe I can even get a half hour. Those naps aren't real sleep, but they help.

In some respects, he is quite right in saying that these brief naps are not "real sleep." There have now been a number of studies that have looked at what we can label "on-call sleeping," or the kind of rest people get when they try to catch bits of sleep whenever possible. In some studies, people sleeping on call (nurses, medical interns, fire fighters and paramedical emergency response workers) had special monitors attached to them that allowed researchers to measure their sleep stages. The results were not encouraging. The nature of the sleep patterns was not normal. The slow-wave deep sleep, which is believed to be the most restorative component, was much shorter and sometimes not even present in these on-call naps. Furthermore, the body never fully relaxed. The average heart rate of the on-call sleepers was higher, almost as if they were still active in some sense, still keeping themselves in a state of preparation for some alarm or call to medical duty, which they knew would eventually come. Overall, their sleep was very fitful, with many brief awakenings, as if they were still checking the environment and not relaxing enough for normal sleep to occur. If you have ever tried to nap while waiting for an important phone call, or while waiting for someone to come home, you may have experienced this type of sleep. You probably remember just how fragmented and shallow any sleep you got at that time was. In effect, you were sleeping on-call.

The blonde doctor was still talking in his halting, fatigue-soaked manner to me. *"You get so damned depressed sometimes, especially when things heat up in the ER, like on "Welfare Wednesdays."* [In that jurisdiction welfare checks are issued on Wednesdays. Some welfare recipients cash their checks and go on a drinking binge immediately thereafter, meaning that the hospital then receives a large number of cases where people have been hurt in brawls or street fights involving alcohol. Other welfare check recipients are often attacked by thieves who know that the money arrives on Wednesdays; many of these injury victims also end up in the emergency room for treatment.] *Last night we were just swamped. I would get finished with one Gomer and the nurses would be putting another in his place."*

"Excuse me, but what's a Gomer?" I asked.

A slim Chinese resident broke in to answer me:

Gomer is a sort of label we use for patients sometimes. It comes from "get out of my emergency room." You really don't want to see another patient when you are on call. They take up your time. They keep you from sleeping. They make paperwork. They really don't appreciate anything we do for them. They all complain that the treatment is too slow, that we're not doing enough for them, that we're paying too much attention to other things. They don't understand that we might have been working for 16 hours or even 36 hours with no sleep. Sometimes when that happens, at least for me, my eyes get all blurry and hard to focus. So I slow down and try to double-check things. I want to make sure that I still see everything. But I can't tell Gomer my problems, because if I do he'll think that I can't do my job right, and if anything goes wrong we end up with lawyers and lawsuits. Outside of the ER we sometimes use other labels for patients, which I suppose aren't very flattering either, like "crocks" or "turkeys." When you are feeling wiped out, you don't think of patients as people. They are just objects that have to be moved out of your ward as quickly as possible. Labels like "Gomer," I suppose, make patients more like objects in our minds.

The depression and cynicism in his voice was very apparent as he went on:

You can't even sit down until you've seen all of the patients. With each new one you keep hoping that it is something simple—you know, like a burn that you can turn over to the nurse to wash and dress. Maybe a shallow cut, with only a few stitches required. Nothing complicated. Bone stuff is okay, since you have an excuse to send them off to x-ray for a while. Sometimes, when you get one that is going to take a lot of time—like stabilizing some drug overdose case or something that will probably end up in the internal ward—and it's 3 A.M., you start to wish that the patient will die so that the bed will clear.

"No you don't!" came a loud protest from the only woman in the group. "Too much paperwork!" At that point she gave a tired laugh, and the others joined in.

The blond doctor started talking again:

All you want to do is to get them out of your ward. You don't want to talk to them. We are not rewarded for getting to know patients or for lending them that sympathetic ear that we are supposed to be developing. If you treat them like people, then you are effectively punished for it. First of all, it means that you have to spend extra time with them and that means more time in the ward. If the patients get to know you, then all that happens is that they feel like they can stop you to talk or something when you are trying to sneak out for a nap or trying to get out of the hospital at the end of your shift. Maybe when I go into private practice, I'll start to take an interest in individual pa-

tients, but not now. Now I'd rather sleep. You know, sometimes it gets to the point that you don't even want to spend the time with them to properly evaluate their medical problems. Like the nurse wants you to look at a patient because she sees some change, but you don't want to take the time so you give some instructions over the phone that you hope will keep things calm for the time being.

You develop survival techniques. Like the paperwork. You learn how to do it as quickly as possible. You keep it brief. Sometimes you are too brief. Like once I got a call from the doctor who had relieved me, who couldn't figure out what I had done. I told him to read my entry on the chart back to me. He did, and there wasn't even enough information there for me to remember which patient it was. Fortunately, there was a good nurse on with me, and she remembered enough so that the treatment could continue in an orderly manner. One other time I did some paperwork on a patient and was so sleepy that all I wrote under presenting symptoms was K Y pain and later on for the outcome I entered K P normal. I have no idea what I meant by either of those. The nurse said that I had described it as a routine kidney stone that had passed in the ER. She tacked a note onto the chart for me to see when I picked it up again, so that I could correct my entry to something more sensible. She's a good nurse.

The Chinese resident spoke again:

How much sleep you get is different for the different medical services that you are assigned to. When I was in surgical, I found that there were times that you could catch a few minutes' worth of sleep even in the operating room. After a while you got to be pretty good at it. There is always some slow time. For instance, when you are cooling down a patient for some procedures or rewarming them in open heart surgery. At those times the bath or bypass equipment is doing the work and you can be there for 15 or 20 minutes waiting. Why not catch a few minutes sleep then? There are always other people in the room, and one of the nurses or other doctors will usually wake you in time.

There was once, though, that I really got skinned. I was supposed to be watching this procedure and assisting. It was a really complicated liver procedure, but, from what I could tell, it was complicated because you had to do the same thing dozens of times at different locations around the organ and you had to make sure that you had them all. After I had seen it done two or three *times, it began to look routine. When you are down on sleep, it is always the routine things that you find hardest to deal with. If the patient had started to go into crisis, then there would have been enough adrenaline to keep me awake and alert, but this was just dull. Anyway, I think that I must have just fallen asleep standing there next to the table. The next thing I know the nurse is jostling me and R_____ [the surgeon doing the operation] is telling me to close. Well, I pull together the incision and close things off and then go out to wash up. R_____ is writing out some stuff, and he turns to me and says, "You know, I'm disappointed in you. I thought that at least once you would have had the courage and understanding to take my offer to do one." I didn't even know what he was talking about. He turns his back on me and walks out, and I asked C_____ [the anesthesiologist] what that was all about. He says to me, "Dr. R_____ kept saying to you that if you thought that you understood what was going on and if you thought that your hands were quick enough, you should tell him and he would let you try one. He must have said it two or three times, and you never said anything. Sometimes interns get that way on their first major OR [operating room] procedure. They just stand there and stare, too scared to say anything. We were all surprised. We thought you were past that." I never said anything because I had been just leaning on the table sleeping. I never heard R_____ offer anything. Ever since, when I am working with R_____ or C_____, I make it my business to try to appear as competent as I can, but I still feel pretty uncomfortable and stupid around them.*

The woman resident was smoothing down her hair, with hand movements much like those one might use to pet a dog. She now reentered the conversation:

I don't know how we are supposed to learn new things under these conditions. We know that we are supposed to be reading journals, studying texts, and that sort of thing, but I'm so tired all the time that if I sit down to read a text, I just fall asleep. We've got these conferences where we discuss cases and procedures and then there are "Grand Rounds," which are talks where superstars come in and give a lecture. We all agree that we will attend all of these, but a lot of times if you have a choice of spending an hour in conference or sleeping, you choose the nap instead. Even when you do go, your mind isn't in any shape to take in any new information. The room that we use for most conferences has these really nice soft chairs, and I think that that is a mistake if they really want us to learn anything there. All of the residents and interns sit in the back three or four rows. We call it the dormitory because the moment the lights go out so that the speaker can use the slide projector, we all go to sleep back there.

She gave a friendly poke at the blond resident with her elbow and said, "As soon as the lights go out, he always says, 'Wake me if I start to snore.'"

I turned to the fourth resident, a dark-haired, narrow-faced young man with wire frame spectacles. He had not said anything since we started to talk. In front of him was a cup of coffee, and resting on his lap was a sweet roll with one or two bites missing. His head was slumped on his chest and his regular breathing was a clear indication that he, too, had been working with a major sleep debt and that it was demanding payment now. The Chinese doctor slowly stood up and said to me, "Don't worry. I'll make sure that he gets home okay, but I think that we all better head for bed."

One of the most striking things about these doctors was their hard-edged cynicism and their overall sense of depression. I have now been told by many people in the health care field that after 4 years of medical school most newly qualified doctors are looking forward enthusiastically to actually working more freely with patients and to having a staff job with the official title of "Doctor." Yet by the end of the first year as an intern these attitudes have significantly shifted. Gone is that original enthusiasm; gone is the feeling of dedication to helping the sick. In their place are bitterness, pessimism, sarcasm, and a low level of hostility. Even worse is the fact that so many also develop a degree of indifference to the quality of medical practice. These mood shifts are completely consistent with the kind of mood changes we know occur in sleep-deprived people, and these doctors are definitely sleep deprived. As one former president of the Canadian Association of Internes and Residents put it, "The biggest drawback to being a member of the house staff is the almost callous disregard by the senior medical staff, and to a lesser extent the nursing staff, of the need of residents and interns to sleep."

There have been a number of studies that have looked at how a sleep debt can alter the mood of doctors. After a long duty period or a night on call, we would expect the doctors to feel fatigued and tired, and they do. However, a number of studies have also shown that at these times the doctors also show an increase in irritability, anger, restlessness, and generalized tension. Many describe themselves as lacking in verve or vigor and feeling hesitant and unsure in their daily actions.

One study by C. V. Ford and D. K. Wentz followed 27 interns through their first year of medical service.[1] They set up interviews and testing periods at four different times during that year. They found during that year that 56 percent of the interns suffered from at least one episode of depression severe enough to be considered clinically significant. As the year progressed, the interns' feelings of anger, fatigue, depression, and disordered thinking grew. The best predictor of whether they would be depressed and in poor psychological shape was the amount of sleep they had had in the previous few days. The less sleep they had, the lower their mood was and the more likely they were to show psychologically disturbing symptoms.

If the problems caused by sleep debt only impacted on a doctor's mood, this would be bad enough, but I would not want to be treated by a doctor who feels the way one resident admitted to me that he felt late in his shift:

After 18 hours of straight duty, like tonight, I just don't give a damn. I find myself getting annoyed at the patients that complain about pain or discomfort. Hell, I'm uncomfortable, too, and they can damn well put up with it, like me. When I feel like I do tonight, everybody better stay out of my way and let me do my work. I won't put up with any nosy nurse whining "Oh, doctor, could you check this drug dose? It doesn't look right to me." Shit, I don't care if it looks right to her. I'm the damn doctor, and she has no right to question my judgment. I won't put up with them calling me back and whining, "Doctor, do you want to check the dressing before I release the patient?" Hell, if they can't even do a bandage right, why do they call themselves nurses? Don't they know that I don't have time to waste on that crap?"

In this case the sleep deficit not only has generated anger but has created a resentment against the very actions that might serve to pick up errors, such as rechecking prescriptions or responding to the concerns of an alert nurse. Such a doctor might not have impaired logical reasoning or problem-solving ability but could still cause harm by simply not caring enough about the important details of treatment.

Unfortunately, more than mood changes during long medical shifts. Logical reasoning also deteriorates, as does the ability to do the kinds of tasks required by a doctor. There have been many studies that have looked at this. Let's just consider a couple of these. One of the most recent comes out of Tübingen, Germany, where a team working with Dr. Thomas Lingenfelser looked at 40 young hospital doctors, comparing their performance following a night off (with approximately a normal night's sleep) with their performance after 24 hours in the hospital owing to a night on call.[2] They gave a broad range of tests to these doctors in order to look at various mental abilities. Some of these were rather standard tests of mental abilities, while others were based upon actual skills needed in day-to-day hospital activities. The standard tests measured thinking speed and sustained attention, speed of responding to particular signals, and the ability to continue to work and process information when there are distractors around. Across these three tests, the doctors who had been on call and were sleep deprived scored an average of 5 percent more poorly. This means that, in general, the thinking ability of these doctors had deteriorated because of an immediate lack of sleep.

When Lingenfelser and his associates looked at the doctors' responses on actual hospital-related tasks, the effect of sleep loss was even more severe. One of these tasks involved the kind of memory task a doctor normally has to engage in while diagnosing and treating a patient. When examining a patient, the doctor usually sets up a mental check list of things to do. Thus, noticing a head bruise, he might immediately think of checking for pupillary responses and three or four simple reflexes. He would make sure that the patient is thinking clearly, and he might even want a skull X ray to look for fractures in the skull. This might be followed by an electroencephalogram to measure brain function if a closed head injury is suspected. To take another example, bad bruising on the chest clearly calls for a check of breathing clarity with a stethoscope and some routine chest X rays and . . . Notice that the list of things to do grows quickly and that all the items must be kept in short-term memory. If any item is forgotten before it is performed, an important piece of clinical information might be lost.

When doctors were tested on a version of this common clinical task, it was found that the doctors with the sleep debt did 8 percent worse than those who were not sleep deprived. This means that if the list of things to check on a patient has around 12 items, we would expect the sleepy physician to forget at least one of them before it was performed.

It is interesting to compare this result to a study conducted in Edinburgh, Scotland.[3] This study, by Ian Deary and Rosemary Tait, showed that following a night on call a doctor's ability to remember a string of facts, such as results of tests that might have been conducted on a patient, decreases by about 18 percent. This means that one out of every five facts that would be remembered by the doctor when he or she had adequate sleep would be lost to short-term memory under the conditions of sleep debt associated with a night on call. This does not bode well for the patient whose case is complex and who has undergone a number of diagnostic procedures the doctor has to evaluate.

The other major clinical task that the German research group looked at was the ability of doctors to interpret electrocardiograms, which are recordings of heart activity. A special videotape was prepared that showed typical electrocardiograms, some of which were normal and some of which were abnormal. Looking for abnormalities in heart activity is one of the most common hospital procedures a doctor does; cardiac problems by themselves are frequent causes for admission into emergency rooms, and they often appear as complications associated with other aspects of disease and injury. The amount of sleep a doctor has had turns out to be a major factor in his or her ability to detect heart abnormalities. The rested doctors in the study were 14 percent more likely to detect breaks in the normal heart rhythms than were the doctors with a sleep debt after being on call. That means one out of every seven heart problems that a rested doctor would correctly diagnose would be missed by a sleep-deprived doctor.

One of the most interesting studies of the effect of sleep debt on the performance of doctors was done at the Temple University Health Sciences Center in Philadelphia. Dr. Leonard Goldman and his associates actually wired surgeons and continuously monitored their heart rates during the performance of real surgical procedures.[4] A two-camera split-screen closed circuit TV recording was made of 33 operations, and the videotapes were later scored for changes in the heart rate as well as for the competence of the surgical performance of each of the doctors tested. Since increases in heart rate are an indication of stress, monitoring a doctor's heart rate is a way of measuring how stressful the performance of a surgical procedure is for him or her. In the sample of doctors tested, some had been on call and had had less than 2 hours of sleep the night before. Of these doctors, 80 percent showed elevated heart rates, indicating that they were under unusually strong conditions of stress. Stress, as any clinical psychologist can tell you, makes you inefficient, clumsy, and uncoordinated. When the video records of the operations were evaluated, the investigators concluded that the performance of the doctors with the highest sleep debt was inadequate when compared with the performance of those who operated under normal (non-sleep-deprived) conditions. The specifics of this poor performance are frightening. The doctors with sleep debt were extremely indecisive and used poorly planned surgical maneuvers, which filled 30 percent of the operating time. In other words, for nearly one-third of the time the patient was on the table, later videotapes showed, the sleep-deprived surgeons were operating inefficiently, slowing the procedures with wasted motions and performing inadequately and incompetently!

If, as these data seem to show, doctors with a sleep debt perform poorly and may be placing their patients at risk, why are residents and interns still required to put in these long hours? As the hospital administrator quoted earlier suggested, economics probably plays an important role, with residents and interns simply being viewed as cheap medical resources that are currently being exploited. One would think, however, that the health of the patient is the prime concern of hospitals and that certainly people would be willing to pay a little more to ensure better health care. Why, then, does one still see residents and interns working on an average of 4 to 5 hours of sleep a night?

When I posed this question to the dean of a major medical school, he agreed to give me an answer—but only if I would guarantee that he would not be named and that nothing in the interview would be published that might identify him or his medical school. For this reason, some material from the following interview has been deleted or modified. His comments were in response to my question, "Why do you, as doctors and medical educators, still insist on imposing such brutal conditions of sleep deprivation on your residents and interns, especially in light of what we now know about how this affects their performance?"

You sound like one of my favorite characters in medicine. Chevalier Jackson was a laryngologist out of Jefferson Medical School in Philadelphia. He made a number of major breakthroughs in the use of the bronchoscope and the esophagoscope. I think that it was in his autobiography, around 1938, that he wrote, "In teaching the medical student the primary requisite is to keep him awake."

The problem is that you are looking at what is going on as simple education and training or as the simple performance of medical duties. That is not the way that doctors view this. Publicly, doctors tell you that the residents have to put in this time so that they can see as many disease and injury states as possible during their training. This means seeing as many patients as possible. The argument is that no one wants a doctor to be treating them if their only knowledge of a condition is from a book or classroom. The only way to stuff this information into the young doctor is through long hours. Furthermore, the argument goes, this is a toughening process by which the doctor learns to make decisions under stress. The stress here may be due to too little sleep, but the experience and toughening will carry over and make the doctor stronger when the stress is due to a patient whose condition is facing imminent collapse on an operating room table.

I call that the "skill improvement theory." It's really claiming that the difficulties associated with long hours and heavy patient loads are actually a necessary and sacrosanct part of medical training. It's all part of the character development of the young doctor. There are many people in medicine who not only agree with this but believe that rather than making conditions better we should intentionally make them difficult. I have heard senior physicians say that lack of sleep has its benefits. These benefits include toughening the young intern and conditioning him for later medical practice.

Many doctors view the period of being on house staff as something like part of an epic journey that the medical student must make. It's the epic of Orpheus, Dante, or Hercules all over again. In this story the traveler (who is going to become a hero) has already accomplished many things and completed many quests (such as his passage through medical school). Now he is faced with a new challenge—the final challenge. Now he has to pass through hell, and in this netherworld he will confront his own limitations, suffer pain, strive against adversity. In the end, this traveler emerges from the under-world, and he has evolved to a new level. He is now enlightened, and he is now worthy of honors. He may now retire to quiet service of the state and the population, and he will never be called upon to undertake such a mission again. Well, this epic journey, for the young doctor at least, is the year of in-ternship and the years of residency.

Don't think that I am getting all starry-eyed about this way of thinking. It is really quite a powerful metaphor for the way we think. Every sword and sorcery book has some aspect of this quest, and so does every computer game that my son seems to get involved in playing. Having the netherworld be a hospital isn't all that strange. Samuel Shem's book, House of God, *uses this imagery. In the quest he describes, the hell that must be survived actually is a big city hospital. I don't doubt that some residencies may be an underworld experience that is not qualitatively different from those described in some of the epics. Here the traveler is trapped by his acceptance of the challenge. He cannot escape either mentally or physically. Here he must battle the monsters of illness and trauma. Here he must confront the great demon, Death. Yet, ultimately, he emerges. He is blood stained, yet he has overcome and won through. He has confronted, not avoided, every obstacle.*

I may be putting this in epic form, but actually some of our practices are simply examples of historical inertia. Before World War I the way that you obtained your graduate medical education was through an actual apprentice-ship. You could say that the medical hierarchy was quite selective and exclu-sionary, and the gateway to the profession was the internship. There is a real view among many people in the medical profession that medical training was more difficult in those bygone days. The doctors of yore, like William Osler and those others, are viewed as serving "in the days of giants." To be like them we must suffer the same kind of difficult training, and in so doing we will become "the men of steel." This means that the profession dictates that you must make the training really hard and the hours really long so that it serves as an effective barrier screening off the domain of the practicing physi-cian. This will serve to limit the number of trainees who actually make it to the status of full-fledged physician. If you survive the long hours, the work, the lack of sleep, then you have shown that you, too, are a hero with super-human qualities. As a hero you can now join the ranks of the other heroes, those who, like you, have bested the challenge and have been rewarded with the honorific title of "Doctor."

My view may be somewhat more elevated than that of many of my medical compatriots, however. Some doctors flatly deny that there is any problem at all. Their memories may simply be repressed. It's the same phenomenon as when women deny that there was much pain associated with childbirth even when the people who were there with them when they were delivering remember vividly their screams of pain. Some of my other medical associates simply view internship and residency as the medical equivalent of boot camp or maybe of a fraternity, where internship is just part of a hazing ritual. If you want to get into the fraternity, you have to go through the initiation. I have heard doctors say, "I went through it. I don't see why they shouldn't have to go through it, too." I even heard of one incident in which a senior physician shouted at a surgical resident, "What kind of doctor do you think you are going to turn out to be if you can't operate when you are a little bit short of sleep? Don't give me that crap about being so sleepy that your hands shake. A real surgeon can cut through that 'sleepy business' just as effectively as he can cut through anything else." I think that this may have been a bit harsh, and it certainly could have been presented in a more diplomatic way, but I do think that the surgeon was right. If we can't trust the resident's performance when he is finishing a night on call and is a little sleepy, then maybe that resident wasn't really cut out to be a doctor in the first place.

I really don't think you should view sleep loss as some casual side effect due to hospitals overworking the house staff. I view it as a sort of trial by fire. I think that patients really benefit from doctors that have been toughened and tested this way.

I thought to myself, "The patients that survive may benefit, but how about the others?" A line written by the Greek physician Galen, who lived during the 2nd century came to mind: "That physician will hardly be thought very careful of the health of his patients if he neglects his own." What, then, of a system that forces doctors to neglect their own health by depriving them of the sleep needed to restore their bodies and minds to full functioning? What does such a system think of its patients? After all, this is the system that has renamed all of us who are its patients. We are, remember, just Gomers.

Asleep on the Night Shift ✳

By my watch it is just past 3:30 A.M. I am walking across a factory floor. On either side of me are long conveyor belts carrying stamped and pressed bits of metal that will ultimately become parts of an automobile or a truck. Workers are engaged in various activities at several stations beside these belts. The man I am about to visit is just being relieved so that he can have his "lunch break." He is working the midnight-to-8 A.M. shift. He greets me, and we stroll in the direction of the employee eating area. As we move across the shop floor, I notice one man sitting on a high stool. In front of him is one of those big magnifying glasses that are surrounded by a circular fluorescent lamp to illuminate what is being looked at. A small plastic sign next to it reads INSPECTION STATION 7. The man, however, is not looking in the magnifying glass; his head is resting against a nearby metal support, his eyes are closed, and he is breathing quite regularly. Meanwhile, dozens of bits of stamped metal that may be important for the safety of a car that you or I might someday buy go slowly by in a continuous and unending flow.

It may well be that the second-greatest thief of sleep, after Edison's electric lightbulb, owes its existence to the invention of the production line and the continuous conveyor belt. This culprit is the "shift work" system. It all started with Eli Whitney, who is probably best known to us as the inventor of the cotton gin, a device for removing the seeds from cotton balls. Whitney had another invention that was not patentable but was infinitely more important: he invented the concept of machine tools and interchangeable parts—when he accepted an order to make 10,000 muskets. Prior to Whitney's invention, muskets were built by having a skilled workman fashion the entire weapon, forming and fitting each part. This meant that each musket was unique. If a part broke, its replacement had to be individually fashioned for that weapon. What Whitney did was to design machine tools to make individual parts that conformed precisely to a model. Unskilled workmen could operate the machines, and assembling all the various parts resulted in a musket. Since any part from one musket could fit into the corresponding location of any other musket of the same design, the muskets were easy to repair. Since the parts could be rapidly produced in great numbers and since final assembly was a matter of only a few minutes, many muskets could be constructed quickly and cheaply. In 1801 in Washington, D.C., in front of President-elect Thomas Jefferson and a number of government officials, Whitney demonstrated the results of his new system. From piles of disassembled musket components, he had them randomly pick out parts, and he quickly assembled them into muskets. Jefferson and the others did not know it, but they were the witnesses at the inauguration of what has come to be known as the American system of mass production.

Next came the assembly line and the continuous conveyor belt. It is somewhat amusing to note that this innovation really began as a "disassembly line." A meat processing plant in Cincinnati, Ohio, started it as a system of overhead trolleys that moved the carcasses of cattle and pigs from worker to worker. Each worker removed a particular organ or part for further processing. These trolleys were connected with chains, and a power source moved them past the workers at a steady pace. Each worker remained at a stationary post and each concentrated on one task, an arrangement that minimized unnecessary movement. It also allowed the pace of work to be dictated by the machine. The end result was a dramatic increase in productivity.

In 1914 the automobile manufacturer Henry Ford successfully combined the principles of machine tools, interchangeable parts, the assembly line, and the continuous conveyor belt. Using the old system, in which parts were carried to a fixed assembly point, it took 12½ hours to assemble an automobile chassis. By using a chain drive conveyor and stationary locations for workers, with each location containing stock-piles of appropriate components, assembly time fell to 93 minutes of actual work time. The positive outcome of this for the common work-ingman was the drastic drop in the price of automobiles, thus making them affordable for the average family. The negative outcome was that shift work—enabling factories to operate 24 hours a day, with a differ-ent group of workers covering each work interval—was now about to become an institutionalized policy across the world.

For most manufacturers, the capital expenses involved in creating machine tools and automating plants is so great that they simply can-not afford to use them only 40 hours a week (just one-quarter of the 168 hours in a week). By instituting 24-hour-a-day operations, manu-facturers can increase the productivity of their plants fourfold. Some-times the very nature of the assembly line makes it impossible to stop the process efficiently. For example, some stations may have just com-pleted processing that requires that the next step be done within a few minutes; if the line were to stop at this point, many units of the prod-uct might be lost. In addition, it was now quite possible to continue manufacturing through the night since Thomas Edison's electric light-bulb had permanently banished darkness from the workplace.

Since people working shifts in factories also need retail goods and services, other businesses have altered their times to accommodate them, meaning that many such businesses are open 20 to 24 hours a day. This includes not only providers of basic necessities, such as food stores, but many services as well. I recently noticed an advertisement for an apartment complex that made the following claims: "Twenty-four-hour services are available in our always open mall. You can get your hair done, your clothes cleaned, your TV or other appliances fixed, see a stockbroker, or just drop by to pick up some fresh-baked pastries—even if your watch reads 3 A.M." This means that there are hairdressers and appliance repairmen and many other people working something like a midnight-to-8 A.M. shift in this mall, even in the ab-sence of a continuous production line.

In the United States over 26 million people are shift workers, if we include all those people who work a scheduled workweek outside the daytime hours of 7 A.M. to 7 P.M. The shifts these people work are either fixed schedules (something like permanent night work) or rotating schedules. A rotating shift can include all three shifts (namely, day, evening, and night) or two of the shifts (usually day and evening for businesses that are not on a full 24-hour schedule). In the United States over 27 percent of male workers and 16 percent of female workers have rotating shift work schedules.

The problem with shift work is that human beings are endowed with a biological clock designed to prepare both the body and the mind to be active in the daytime and inactive at night. We have set up our society and our cultural institutions along these lines. Thus the "natural" pattern of human behavior is work during the day, recreation during the evening, and sleep at night. Because of this, shift work is a remarkably efficient device for disrupting an individual's normal sleep–wakefulness pattern. It does this, in part, by disorganizing our circadian rhythms, since workers required to be on duty at unusual hours are fighting against their own internal clock. Shift workers also find themselves out of step with the rest of the world, so they have little opportunity to have a social life. The process is so disruptive, and the stress of working rotating or night shifts is so great, that it is estimated that around 20 percent of workers simply can't tolerate this kind of work and give up their jobs.

Workers on night shifts and workers on rotating shifts usually suffer from sleep deprivation and, over time, may build up a considerable sleep debt. Compared to day-shift workers, people on evening shift tend to sleep an hour less per night while people on night shift tend to sleep 2 hours less. Shift workers also sleep poorly. They spend most of the night in the lightest stages of sleep and only a tiny fraction of the normal time in the more refreshing deep sleep stage.

There are several reasons for reduced sleep time and sleep quality for the night worker. One is that daylight hours are inherently more noisy. Traffic picks up during the day, and street noises can be quite intrusive. If there are children in the house, or even in adjacent homes, their playing is apt to be loudest during the day. In addition, unless the night worker has installed light-blocking "blackout" curtains or is resorting to a sleeping mask of some sort, light will flood into the bedroom. The presence of light suppresses the production of melatonin. (You may remember that melatonin is a hormone secreted by the pineal gland, but only in darkness.) The direct effect of an increased amount of melatonin in the blood is to make us sleepy, perhaps by making it easier to create serotonin and other chemicals associated with sleep. Thus, a bedroom lit by the morning or afternoon sun interferes with our normal internal chemical cycle and makes it harder to fall asleep and to sustain sleep.

Another reason shift workers end up sleep deprived is that their internal clock is out of step with their actual daily activities. The bouts of sleepiness that reach their absolute peak in the late evening are really designed to prepare us for sleep. Our biological clock causes our mental and physical systems to start to wind down, and in this more relaxed state it is easy for us to sink into sleep. Suppose, however, that you have just returned from the night shift at 9 A.M., and now you try to go to sleep. Your body is placed in a state of confusion. Your internal temperature is starting to rise, telling your brain and other organs that you are entering a period of wakefulness, yet here you are trying to put yourself to sleep by lying in bed.

Torbjorn Åkerstedt of the National Institute for Psychosocial Factors and Health at Karolinsk Institute in Stockholm, Sweden, and his associates have demonstrated what happens when we try to sleep at odd times in the circadian cycle.[1] In one series of studies volunteers were deprived of a full night's sleep. They were then allowed the opportunity to sleep as long as they liked. When they were allowed to go to sleep at 11 P.M., when their biological clock was winding down, these sleepy volunteers immediately fell asleep. They slept well over an hour longer than their usual sleep length and had plenty of deep slow-wave sleep. Most awoke feeling quite refreshed. For other volunteers, however, who were not allowed to go to bed until 7 A.M., when their biological clock was on the rise, the result was quite different: despite the fact that they had been deprived of a full night's sleep, these volunteers actually slept a shorter length of time than was their normal custom. Their sleep was not as deep as that of the volunteers who went to bed in the evening, and their total sleep length was actually only half as long. This group awoke feeling sleepy and still fatigued. Their inefficient sleep was simply due to the fact that they were trying to sleep when their internal clock indicated that they should be awake, regardless of their current sleep needs.

If you stay on a particular shift long enough, your internal clock will eventually adjust to it. Unfortunately, some people on night shift never allow their body to make this adjustment because they don't give it a chance. If you are working the night shift, then weekends (or other days off) may be the only time that you can normally interact with your family and friends. If you want to take the kids to the zoo, for instance, you must do it during the daylight hours, when the kids are awake and the zoo is open for visitors. If you want to have a barbecue and invite your friends and family, you will have to plan it for the afternoon or early evening, just as other people do. Because you are asleep when your family members are awake and you are at work when they are relaxing at home in the evening, you may make a special effort just to wake up with the family to go to church or have a Sunday morning breakfast with them. The end result of these very understandable attempts to lead a normal family life is that you will have effectively undone all of your body's attempts to readjust your biological clock to the conditions of being awake at night and asleep during the day. Thus, when Monday comes and you start your night shift again, you have a biological clock that is still out of synchrony with your work schedule. Under these conditions your sleep disruption may become quite chronic, and your sleep debt will continue to build up over a period of weeks. During this whole time you can expect to suffer from excessive fatigue, reduced work efficiency, and tendencies to be irritable, depressed, and generally unhappy with your life.

The actual degree of sleepiness shown by shift workers is much larger than most people recognize. For example, Åkerstedt reviewed data from police, steel workers, railroad workers, and other shift workers and was startled by the results. He found that approximately 75 percent of shift workers experience noticeable sleepiness *on every night shift!* Furthermore, the data indicated that at least 20 percent of the workers on any given night shift experience at least one episode of sleepiness that is severe enough to actually cause the individual to fall asleep while at work. One police officer described his own situation in this way:

When they rotate us onto night shift, things sometimes get a bit hairy. It takes a while to get into nights, and I'm never very comfortable at it. My wife says that I am really bitchy around the house when I'm working nights, but I just can't seem to get enough sleep during the days. Usually, sometime around 3 A.M. we turn the squad car into an alley, and my partner and I coop for a half hour or so. [Cooping turns out to be a term used to mean taking an unauthorized nap in the patrol car while on duty.] *It's not like we plan it in advance. It's just when things are slow, you start yawning and coffee just doesn't seem to work. If I'm driving and I see my partner with his head hanging and his eyes closed, I reckon that it's time to pull off the street and coop a while. We leave the radio on, of course, so that if a call comes through for our car, we can pick it up. We get pretty good about waking up when our call sign comes over the air. Usually we can get 20 minutes, maybe a half hour, of sleep out of it. Sometimes we've even pulled off an hour if nothing was happening.*

There was one night, though. We had just shifted back to night shift—and I never sleep very well the first few days after the shift. We were both pretty washed out, and we stopped in a parking lot to rest a few minutes and to drink some coffee. It was around 2 A.M. or so, and I suppose that we both just fell asleep there. Next thing we know there's all this noise on the radio. Someone is yelling, "Officer down," which means a cop has been hurt. He's also yelling, "Where the hell are you? I need back up now, damn it!" Well P_____ [his partner] *calls in and asks where this is happening. The controller tells him that they've been calling an "All units in the vicinity" for the past 5 minutes. It turns out that we'd been sitting there the whole time just two blocks away. We got our asses over there fast, and it was a mess. Some bikers had tried to beat up on a longshoreman, and the whole dock had emptied to give him some help. There was a truck burning. One of our guys was lying on the pavement next to his car with his partner kneeling over him with his shotgun out. He's still yelling into the radio. The guy down had been hit pretty hard a bunch of times with a stick or a bat. Broke some bones, gave him a concussion—all of that. Good thing nobody had guns or who knows what would have happened. Anyway, we were still the first back up to arrive. The others got there a couple minutes later. Hell, we were just 30 seconds away! We could have been there before our man even got hurt. It's just we were sleeping. Now, every time we're on night shift and we get something that looks like trouble and we have to call for back up, I get a little scared. I keep wondering whether anyone out there will hear us. I keep worrying that maybe they won't because they're all sleeping in their cars they way we were.*

Tradition is a major contributor to the havoc we see in the sleep cycles of shift workers. For no logical reason, when rotating shift work was first introduced, the decision was made that shift changes would go in a counterclockwise direction. That is to say, when you changed shifts your next shift was 8 hours earlier. Thus, from day shift (say, 8 A.M. to 4 P.M.) you go to night shift (midnight to 8 A.M.) and then evening shift (4 P.M. to midnight) and then back to day shift. This turns out to be exactly the wrong direction to shift. The body's internal clock, you may recall, has a day length that would run naturally at about 25 hours per day, if it were not reset each morning by exposure to light. This means it is much easier to extend our days by putting off going to sleep until later, rather than trying to go to bed earlier. Our internal clock resets itself in about half the time when our work schedule shifts in a clockwise direction (for example, from days to evenings to nights) rather than in the traditional direction (from nights to evenings to days).

Tradition is also responsible for the fact that workers change shift every week or two. The problem with this tradition is that it is wrong for our bodies. If shifts are rotated after 5 or 6 days of work, with one or two days off in between shift changes, this often means that our internal clock will never catch up with our work schedule. If we make the traditional 8-hour counterclockwise shift change, it will take around 16 days for our biological clock to adjust to the new work time. This means that with a shift rotation every week or two our internal clock is always out of step with our daily activity cycle. This was shown by Michael Paley and Donald Tepas of the University of Connecticut in a study of firefighters.[2] Even on the last day of 2 weeks on the evening shift, the firefighters were still describing themselves as "not fully alert," "foggy," and "let down." Their sleep patterns were a mess. Over the three shifts these men averaged around 6 hours and 20 minutes of sleep a night, and this dropped to only 5 hours a night when they were on night shift. The night shift was the most difficult: the mood of the firefighters deteriorated from the first shift on night duty and continued to be poor over the whole 2-week period.

The importance of the direction of shift rotation and the length of time at each shift was dramatically illustrated by Dr. Charles Czeisler of the Brigham and Women's Hospital of Harvard University Medical

School. In 1986 he was asked by the U.S. Fraternal Order of Police, a national police union, to devise a new work schedule for the police officers in Philadelphia. When surveyed, 45 percent of the police force in that city complained about sleep problems. They were using a very traditional shift system, which involved an 8-day counterclockwise rotation. The night shift was the most difficult, as might be expected, and police records showed that those officers working nights were having four times as many accidents as those working days. The new schedule that Czeisler devised involved a longer time on each shift (18 days) and a clockwise rotation direction. These simple changes produced incredible benefits. There was a reduction of 25 to 30 percent in the amount of sleeping on the job and a 40 percent overall reduction in accident rates. When surveyed after the new shifts had been put in place, police officers reported that their sleep quality was better (and many fewer reported using sleeping pills or alcohol to try to get to sleep). Furthermore, the police reported improved family relationships and general satisfaction with their social lives.

As a group, shift workers are chronically unhappy, continually irritable, and always complaining about fatigue. For this reason, many different systems of shift scheduling have been tried. Some seem quite counterintuitive. For example, one of the conventional practices in some European countries seems, at first glance, to be a deliberate and brutal assault on the typical human biological clock. It involves quickly rotating workers from one shift to another. Thus, a worker might begin with 2 days on day shift, then go to 2 days on evening shift, then 2 days on night shift, then 3 days off; then the cycle repeats itself. The notion behind this kind of scheduling is this: a rapid shifting won't give the workers any time to start adjusting their circadian clocks to the new schedules, and in this way some of the fatigue and sleep disruption that accompanies shift changes might be avoided. There is considerable controversy about whether this system works, however.

An example of how rapid rotation of shifts can cause problems comes from Dr. Patricia J. Sparks of the Department of Health Promotion and Preventative Medicine of the Providence Medical Center in Seattle.[3] She looked at the performance of masters, mates, and pilots on her state's ferry system. Most of the ferry runs have a standard shift rotation, but one of them has a rapid shift rotation similar to the schedule that is common in many European countries. Dr. Sparks found that twice as many of the ferry officers on this short shift rotation were unhappy with their work schedule. Short rotation workers were also twice as likely to report poor sleep; in fact, 36 percent of them consulted a physician for insomnia, as opposed to only 7 percent of those on normal shift rotations. Of even more importance than these findings are the differences these shift schedules make in terms of safety: an amazing 64 percent of the short shift rotation crew admitted to making errors of judgment on duty, specifically, errors they felt were due, at least in part, to fatigue. This is nearly four times as high as the proportion of ferry officers on a normal rotation who admitted to making such errors. Furthermore, ferry masters, mates, and pilots on quickly rotating shifts, as compared to officers who had normal shifts, were twice as likely to admit that they had had a near miss in which they had barely avoided a major accident. Obviously, the rapid rotation of the work shifts was causing a major disruption of the circadian sleep–wakefulness cycle in these workers, which, in turn, was causing errors and increased accident susceptibility. In addition, *100 percent* of the short shift rotation crew reported feeling fatigued through at least 2 or 3 shifts every week!

So far, we have only been talking about the standard 8-hour work shift. However, a 12-hour shift is common in some chemical and plastics industries. Nursing staff in many hospitals and community health centers have recently started to work 12-hour shifts. The attraction of this system is the amount of time that workers have off. In a typical schedule the worker might alternate, working 4 days one week and only 2 days the next. Some estimates indicate that nearly 140,000 workers are now on 12-hour shifts in the United States, and about one-fifth to one-quarter of all hospital nurses working shifts have opted for a 12-hour shift length.

There are problems, however, with the 12-hour shift, as has been shown in a series of studies by Roger Rosa and Michael Ciolligan of the U.S. National Institute for Occupational Safety and Health in Cincinnati. When they compared the performance of control room operators who worked a 12-hour work shift 4 days a week to the performance of operators working rotations of 5 to 7 days with only 8 hours per shift, there were obvious differences. Over the four 12-hour days, workers built up a considerable sleep debt, probably because of nonwork activities. Consider the fact that traveling to and from work, eating, maintaining personal hygiene, and joining family activities all have to be squeezed into 4 hours if workers are to get a full 8 hours of sleep in a day in which they work a 12-hour shift. For workers on this shift, sleep time actually decreased between the 1st and 4th day by about 45 minutes. Feelings of fatigue and decreased alertness were common over each 12-hour shift, and these became worse over the course of the workweek.

Several pieces of research have shown that performance also begins to deteriorate and the number of errors tend to increase when people are working a 12-hour shift. In one study, the number of errors doubled over the 4-day workweek. The greatest effects, however, are found within the 12-hour shift itself. Studies have shown that workers are responding more slowly after 10 hours of continuous work and are missing bits of information they had no difficulty processing earlier in their shifts. They are also making many minor errors in judgment.

Errors late in a long shift might have been the cause of a mishap at the Kennedy Space Center. On one space mission, console operators had been working 12-hour shifts. At approximately 11 hours into their shift on the third consecutive night of work, information flashed on their consoles concerning a valve failure in the fuel system of the space shuttle. Apparently, one operator misinterpreted this information and instead of simply closing off the next valve down the line, the operator pressed a button that caused several vent and drain valves to open. This resulted in the dumping of 18,000 pounds of liquid oxygen from the space shuttle's fuel tanks. This was just 5 minutes before the spacecraft was scheduled to take off. Fortunately, there are numerous safety monitors in the system, and these immediately began to issue warning signals. The operators, apparently suffering from sleep debt, were still too foggy to understand what was happening and did not immediately respond. It was not until a mere 31 seconds before liftoff that the launch was finally stopped. During the investigation that followed, one official said, "They had lost enough fuel so that they would probably have not made it into orbit. I hate to think what might have happened if the burnout came without warning, when they were still on their way up." The investigation concluded that the major cause of the problem was console operator fatigue.

The event just described occurred less than a month before the space shuttle *Challenger* exploded during its takeoff in January 1986, killing all of its crew. The Kennedy Space Center management had apparently not yet learned of the dangers of long shifts and cumulative sleep debt. If a shift system allowing long hours is in place, it is common to abuse the system. When there is an unusually high workload or external time pressures or when unexpected events slow progress, it is easy to begin to ignore scheduled time off and just continue people on their shifts for as many consecutive days as are needed to accomplish the task at hand. According to the report of the presidential commission appointed to investigate the *Challenger* disaster, this was a major factor in causing the accident.

The pressure placed on the Kennedy Space Center came from the agency funding it. The U.S. National Aeronautics and Space Administration (NASA) was trying to establish the fact that the space shuttle program was valuable and reliable and could handle a large workload. To do this, they were trying to increase the frequency of shuttle flights and had plans to fly more than one flight per month. In order to achieve these goals, heavy pressure was put on the ground crew of more than 5,000 workers as well as on the engineers, scientists, and launch control officials who were in charge. For example, during the 2 months preceding the launch the average shift length was 10 to 12 hours, with work periods ranging from 10 to 18 days in a row—without time off. The investigating commission found one worker who had put in 50 such days in one continuous run without a single day's rest! As might be expected, those individuals with critical skills, whose judgment was most relied upon, often put in the longest shifts. The leader of one of the mechanical teams worked for 26 consecutive days. Two of these involved 8-hour shifts, but the other 24 ranged in length from 12 to 16 hours. The report of the commission commented that this sort of schedule was "extreme but by no means isolated" and that it illustrated "a frequent pattern of combining weeks of consecutive work days with multiple strings of 11- or 12-hour days." Such schedules are wearing and cause fatigue, inefficiency, and discontent. James Beggs, a former

NASA administrator, later speculated that the continuing pressure of such work schedules might be one reason so many of NASA's most skilled and experienced people were forgoing the glamour and excitement of being associated with the space program and resigning.

It may well be that the final set of errors was made in a meeting—actually, a telephone conference—the evening before the launch. This meeting involved 13 key managers, including personnel from the company that manufactured the shuttle's solid fuel rockets. Later investigation showed that the accident was caused when an O-ring seal on one of these boosters failed. A number of scientists and engineers have claimed that there was adequate information available at that meeting to predict this failure, although that information apparently went unnoticed at the time. The commission investigating the accident blamed this inattention to crucial details on the fact that so many of the personnel were suffering from severe sleep debt. When the teleconference started at 7 P.M., most of the managers had been on duty for 12 hours (and many for more than this). Two of the managers had been awake nearly 19 hours and had had only 2 or 3 hours of sleep the previous night. The average length of sleep for the rest of the group was around 6 hours.

Things did not go well at this meeting. There had already been one launch delay that morning. At the conference there were heated arguments about whether to launch at all. The commission's analysis of the situation was that the long hours of work and short hours of sleep contributed to what they called "*a lack of effective communication and a failure to adequately exchange information during the teleconference.*" Sleep researcher William Dement has publicly stated, "*My own speculation is that in their severely sleep-deprived condition, these managers weren't able to assess the full impact of the O-ring data they were receiving from the manufacturer, Morton Thiokol.*"[4] The result of the cumulative sleep debt of many people was the tragic and fatal decision to launch the shuttle. In addition to the grievous human loss, it is estimated that the actual dollar costs from the delays, lost contracts, astronaut training, increased insurance, and the loss of the space vehicle itself must be measured in billions of dollars.

Long shifts are at the root of many accidental deaths. One example comes from Firozabad, India. In September 1995, a railroad switchman gave the green light to an express train traveling 100 kilometers an hour, thus causing it to slam into a stationary passenger train. The resulting death toll was 348 people, making this the worst train accident in India's history. The switchman was on a 12-hour night shift and had a schedule that involved seven nights on and one night off. The accident occurred at around 2:45 A.M., which would place it somewhere near the lowest point in the daily alertness cycle. Whether the man was literally asleep at the switch may never be known, since he fled in the confusion following the accident, taking his family with him.

There is really little to separate work-related from non-work-related effects of shift work. The sleep debt associated with shift work can account for both on-the-job and off-the-job problems, including accidents. This was shown very clearly in a study of 635 Massachusetts nurses. The study was done by a team of researchers headed by Dr. Diane R. Gold of the Brigham and Women's Hospital of Harvard Medical School.[5] They directly compared the performance of nurses on rotating work shifts or night shifts to the performance of nurses on regular day shifts. The nurses on rotating shifts were nearly 3 times as likely as those on regular day shifts to report poor quality sleep, confirming what we already know about the effects of shift work on sleep, and made many more errors on the job. For instance, they were 83 percent more likely to make medication errors than were the nurses on regular day shift. Moreover, they were also in greater jeopardy from off-the-job accidents. Nurses with sleep debts because they were on rotating shift work were 4 times more likely to report that they had a tendency to nod off while driving their car to or from work and were 163 percent more likely to report having had a near miss when driving their car.

We have seen that the sleep debt from working long shifts and rotating shifts can lead to poor judgment, reduced alertness and concentration, and higher susceptibility to accidents. There is also another problem that sleep debt can lead to, namely, night shift paralysis. An incident involving this was graphically described to me by one airport flight controller:

I was working at [a large high-traffic airport] *at the time and had been there about a year. The traffic rate had been going up, and we were handling about 80 flights an hour at peak times. We were really understaffed. I think that the aviation administration recommendations called for over 200 con-*

trollers, and here we were working with a crew of about 140. It was worse with the tower controllers, though. They were supposed to have around 40 people up there, and they only had around 25. All of us were working long hours and overtime. What that meant was that sometimes when we rotated shifts, we did it without any time off in between the schedule change. That's what I had when it happened. When it's set up the usual way, we call it an "M-N shift." That's because you work the morning shift and then the night shift the same day. Believe me, you don't get much sleep that day. I must have had only 4 or 5 hours, and I was feeling pretty bagged—really sleepy. It was around 4 or 5 A.M.—not capacity traffic but always something moving. There was one particular plane that I was working, and I had set him up for approach. It was time to turn him over to tower control for landing. I also had to warn a private [a privately owned noncommercial plane] that he was drifting too close to the landing approach. I went to reach for the switch to turn the radio to the private's channel, and I couldn't move my arm. I tried my other arm and it didn't move, either. I tried to stand up, and that didn't work. My arms and legs were kind of numb—not cold so much as stiff and heavy, like they were made of stone. I could see and hear everything around me; I could see my hand on the console, and when I tried to move my arm again, I could see my fingers move a little. That kept me from totally freaking, because I believed that it meant that all the nerves weren't gone. As I was sitting there trying to move, I noticed the screen again, and the private looked like he was on a convergence with the heavy [the large passenger plane]. I did panic then. I let out a yell. That's when I knew I could still talk. I shouted for the supervisor to take this one because I had a problem with my board. He took over and separated the planes. They were close enough to get officially counted as a near miss. A couple of minutes later he came over to find out what the problem was. By that time I could move again. It had only lasted a couple, maybe 3, minutes. I didn't know what to tell him. I didn't want to tell him the truth because it might mean my job. So I lied and told him that the display was unstable for a couple of seconds, and I couldn't monitor accurately. I told him the display was okay now, but he had it checked out, anyway. They didn't find anything, of course, and just assumed it was some kind of temporary glitch.

As the expression *night shift paralysis* suggests, this problem seems to occur most frequently in flight controllers who are working night shifts.

Simon Folkard and Ruth Condon of the University of Sussex gathered anonymous reports on this problem. Their data included reports from 435 flight controllers in 17 countries. They found that the problem is not limited to the night shift and that about one-quarter of the incidents occur on other shifts. According to these researchers, flight controllers say that these incidents typically last less than 2 minutes, although the data show that 11 percent last over 5 minutes. The likelihood of an attack of paralysis seems to be increased when the flight controller works the morning and evening shift on the same day, as in the incident described above. However, attacks become more frequent in those who work successive night shifts and also in those who seem to be suffering most from sleep debt.

This problem is not exclusive to flight controllers, however. I have spoken with nurses who work 12-hour shifts who also report similar experiences. One reported finding herself rigidly standing beside an intravenous tray setup that she was supposed to be attending to. She claimed that she was simply unable to move for a minute or more. Another nurse found herself sitting paralyzed at the nursing station, unable to move her arms to reach for a ringing phone. Like the flight controller quoted earlier, neither nurse reported the incident to superiors for fear of losing her job.

There are suggestions that shift work may damage workers' health. There have been some reports that shift workers are more likely to have heart problems, pulmonary disease, and some stress-related psychiatric and neurological diseases. However, this research has not been conclusive; it is difficult to compare shift workers to day workers because shift workers are more or less self-selected. They can, in effect, cease being a shift worker at will. There is a lot of evidence that many people do stop working nights and rotating shifts when they are stricken with physical or psychological problems. Often, when they do this, they feel considerably better; this means they will try to find work that does not involve such shifts. While this is good for the individual, it is not so good for researchers, since it means that the very people they are looking for, the ones most vulnerable to these problems, are disappearing from the research population.

There is, nonetheless, one group of medical problems that is consistently found in shift workers: gastrointestinal disorders. These include indigestion, heartburn, gas, constipation, abdominal pain, and feelings of extreme fullness after a meal. More severe complaints from shift workers involve problems in which the stomach lining (mucous membrane) becomes inflamed, such as in cases of gastritis. Peptic ulcers (the general term used to describe actual damage or disruption of the mucous membrane lining the lower esophagus, stomach, duodenum, or, more rarely, the small intestine) are also more likely in shift workers. The magnitude of this problem is really quite extreme: some research suggests that shift workers may have 6 times the susceptibility to gastrointestinal problems that day workers have.

It is known, for example, that shift work causes a noticeable change in the chemical cycle that involves the digestive hormone *gastrin,* part of whose function is to trigger the secretion of gastric juice (primarily hydrochloric acid) by the stomach wall. Gastrin also increases the rate of stomach contractions and hence is responsible for the churning action that moves the contents of the stomach around. The resulting increase in stomach acidity and mechanical action may help to explain why workers on rotating shifts are 50 percent more likely to have peptic ulcers than workers not on such shifts.

The factors that lead the shift worker to have more gastric problems are not clear, but several possibilities seem likely. Shift workers tend to have more erratic dietary habits, eating meals at times that depend upon their shifts. Often, the timing of meals will then be out of synchrony with the circadian rhythms that cause certain intestinal enzymes to be secreted at regular times in the 24-hour cycle. Whatever the reason, several studies suggest that one of out of every two rotating shift workers may be suffering from gastrointestinal complaints.

A large study looked at shift workers employed by the petrochemical company Exxon. In addition to confirming the workers' gastrointestinal difficulties, this study indicated another problem: if the worker had a preexisting systemic disease, such as epilepsy, insulin-dependent diabetes, or a neuropsychiatric problem, shift work seemed to make the problem worse and seemed to increase the severity of symptoms suffered by the worker.

Is there any solution to these shift-work-related problems? This is a current area of controversy and research activity. Some researchers have begun to investigate the effects of naps on shift work tolerance.

In some instances naps are taken immediately before the shift, in effect storing a bit of sleep for the work interval; in other cases naps are scheduled as part of the shift activities, somewhere in middle of the work period. Both of these techniques have reported modest success, but both have been difficult to implement. Employers tend to consider the scheduled naps during the work period as merely paid time off for the employees. This seems like an unwarranted expense to many managers, especially at a time when there is pressure to cut costs. They argue that shift work is already expensive enough, with employees on night or rotating shifts often commanding higher salaries than workers doing the same job on fixed day schedules.

Nor has the idea of prophylactic naps, taken before the shift in order to stave off later sleepiness, been accepted well by workers themselves. They and their unions have argued that such naps take away from their free time, which would otherwise be used for recreation, family activities, or basic home and personal maintenance. They maintain that if the nap's purpose is to maintain worker performance, it ought to be on company time. They want shifts to be appropriately shortened to compensate for the nap or to be paid for the time spent napping on their own time. Several studies have shown that even if workers agree that the naps make them feel better and less sleepy during the rest of the day, most workers do not voluntarily continue to take them. Within a few weeks workers on voluntary, unpaid, supplementary nap programs tend to abandon them, using the time for household and personal projects instead.

The one procedure that seems to provide the most benefit for shift workers involves adopting a permanent nonrotating shift schedule. This was demonstrated in a study headed by Dr. Barbara Phillips of the Chandler Medical Center of the University of Kentucky.[6] The Police Department of Lexington, Kentucky, implemented a permanent shift system on the basis of a vote taken by the members of the police force. Although the times of the three shifts were kept the same as they had always been, the police officers had the opportunity to select their shifts, which then became their permanent work schedule. Most (88 percent) got their first choice. The results showed a dramatic improvement in performance and self-evaluation for the officers. There was a general feeling that the quality and efficiency of sleep was improved, sleep and waking times became more regular and predictable, there were fewer disruptive wakenings, and less time was spent lying awake in bed. Moreover, there were significant changes in the psychological well-being of the police officers. Mental fitness was measured on a scale that looked at 10 categories of psychological problems, including depression, anxiety, hostility, fearfulness, and vague physical symptoms. Not only was there a drop in the number of psychological problems the officers reported, but the overall severity of the problems was also lower after the introduction of permanent work shifts. Perhaps the best single indicator of the benefits of the fixed schedule was the fact that absenteeism dropped nearly 37 percent over the course of the study.

Unfortunately, permanent shifts are not possible in many industries. Also, there are often social and family obligations that cannot be met if a worker is permanently tied to a night or evening shift. For these reasons, shift workers will continue to rotate their shifts and to rack up dangerously high levels of sleep debt.

Asleep in the Sky 🚁

Of all of the industries that are subject to developing sleep debt and paying for it with accidents and even death, perhaps the highest risk is to transportation companies. We have already seen this in the case of truckers who put in long hours and build up a sleep debt. However, the airlines, railroads, and shipping companies are not far behind. In the case of these industries long hours and constantly rotating shift work combine to make the operations unsafe. If an individual trucker runs off the road and hits a tree, one truck and one life are lost. If the truck hits another vehicle, even more lives may be lost. However, if a pilot of a 767 falls asleep, it could cost the lives of 450 passengers and of others on the ground. A railroad accident or loss of a passenger ship or ferry can also cost hundreds of lives. Thus, the scale of the damage done by sleep-related errors is much greater for air, rail, and sea transport than for highway transport.

In the United States commercial transportation accidents are usually investigated by the National Transportation Safety Board (NTSB). I spoke with one accident investigator from the NTSB, who told me the following:

I know that you are interested in the effects of sleep loss on safety, but it's really not easy to give you answers about this issue. In around 60 percent of all transport accidents the underlying cause is human error, and human error is a contributing factor in another 25 percent of accidents. Our problem is in determining what the nature and cause of that error was. You see, if there is metal fatigue in a vital part of a plane, our teams can find it and determine if it caused the accident. But suppose that the fatigue was human and that someone just screwed up and misread an instrument or missed a cockpit warning signal until too late. How are we going to know? There is no real physical evidence; everything will just be circumstantial.

Most of the evidence that we have about the effects of pilot's sleep needs or fatigue comes from the near misses, where there are survivors. If we've got witnesses, one of them can say, "The pilot was asleep" or "The number one officer had his eyes closed, and he was snoring." Without witnesses we don't have much. Even with survivors we don't always get the whole story, since the people who were actually doing the sleeping aren't very likely to "fess up" about it. The crew will often leave out details like that to protect the careers of their friends, or maybe because it can be hard to tell if someone is asleep. I think that there is a sort of unwritten policy that the public really shouldn't be exposed to horror stories about pilots asleep on duty unless there was conclusive physical or electronic evidence. I'm not even sure that I know what conclusive physical or electronic evidence of the crew being asleep would be.

While the NTSB may be reluctant to attribute accidents directly to pilot fatigue, there are times when this conclusion seems to jump out at you as the only reasonable explanation. This is especially the case when you see the workloads taken on by pilots and the rapidly changing and erratic shift scheduling that we already know has disastrous consequences on our circadian rhythms and our natural sleep patterns. Consider the case of Eastern Airline Flight 212 from Charleston to Charlotte, North Carolina, on September 11, 1974. This flight crashed killing its pilot, Captain James Reeves, and his crew of three, as well as all of the 68 passengers on board. The official investigation blamed the crash on "pilot error." The report specifically notes that the pilot and the crew were not paying attention to their altitude. We are not told why there was this attention failure, and, as the NTSB suggests, we can only speculate on the basis of circumstantial evidence that fatigue from sleep loss was a factor. However, there is enough evidence to warrant a very strong suspicion in this case. First, there is the underlying cause itself, namely, failure to pay attention to important details. Lapses in attention are one of the first symptoms of a sleep debt. Why should Captain Reeves be running a sleep debt? Well, consider his work schedule the week before the crash: the week began with his getting up at 4:15 A.M., and he made five flights that day. The following day his work began in the late afternoon, at 4:45 P.M., and he made three flights. The next day at 3:30 P.M. he started a series of four flights. There was one day off, and then Captain Reeves went back to early mornings on the 5th day, when he got up at 6:45 A.M. for four flights. After another day off, the captain was up again at 7 A.M. The day of the crash he was up at 3:30 A.M. The long hours of flight, the erratic start times, the shift from early morning to evening work—all this seems almost deliberately designed to scramble a person's circadian rhythms and to make it virtually impossible to get enough continuous and refreshing sleep. Reeves had voluntarily chosen this schedule because he wanted to get all of his flying done early in the month in order to have the rest of it off. However, the effects were obvious and devastating. Just a half hour before the fatal accident Reeves checked in with a control tower. The conversation was taped, and it was entered into evidence at the hearing. The voice on the tape is that of Captain Reeves. He sounds tired and depressed, and he is saying, "Rest. That's what I need is rest. I don't need all of this damned flying." I am not a member of the NTSB, but to me all of the evidence seems to add up to a pilot microsleeping or dozing, because of lack of sleep caused by shift-work-induced disruption of his internal clock, while his plane loses altitude on its way to destruction.

I did manage to find a commercial pilot who was willing to talk to me about some of his own experiences. He was in his 50s and was nearing the end of his active commercial flying days. We met in an airline lounge and talked for several hours.

Flying a plane is just shift work in the sky, and some of the shifts are pretty brutal. I often do a run from _____ to _____. As soon as I had the seniority, I went for that one. It's got really long hours on, but you get a lot of days off in a row because of it. It's not unusual to work 12 to 14 or maybe even 15 hours straight through. There was this NASA study that found that one-third of a pilot's duty days are over 12 hours long. I can believe it. If we have a rough flight, it's even possible that we'll be landing after being awake for 24 hours straight. When you go without sleep that long, it's not unusual to give all kinds of wrong info to the flight controllers. A few months ago my first officer was so sleepy that he even got the destination of our flight wrong on a check-in.

A day off at home doesn't really seem to help. You arrive home at odd times, not necessarily night. You're tired but just can't seem to get to sleep. Worse, you look and act really dumb right after a long shift. Like one time, I got home from a long series of flights, and I felt miserable and fatigued. Now one of the stews [flight attendants] had been been on my case about the food that I was eating, and she thought that I would feel a lot better if I ate more healthy stuff. Well, I knew that my wife kept some kinds of healthy breakfast cereals in one of the kitchen cabinets. I pulled one out, and I remember looking at the label and noticing it had lots of vitamins. I poured myself a bowl and started to eat it. I was not impressed with either the taste or texture. When my wife walked into the kitchen I asked her, "How can you and the kids eat this stuff?" She looked at me really strangely and told me, "We don't. You're eating a bowl of hamster food." Now, I remember looking at that label, but I must have been so groggy that I didn't see the big red letters that said HAMSTER CHOW on the box.

Sometimes the crew just dozes off in flight. It's against the rules but on long flights there are two pilots and sometimes even three pilots on board, so you feel that there will always be someone to cover for you. It doesn't always work that way, though. I was once on the _____ to _____ haul and went to sleep for maybe 15 minutes. When I woke up, I looked around and everyone in the cockpit was asleep. The only reason that we didn't get into trouble on that one was because we were between checkpoints [where pilots call in their location and status].

If you ask me, one of the real problems has to do with the planes themselves, not just the schedules. You get a nonstop flight of 18 hours or more, and during most of it there is just nothing to do. They have completely automated the cockpit. The original idea was that computerizing the whole operation would make things easier on the pilots and safer for the passengers. Another reason for all of the automation is economic, since you can get away with a smaller crew. The flight computer is certainly better at making routine adjustments; it's always paying attention and never needs sleep. Flight computers aren't perfect, and they do sometimes hang up, which can be a real mess. Also, if there is some emergency, that's when you need a human pilot to find the creative solution that will get everyone down safely.

*The problem is that there aren't enough emergencies to keep us awake. We sit
there in the cockpit with an autopilot going and nothing to do except check
the flight computer and the instruments now and then and do voice checks or
watch the weather. At night the whole thing is set up to make us sleepy: the
lights are dim, the engine noise drowns out stray sounds. Coffee just doesn't
work. At around 2 A.M. you end up sitting there slapping your face and trying to stay awake because the rest of the crew are all yawning and look like
they are going to fall asleep.*

*One of the ways that I try to stay awake is to actually fly the plane. I take
it off of auto and fly awhile, just to feel like I am a pilot again. Some of the
guys believe that the automated cockpit is making us lose our skills as pilots
since we get in so little real hands-on flying time anymore. I don't know
about that. I do know that being on autopilot bores a lot of us to sleep. I think
that it's when there is nothing to do and you haven't had a lot of sleep that
you really feel your sleepiness. I mean it gets to the point where I know that
I'm fighting falling asleep but I know that I'm losing.*

*Let me give you an example of an incident that I believe resulted from long
flight shifts and an autopilot that lulled the guys to sleep. This one wasn't me,
though. A few years ago there was this [Boeing] 707 that was supposed to
land at LAX [Los Angeles Airport]. Well, it comes in at about 32,000 feet,
and instead of contacting flight control and going into its landing pattern it
just kept on going straight out over the Pacific Ocean. Turns out the plane
was on autopilot. Also turns out that there were three pilots on board, and all
three of them were fast asleep. Well, the plane just kept flying out over the Pacific. They could have ended up in the drink except they were bloody lucky.
They must have been around 100 miles out to sea when some hotshot flight
controller figured out what must be happening. He fooled around and found
some way to wake those guys up by setting off the cockpit alarms. That must
have been one hell of a rude awakening!*

The other major problem confronting pilots is jet lag. This is a problem that comes about because transportation is so fast that we can now
travel over many time zones in a single day. The end result is that our internal clock is completely out of synchrony with the external time.
When we cross several time zones we are, in effect, asking our bodies to
adjust to a new time and to do it *right now!* All of the things that help
synchronize our circadian rhythms are now wrong: the light level is inap-

propriate and we are being asked to eat or to sleep at times when our body is not ready for these activities. The result is a collection of symptoms, including headache, fatigue, lethargy, irritability, depression, trouble concentrating, difficulty making decisions, and slowed physical and mental reactions (and sometimes also loss of appetite, earache, and diarrhea). On top of all of this, we have difficulty sleeping and what sleep we get is often fragmented and not very restful. The severity of these problems really depends upon the number of time zones you cross. Crossing eight time zones, for example, is the equivalent of changing your work shift by 8 hours with no time off in between.

A series of studies has been conducted by NASA at Ames Research Center in California. Researchers looked at the effects of jet lag on flight crews. Generally speaking, the effects are quite disruptive and result in a massive loss of sleep. For pilots of long-haul flights (greater than 8 hours in length), the effect of crossing many time zones is to totally disrupt the normal sleep-wakefulness cycle. Some studies have had pilots keep sleep logs and have noticed that their daily sleep is often reduced to less than 6 hours a night. The pilots were asked to monitor all sleep episodes, and they were promised that the information would be kept confidential. A large number of the pilots admitted that they took naps when they were on duty. Napping on duty is strictly forbidden under current U.S. regulations. The average amount of time spent napping was around 46 minutes, but naps ranged from short ones of only 10 minutes' duration up to much longer sleeps of 2 hours and 10 minutes. Research observers who accompanied a number of these flights noted that there were many crew members who napped and did not actually note it in their sleep logs.

Part of the problem with jet lag is that *all* of the body's rhythms go out of synchrony. Recall that our circadian rhythms involve a number of daily physical cycles. After jet lag, all of these have to catch up to local time and each does so at a different rate. The heart rate cycle adjusts at about an average rate of 60 minutes a day. Body temperature adjusts at about 40 minutes a day, the urinary rhythm readjusts at about 90 minutes a day, and the steroid cycle may only readjust at 30 minutes a day. This means that if you cross 3 time zones, it will take your heart cycle 3 days to adjust, body temperature 4 days, urinary cycle 2 days, and steroid cycle a full 6 days to accommodate to local time. Jet lag can have dire consequences for air crew who end up with such disordered internal cycles.

It is odd, but the Federal Aviation Administration (FAA) does not seem to pay any attention to jet lag or the internal cycles of pilots. Remember Captain Reeves and the Flight 212 crash? The schedule that this pilot was flying was in perfect accord with FAA rules, which require pilots to have at least 10 hours of rest (or at least time off) per day. These rules were put into place to prevent fatigue from long work shifts. They were, however, introduced in 1934 and have been unchanged since. What they fail to take into account is that recent research has demonstrated that *when* a pilot rests is as important as *how long* he rests (which is something that we saw when we discussed shift work). At certain times in our daily cycle, even though we are tired, it is virtually impossible to fall asleep. The FAA makes no provision for the fact that the body must first be in a receptive state for sleep and that if it is not, attempts to rest are at best only partially effective.

Although the FAA does not seem to make allowance for effects of jet lag on commercial pilots, there is another branch of government that does seem to be sensitive to the problem. This is the diplomatic corps. I had an interesting conversation with a recently retired member of the U.S. State Department:

When I first started with State, you never heard anything about jet lag. It all started a couple of years after I began working there. Eisenhower was president then. The way I remember it, it was around 1953, or maybe the year after. [John Foster] Dulles was the secretary of state at the time. He was a tough man, always in control, brilliant, religious—hated communism. [Gamal Abdel] Nasser had Egypt and was planning to put up the Aswan Dam. There were going to be millions of dollars in contracts involved, and there were already noises about requests for aid to finish the project. More important in the long run was the fact that the Soviets were trying to use the dam project as a means of gaining some political control in the Middle East. Now Dulles was usually fantastic at negotiating things and at reaching favorable agreements. [President Woodrow] Wilson had him on the delegation that went to Versailles to set up the peace after the war. He was on the War Reparations Committee. Afterwards he helped prepare the U.N. charter. He was mainly responsible for SEATO [Southeast Asia Treaty Organization]. He helped negotiate the borders of Austria and also Yugoslavia. He was good. So he decided to take a team down to Egypt to negotiate Aswan. The way I heard it, they got off of the plane tired and with 8 hours of jet lag. Then they went right into negotiations after the minimum amount of ceremony. It just didn't work. Dulles was sullen and irritable. He was not in the mood to be subtle or forthcoming. He ignored important details. He played fast and loose with protocol, and I think he insulted a lot of people. One of the people present at the negotiations said that Dulles was spitting out instantly formed opinions and using really strong language for a diplomat. Some of his staff said later that it appeared that he never even gave himself time to think about what was happening. At one point I was told that he exploded at one of the Egyptian speakers. He rudely interrupted him to an-nounce something like, "I disagree with your point utterly and entirely." Well, the speaker replied that he had made two major points, and he politely asked which of the two Dulles disagreed with. Dulles suddenly looked confused and lost and mumbled, "Well, if you repeat them, I'll tell you which one I disagree with." So Moscow got Aswan and Egypt, and the Communists had their toe-hold in the Middle East.

The word in the department was that Ike gave Dulles hell when he came back. Chewed him out about doing important business right after a long-distance trip. Eisenhower had a thing about that. He would always try to ar-rive several days early so he could work through his jet lag before he actually had to meet with any foreign leaders. Well, after that it was Dulles himself who set up policy recommendations about not negotiating when you are jet-lagged.

Nowadays a lot of diplomats do take jet lag into account. Some of the Rus-sians, I know, had strict rules and used to do what Ike did. We had to arrange to give them a couple of days before doing anything significant when they vis-ited Washington. Now when [Henry] Kissinger took over State, he had a dif-ferent trick. I think that he believed that it was impolite to hang around the other leader's capitol and not talk to him or do any work. So he would try to do his adjusting while he was still here. I think that he had the notion that you could stock up on sleep and that this would carry you through your jet lag. The way I understand it, the week before he had to travel, Kissinger would start to go to bed an hour earlier and wake up an hour later. [There is actually no scientific evidence that indicates that this kind of regimen works. How-ever, there is evidence that if you are already sleep deprived, the symp-toms of jet lag hit you much harder. It may well be that what Kissinger was actually doing here was making up the sleep debt that he normally had because of his busy schedule. His experience of jet lag would then have been less onerous once he was fully rested.]

I suppose that the diplomat that handled jet lag best was LBJ [President Lyndon Baines Johnson]. He set his watch for Washington time and never changed it. When he went on a long-distance trip, he just informed everybody that he was going to stay on his own regular schedule. That meant that he ate dinner at Washington time for dinner, went to sleep at Washington time for bed, ate breakfast at Washington time, no matter what the local time was. He had real brass. If the foreign leaders wanted to meet with him, it had to be at an hour that would be convenient to someone on Washington, D.C., time. He didn't care that he was in their country or that the time might be inconvenient by regional standards. One of his aides told me that LBJ once told his staff, "Jet lag gives me indigestion, and I won't put up with it. They [the local government officials] can go to bed a few hours later if they want to talk to the president of the United States." I suppose that he was right, because they certainly did.

Jet lag seems to affect everyone who does much traveling, including professional athletes. I was recently told an odd story by a sports-minded colleague of mine who knew I was interested in sleep and jet lag. The story is about Bronko Nagurski, a Chicago Bears football player who eventually was immortalized in the football Hall of Fame. He was well known for his strength, stamina, and versatility. During the 1943 season, when they were heading for another National Football League championship, the Bears had a schedule that took them from one game out west directly to another on the east coast. After one such flight the whole team was obviously rather jet-lagged. Although the team had arrived several days before the game to allow them to adapt to the local time, reporters wanted to interview the stars of the team as soon as they got into town. A press suite was arranged on the second floor of the hotel, and various reporters began interviewing team members the morning after their arrival. Nagurski was sitting on the sill of an open window while reporters were gathering, and in his jet-lagged state he apparently simply fell asleep and tumbled one story to the ground, landing in front of the hotel. A small crowd quickly gathered, and a policeman pushed his way to the front and asked, "What happened here?" Supposedly, the indestructible Nagurski picked himself up from the ground and replied, "I don't know. I just got here myself."

People in the entertainment business also complain about the effects of jet lag, especially musical performers, who often go on concert tours where they may give three or four concerts a week in different cities, some often separated by many time zones. The Polish-born concert pianist Josef Casimir Hofmann, who also composed music under the pen name Michael Dvorsky and had been director of the Curtis Institute in Philadelphia, told a story about one of his own experiences late in his career:

I had just finished a long concert tour that had taken me from New York to San Francisco, and I had just arrived back home in Philadelphia, where I was expected to give a recital. I am not as young as I used to be, and it seems that travel that involves many time changes now takes a heavy toll. This performance certainly proved this. When I sat down at the piano to play I did not know what to do. Fortunately, I was playing in a small auditorium, so that I was within nearly touching distance from the first row. I was most embarrassed when I had to bend over to a woman in front and ask her, "May I please see your program, madam? I forget what comes first."

TWELVE TIPS TO COMBAT JET LAG

Whole books have been written on coping with jet lag. Some contain elaborate pretravel dietary and sleep schedules. There are even computer programs in which you enter the specifics of your trip and get a personalized schedule indicating when you should eat, sleep, and exercise. In the absence of such aids, here are a few tips that seem to help travelers quickly adjust their biological clock to their new time zone.

1. Get a full night's sleep before the trip. The effects of jet lag are considerably greater if you are already running a sleep debt. So avoid the bon voyage party.

2. Book your flight to arrive in the late afternoon or early evening. This gives you time to eat a light meal and then go to bed by no later than 11 P.M. local time. The rule of thumb is "Travel east, fly early. Travel west, fly late."

3. Anticipate your new time zone. If you are flying when it is nighttime at your destination, try to sleep on the plane. If it is bright outside, use a sleep mask or close the window shade and bury your face in a pillow. If it is daytime at your destination when you fly, stay awake. Read. Do isometric exercises at your seat, such as pressing the palms of your hands together hard or stretching your arms or legs. Walk up and down the aisles.

4. Avoid alcohol. It causes dehydration, which makes jet lag symptoms worse and also disrupts your later sleep. Do drink lots of other (non-carbonated) liquids.

5. Avoid caffeine if it is night at your destination. If it is daylight there, you may have some caffeine but not within 6 hours of your anticipated bedtime.

6. Immediately adopt the new time pattern. Go to dinner at local dinnertime, sleep at local bedtime, and, most importantly, awaken at the local wake-up time.

7. Some milk, a light carbohydrate snack (such as bread, crackers, or cookies), and maybe a couple of aspirins just before bed may help.

8. Some researchers suggest taking a few milligrams of melatonin right before bed. This sleep-related substance is available as a nonprescription product in many health food and vitamin outlets.

9. Watch your body temperature. Keep the room a little on the cool side when you sleep. Try to warm up in the morning with heat-preserving clothes and a hot breakfast drink.

10. On awakening in the morning, get out into the light. Exposing yourself to sunlight is one of the best ways of resetting your internal clock. If the outside light is dim, turn on every light in your room.

11. Exercise in the morning when you awaken. Some calisthenics, a short aerobic workout, or even simply running in place for 5 or 10 minutes will help reset your biological cycles.

12. Eat lightly the first few days at your destination. Your daily digestive rhythm may take a while to match local time.

The Cost of Sleep Debt

$\mathcal{I}$ remember once working late into the night with a graduate student. She desperately wanted to finish her doctoral thesis so that she could receive her degree at the spring graduation ceremonies. This was really important to her because she had been offered a 2-year postdoctoral fellowship in the laboratory of a major Canadian psychological researcher. However, the fellowship required that she complete her Ph.D. before September. She had been working very hard at finishing; she was putting in long hours writing and doing statistical analyses. Unfortunately, a snag had arisen. At a meeting of her doctoral committee her thesis supervisor and I noticed that she needed one further set of measurements, which required testing an additional 10 people on a device called a tachistoscope (which can present visual images to people for times as brief as one-thousandth of a second). We had two tachistoscopes in my laboratory; at that point in time neither was in active use, so the graduate student had access to one of my apparatuses for her final study.

Before she could actually take her measurements, however, the device had to be programmed, the complex optical pathways had to be aligned, and all of the light levels had to be measured. This was a process that normally takes 3 or 4 working days. Because of the time pressures, however, I decided to stay late with her in the hopes that two people could finish the programming and calibration in one long workday. My student was obviously drastically sleep deprived. She complained of having had only about 5 hours of sleep each night for the previous week, and I had been filling her with coffee in an attempt to keep her alert. It was like a scene from a formal sleep deprivation experiment: my student was continually missing the instructions I gave to her and reacting slowly when she was called upon to do something, and her mood was depressed. There is one place in the optical alignment procedure where one person has to look through the viewer while another person adjusts the optics until two lines are perfectly on top of one another. I had asked my student to be the observer while I adjusted the mirrors. However, that didn't work, for she responded so slowly that each adjustment had to be repeated several times (she was also complaining that her eyes weren't focusing very well). In some desperation, given the late hour, I decided that we should switch places; she would make the adjustments, and I would monitor the alignment. She climbed up on a chair next to the apparatus and bent over it, with her head near the top surface and her hand on the adjustment screw. I called for her to adjust one revolution of the screw, and she complied. I had just stopped for a moment to make a quick calculation when I heard a dismaying cracking sound. I jumped out of my chair and saw my student sprawled across the top of the tachistoscope with her eyes closed. One of the tachistoscope's thin metal legs, not designed to carry the weight of an adult, had buckled, and the apparatus had pitched to the side and slid off the table. One corner struck the floor with a sickening thud. I grabbed my student in time to keep her from hitting the floor a moment later. "What happened?" she wanted to know. "I was just resting there and decided to close my eyes for a few seconds while you made the calculations, and the next thing I know you're picking me up off my knees."

What happened was obvious. Given the lateness of the hour, the pressure to sleep simply became irresistible in her sleep-deprived state. She had entered the beginning of a microsleep episode, causing her full weight to drop onto the apparatus. She was sound enough asleep that I vividly remember noting that her eyes were closed even though her body was sinking rapidly toward the floor along with the device she had been resting on. I terminated our work session and drove her home, giving her instructions to sleep until she awoke naturally (no alarm clock) the next morning. When she arrived at the university the next day, it was already lunchtime. I had spent the morning surveying the damage. Several of the optical components in the device were broken, and one of the viewing channels had actually cracked open. Although my student eventually finished her research on time using the other tachistoscope, it cost my laboratory several thousand dollars to repair and replace the ruined optical channel. This cost would never show up in any accounting as a sleep-related expense or a sleep-debt-induced accident, yet the costs were real and destroyed my plans to hire an extra student that summer to work in the laboratory.

The direct monetary cost of sleep deprivation and the accidents that it produces is much greater than most people can possibly imagine. For example, Dr. Damien Leger prepared a report on the cost of sleep-related accidents for the U.S. National Commission on Sleep Disorders.[1] The results of his calculations are sobering and astounding. Leger reports that in 1988 the cost of motor vehicle accidents caused by sleepiness was $37.9 billion; to this we must add the costs of sleep-induced accidents in public transportation accidents, which is another $720 million. The cost of work-related accidents caused by sleepiness was $13.34 billion. Accidents in public places, including falls, that were directly due to sleepiness came to $1.34 billion while accidents around the home due to sleep deficits resulted in a cost of $2.72 billion. The total cost of sleep-related accidents in 1988 was $56.02 billion.

Although the dollar cost is appalling, the human cost is even more significant. In 1988 a total of 24,318 deaths resulted from accidents related to sleepiness. In addition, there were 2,474,430 disabling injuries resulting from accidents in which the decreased mental efficiency and attentiveness due to sleep loss was the major underlying factor. Sleepiness-related on-the-job injuries resulted in 29,250,000 workdays lost in 1988 (with 13,650,000 days lost owing to the accident itself and 15,600,000 days lost owing to complications and long-term effects of the accident within the first year). Off-the-job accidents took a toll of 23,400,000 workdays lost, giving a total of work plus non-work-related accidents of 52,650,000. All of this was the time lost in 1988, the year the sleep-related accidents occurred; of course, when accidents are severe and disabling, they often continue to have an im-

pact on the person's life for years to come. Pain, complications, resul-
tant diseases, and late-occurring effects may cause work loss for years
after an accident. Using Leger's figures we can estimate that the accidents that occurred in 1988 will have later time lost on the job
amounting to 152,000,000 workdays. If we total the time lost in 1988
due to sleep-related accidents plus the future time lost due to these
same accidents, we end up with the astonishing figure of 204,650,000
days of productive work lost to the United States economy because of
only one year's worth of sleep-related accidents.

Moreover, the dollar figures for the cost of sleep-related accidents
($56.02 billion) for 1988 is, although quite astounding, probably an un-
derestimate of the actual costs to individuals and society. The cost figures that we used were based upon doctor fees, hospitalization costs,
pharmaceutical and drug costs, and rehabilitation and other treatment
expenses, which make up the direct cost of the accident. The only indirect costs counted have to do with the lost productivity of the person
due to disability or with a premature death due to an accident. Thus,
the cost estimates for an automobile accident, for example, would not
include the damage to the car itself or to any building, highway facility,
or other vehicle involved in the accident. In an individual accident
these costs may not be extremely high, but the sum of such costs from
the thousands of accidents each year would raise our cost estimate by
millions of dollars.

The cost becomes even greater when we are dealing with accidents
in the public domain, such as a commercial transport accident. If a passenger plane, for example, goes down because the pilot fell asleep or
made a sleep-related error, not only is the pilot's life lost but so are the
lives of all the passengers and the rest of the crew. The totals that we
have considered took the cost of personal injuries into account; however, it did not include the value of the plane itself (often worth millions
of dollars). There is also the additional cost of insurance payments, accident investigation expenses, damage to ground structures, and, finally, court costs as litigations arise from the incident. These factors
are simply too complex to add to our estimates.

Consider the case of the largest oil spill in the history of the United
States, the one involving the tanker *Exxon Valdez*. Most of the public
and press coverage about the incident focused on reports that the cap-

tain was drunk in his cabin and was therefore not on duty on the bridge. The real culprit, however, seems to be a case of sleep debt due to long shifts, which finally produced an inescapable sleep pressure at the low point of the daily activity cycle for the man who was on the bridge. According to evidence at the hearings, Exxon had been making personnel cutbacks in all areas, including their merchant marine staff, as a corporate response to difficult economic times. The results were predictable. With relatively understaffed crews, longer work shifts became necessary. On the *Exxon Valdez,* work periods of 12 to 14 hours a day became quite routine. The inevitable disrupted sleep patterns caused an increasing sleep debt, and the crew was continually complaining about fatigue. It was in the small hours of the morning of March 25, 1989, that the third mate was at the wheel of the ship. Just shy of 1 A.M., an hour approaching the low point in the circadian cycle, the third mate seems to have fallen asleep. The result was that the ship ran aground on a reef of the Alaskan coast. It spilled around 240,000 barrels of oil, which then washed up on the coast, destroying what had been a "beautiful and pristine fjord." We will never know the full cost of this accident. Exxon paid fines and hundreds of millions of dollars in direct costs. Workers and volunteers took months in the cleanup. Loss of wildlife and damage to the environment was massive, and the effects will continue for years. Although we can't calculate the actual costs, we can safely say that the outcome made the third mate's nap one of the most expensive in history.

The cost factors can skyrocket in a major disaster. There have been many field studies that have implicated shift work and daily fluctuations in alertness and sleepiness as causes of industrial and performance errors. For example, one of the most extensive field studies ever conducted extended over 20 years and was carried out by a Swedish gas company, which tabulated every gas meter reading error over that period and collected some 74,927 of them. When the researchers looked at the way these errors were distributed over the 24 hours of the day, they found, as we might have expected, that the greatest errors were on the night shift, between 2 and 4 A.M., and that there was also a smaller increase of errors in midafternoon, between 2 and 4 P.M. An error in reading your gas meter due to a sleepy employee has little real effect on your life. One month's gas bill might be wrong, but it would quickly be corrected in the next month or so, when the next meter reading occurred and the numbers were balanced against one another. Cost and human distress would be minimal. Suppose, however, that the meter being read was not monitoring natural gas flow to a home but, rather, the flow of coolants to a nuclear power plant. In such an instance, the reading error could have consequences in terms of millions of dollars and thousands of lives.

Consider the incident at Three Mile Island in Pennsylvania. The commercial nuclear power plant located there developed a problem in the Number 2 reactor on March 28, 1979. The problem started at about 4 A.M., around the low point for the human daily sleep–wakefulness cycle. The crew staffing the plant were on a weekly work shift rotation, which we have already seen wreaks havoc on sleep quality. Furthermore, the crew had just rotated to the night shift only a few days before, so their internal clock was doubtless out of alignment with the activity and alertness requirements of the job. The results were what one might expect from people running a sleep debt: the controllers failed to pay enough attention to notice what was happening for quite a while. When they finally did notice, their judgment was clouded by their condition of sleepiness. The actual event involved the loss of the water used to cool the reactor. The initial problem was mechanical in nature; it involved a simple stuck valve, which if noticed in time and responded to correctly would not have resulted in any emergency at all. Unfortunately, the crew did not notice this problem until conditions had begun to move to a near crisis stage. Then, when they did become aware of what was happening, the corrective action they took was so flawed that it actually made the situation worse and nearly resulted in a reactor meltdown later that morning.

What is amazing is that almost this same scenario has happened several times since in the nuclear industry. For example, on June 9, 1985, the Davis-Besse nuclear power generating reactor at Oak Harbor in Ohio had a similar problem. In response to the incident at Three Mile Island, the nuclear power industry had begun to put automated safety equipment into plants, and such safety equipment existed at the Davis-Besse reactor. At 1:35 A.M. on the aforementioned date an automatic shutdown of that reactor was triggered. The problem, as in the Three Mile Island incident, was loss of coolant water. This time, however, it was caused by the loss of the main water input. The similarity between the two incidents continued, with the situation being made worse by the operator doing exactly the opposite of what the situation called for. Specifically, the sleepy operator, pushed the wrong two buttons in the control room. The buttons he pushed actually disabled the safety function that would have caused an auxiliary source of coolant water to enter the reactor. The situation then became more dangerous when the operator's action caused additional equipment malfunctioning and his responses continued to be inappropriate for the conditions. Fortunately, the arrival of a less sleep-deprived day crew brought with it clearer judgment, and corrective actions were taken before conditions became critical.

One nuclear plant operating engineer described his own experience to me this way:

Well, when I first started working at _____, it was long before the Three Mile Island fiasco. After Three Mile, things started to change, or at least they started to change after the hearings. You see, they came down with this interpretation that a lot of the problem was human and human fatigue. The industry decided that the best way to solve the problem would be to remove the human from the equation almost completely. Everything got put on automatic. When I first started, you still had to walk around the control room and twiddle knobs and turn switches on and off. You set up a timed routine and did the walk-around every, maybe, 15 minutes. It got you up at least and got the blood flowing. Well, after Three Mile they changed all of that. Now there are just three main screens to look at. You sit there, in a big padded chair, and stare at those screens for your whole shift. They've even darkened the control rooms, so it looks like one great big airplane cockpit. They tell us that this is better for us and that we're all real safe because of all the automatic emergency shutoffs. Well, I don't see it that way.

Back in '85, there was this mess-up at Rancho Seco [a nuclear reactor located near Sacramento, California] where the DC [the electrical power to the control system] went down. [This incident officially occurred at 4:14 A.M. on December 26, 1985, only 7 months after the Davis-Besse reactor incident.] Well, the plant ops [the actual crew in the control room] just were so slow in reacting to what happened that they nearly lost it all. My guess is that they were asleep in front of the screen.

They had this expert named Chesler, or something like that [this was, most definitely, Dr. Charles Czeisler], who did this survey on a bunch of us. I don't remember the specifics except for the fact that half of the plant ops admitted that they had fallen asleep while they were on duty. I know that I was one of the ones who admitted to falling asleep. There is just nothing to do most of the time, and if they're right about those automatic safety shutoffs, it shouldn't make any difference, anyway.

It could have been because of that survey that the NRC [the U.S. Nuclear Regulatory Commission] went after Peach Bottom [a nuclear reactor in Pennsylvania]. It seems that NRC inspectors actually caught some of the ops asleep on duty. Well, they just put the ax to the whole operation late in '88. First they shut them down, next they fined the company over a million dollars, and then they hit all of the plant ops with fines of about a thousand dollars each. During the hearings some of the ops complained about the shift schedules and the boring working conditions, but the NRC wasn't in the mood to listen. They just blamed the ops for sleeping and blamed the company for not taking action about their sleeping on the job. Well, they kept Peach Bottom closed for around 6 months; then they reopened it. The company and the ops have promised to be alert and to stay awake, but, as far as I know, they have done almost nothing about the shift schedules or the control room. My guess is that the only additional warning system that they have installed is a wake-up alarm that sounds when the NRC comes around to inspect.

Perhaps the most expensive accident in the field of nuclear power generation occurred at the Chernobyl nuclear reactor in the Ukraine in April 1986. We are looking at the same kinds of factors in this disaster that we found in the near-miss nuclear accidents in the United States. We have a case of rotating shifts, some crew members working extra long hours, and the bodies and minds of the plant operators winding down in the bottom of the daily alertness cycle, when the pressure to sleep is the greatest. The outside pressure that brought about increased shift lengths came from demands on management to complete a series of safety tests before a government-imposed deadline. The tests were scheduled for after midnight, and, as is typical of most people who are carrying a major sleep debt, the crew was not working at top efficiency and were not motivated to check details closely. Specifically, no one bothered to check about the implications of shutting off several safety systems at the same time. In effect, the crew closed down all of the vital automatic safety systems. Then, at 1:25 A.M. there was a problem with an increase of heat in the reactor. In what sounds like a replay of the Three Mile Island situation, the sleepy operators apparently failed to do the most obvious things— like turning the automatic safety systems back on. What followed was a repeat of the Davis-Besse reactor situation: the crew actually did exactly the opposite of what was called for and switched off the reactor's emergency cooling system. A report written by V. M. Munipov accuses the crew of acting like "intelligent idiots" (in the sense that they were intelligent enough to act as nuclear plant operators but not intelligent enough to be aware of the consequences of their actions). It is likely that their temporary idiocy was the simple consequence of sleep debt. The resulting explosion spread hot, extremely radioactive debris from the reactor over more than 2,000 square miles. The result was that 17 million people, including 2.5 million children below the age of 5 years, all suffered some degree of radioactive contamination. Many people near the site of the explosion died of radioactive poisoning and burns soon after the accident. In the Ukraine for 5 years after the catastrophe there was a large drop in the live birth rate and an increase in the death rate. The average life span of the Ukrainian population in the 5 years following the Chernobyl incident has dropped from 74.5 years to 63.3 years. Scientists throughout the world are still cataloging the specific results of this disaster. They have already seen a 700 percent increase in thyroid cancer, and some medical researchers are saying that increased cancer levels may be expected for the next 50 years because of the increased radioactivity of the soil, due to long-lasting radioactive materials, such as cesium 137, that work their way into the food supply. How do we calculate these costs? I am sure that if we could convert these health effects into a dollar amount, the resulting figure would be staggering. All of this might have been avoided if the operations staff had had enough sleep to allow them to react in a quick and intelligent manner.

So can we ever know the true cost of sleep-related accidents? Obviously, we may never have a complete answer. Major disasters like Chernobyl are beyond cost evaluation because of their magnitude and because the results extend for years beyond the event itself. And then there are the numerous little accidents caused by sleepiness, accidents that don't become data entries in any study or government tally because they don't involve direct physical injury but only damage to property or equipment.

I posted a query on the Internet about sleep-related accidents and was swamped with responses. People told me of wrecked garage doors, ruined power tools, broken china, hurt children, burned houses, and more. Perhaps the oddest incident was personally described to me by a man who had a prize pumpkin that

was so big that it was wider than a man with his arms stretched out. We got the seeds from an agriculture scientist in the University of Manitoba along with lots of instructions to make it grow better. Well, I figured that this was a Guinness World Record pumpkin that I had grown, and I was going to show it at the provincial fair. If I was going to the fair I first had to do a lot of work, since we had to finish harvest and all. So I put in some real long days with some real short sleeps. I was really weary but got it all done. We used a fork-lift to put the pumpkin in the truck. A reporter came down and took my picture standing next to the truck with the tailgate down and this monster pumpkin next to me. Well, right after that I got some stuff together and put it in the cab of the truck. I must have been really tired because just sitting there I fell asleep. When I woke up I saw my watch and knew that if I didn't get moving fast I was going to miss the entry time. I turned the ignition and hit the gas pedal, and the truck started forward. That's when I heard Gracie yelling at me. What a damn fool. I was so tired I never even looked in the back of the truck, so I never noticed that I hadn't hitched up the tailgate after the reporter took the picture. When the truck rolled forward, that world record pumpkin of mine just rolled backward and off the end. Broke itself into a dozen pieces.

We have only talked about the cost of sleepiness when it causes accidents that affect property or health. What about the costs of business, or judgmental "accidents"? These might result in money lost by a sleepy investor whose mind was not efficient enough to process the facts that could have told him or her that a particular stock or bond transaction was not financially sound. Sleepiness can result in accounts or contracts lost because of mistakes made when preparing bids or plans. It can result in court cases lost by sleepy lawyers who, believing that they are working in their client's best interests, work late into the night, then miss details or make errors during the presentation of arguments in front of a judge. These judgmental accidents are no different than the judgmental accidents that caused Chernobyl, except that the resulting costs will not appear in any government tally.

Here is the opinion of a busy manager of a mutual fund:

Sleep is a waste of money. The only way to make money is to be awake all of the time. That way you are ready when opportunity comes, and you can make the right decision at the right moment.

Maybe, on the basis of what we see here, we should rephrase his comment. Perhaps it would be more accurate to make the following statements instead:

Sleepiness is a waste of money. The only way to make money is to be rested enough so that you are actually awake when opportunity comes. Only then can you logically select the right alternative at the right moment.

At least if you are wide-awake enough, you won't make the errors that cost money—or lives.

Are We Chronically Sleep Deprived?

It is around 9 A.M. and most people have arrived at or are on their way to work. I am traveling at an altitude of approximately 30,000 feet, heading for a scientific meeting. My flight lifted off the ground in Vancouver, Canada, about 30 minutes ago, and it will touch down in Los Angeles in just over 2 hours. The seat belt sign has just gone off, and I am walking slowly down the aisle, counting as I go. This morning there are 156 passengers in the coach section (scientists never get to travel first-class unless there has been some sort of mistake); 71 of them look as if they are asleep. They have their seats in a reclining position, their eyes are closed, and most are using pillows and blankets provided by the airlines. If I were brash and apt to speculate on the basis of little bits of data, like the proportion of passengers asleep on this flight, I might conclude that around 46 percent of the population I awakened with today are sufficiently sleep deprived as to want to fall asleep even in the strange, noisy, vibrating, and minimally comfortable environment provided by a passenger seat in an airplane. Does this make sense?

Let's run another experiment. It is now 8:30 P.M. and I am sitting in the Orpheum Theatre in Vancouver. It is filled with many of the hard-driving, ambitious people who occupy the upper economic strata of the city. The man to my left is talking about a court case he is working on, two men behind me are discussing a stock issue, and the people in front of me are bent over and talking excitedly, though the only words that I can make out are "patents have been filed . . . if we're in on the ground floor." Obviously, business has not been left behind this night. The formally dressed ushers have closed the heavy doors, and the lights are dimmed. The Vancouver Symphony Orchestra has just started a typical weeknight concert. The melodic sounds of a piece by Debussy fill the hall, and the audience grows quiet and seems to noticeably relax. By the third movement it seems that every fourth person is asleep. At the first intermission I speak to an usher, and he assures me, "The audience isn't really sleeping; they're probably just listening with their eyes shut."

After intermission we return to our seats. My scientific curiosity is now stimulated, and I wait until we are well into a long piece by Mendelssohn. As I look around, I am struck by the resemblance of the concert hall to a nursery school at nap time. The lawyer on my left has his head drooped on his chest, and he is breathing regularly. One of the men behind me who had been talking about stocks is slumped to one side with his arm hanging limply down. The woman beside him has her hands folded in her lap, her head is leaning at a precarious angle over her shoulder, and her eyes are closed.

I have just finished a rough count of one section of the concert hall that is near enough to me to allow me to estimate whether people seem awake or appear to be dozing. Well over one-third of the audience seems lost in slumber, despite the hefty $30 cost of a ticket for the orchestra seat they are occupying. Suddenly, the timpanist emits a loud burst of percussion followed by a cymbal crash. The lawyer beside me visibly jumps in his seat. The piece is now over, and he blinks his eyes and applauds politely. I am thinking to myself that I now understand why symphonies end with a series of loud staccato chords or a big display by the percussion instruments: this is the classical and symphonic version of the alarm clock.

The scene in the airplane and the scene at the symphony are typical. They are merely symptomatic of the conditions in our current lifestyle. At a public meeting in November 1990, Dr. Norman Edelman, dean of the Robert Wood Johnson School of Medicine spoke. He was giving a presentation to the National Commission on Sleep Disorders Research. One of his statements starkly described the current situation when he said, "America is a sleep-deprived society, and [that condition] is interfering with its societal mission."

What kind of data might lead to the conclusion that we are all sleep deprived? There is a lot of data pointing in that direction, but no one has yet put all the pieces together. As Dr. David F. Dinges, a biological psychologist at the Institute of Pennsylvania Hospital in Philadelphia has said, "I can't think of a single study that hasn't found people getting less sleep than they ought to." When I looked at seven of the larger and more recent surveys that measured sleep length in North American and European adults, the average was around 7 hours and 20 minutes. If this is too little, how much sleep should we be getting?

There are a number of ways that we might look for this answer. One of the ways is to consider the sleep patterns of animals that are closely related to human beings. When we do this we find that most of the apes and monkeys have a circadian rhythm that is similar to that of humans, and a sleep–wake cycle that is similar to that of people who live in cultures where the siesta is still practiced. Specifically, these animals have a long sleep at night and a shorter sleep in midafternoon. Let's define total sleep time per day as any nighttime sleep plus any day naps or siestas, rounded off to the nearest hour. For monkeys (specifically, the baboon, rhesus monkey, and squirrel monkey) total sleep time is 10 hours. Of the great apes, our closest evolutionary cousins, the chimpanzee sleeps the same 10 hours as the monkeys, and the gorilla's total rounds off to 12 hours of sleep.

Does monkey or ape sleep predict anything about human sleep? Man and the apes have many more similarities than differences. Apes have the same internal organs and similar nervous systems and brains, can eat similar foods, are susceptible to the same diseases, and even suffer from many of the same psychological difficulties. Recent molecular genetic analyses have shown that the degree of similarity between man and chimpanzee is 98 percent, which, if it were not for the ethical issues involved, might suggest to us that experimental interbreeding across species is possible. Electrically, the sleep stages in man and the other primates is virtually identical. With that in mind we can sensibly speculate that there should also be some similarity between humans and apes in terms of their sleep needs. Given the fact that, without exception, all the apes and monkeys studied to date sleep 10 hours or more each day, we might conclude that human beings are sleeping around 2½ hours less than they should.

There are more direct ways of determining the amount by which we are undersleeping without resorting to data from other species. Dr. Wilse B. Webb of the University of Florida at Gainesville, who has been one of the major pioneers of sleep research, was one of the first to raise the question of whether we are chronically sleep deprived. He concluded that we might be when he looked at data from an earlier era, when time pressures on people were not as great. He found that students in 1910 were actually sleeping around 9 hours per night, 1½ hours longer than a similar group of university students tested in the 1960s.

Dr. Robert A. Hicks of San Jose State University has data that show that the trend toward shorter sleep is continuing still. He found that in the 10 years from 1978 to 1988 average daily sleep length for university students dropped nearly a half hour, from about 7 hours and 18 minutes to 6 hours and 52 minutes. This means that these young adults were sleeping around 2 hours less per night than their counterparts who were tested 80 years ago.

If we look at cultures where there is less time pressure than in the large metropolitan centers of the United States, we usually find people sleeping longer hours. Around 1970, John M. Taub of the University of California at Santa Cruz measured the sleeping patterns of a broad cross section of people living in the Mexican city of Hermosillo, the capital of the state of Sonora, in northwestern Mexico.[1] When the study was conducted, the city had a population of around 200,000 people. The largest employer was the government, as would be expected in a state capital. There was also commerce and light manufacturing, mostly oriented toward servicing the surrounding area, a rich irrigated agricultural land. This means that most of the work and activities of the city occurred during the daylight hours. The press of shift work and the pressures associated with international commerce were quite minimal. The average nightly sleep time for the residents of Hermosillo was 8 hours and 10 minutes, which is approximately 50 minutes more than adult sleep time in North America. This extra night time sleep, however, is not all of the story. Hermosillo still observed the afternoon siesta, as did much of Mexico. The average amount of time spent sleeping during the day was 1 hour and 30 minutes. This means that the average resident of Hermosillo had a total daily sleep time of 9 hours and 40 minutes. This is a value very similar to that seen in monkeys and in North Americans measured around the turn of the century. It is around 2 hours more than the average U.S. city dweller gets today.

There is a very sophisticated way that we might use to estimate the natural length of sleep per day. Suppose we had a situation where people still had work and chores to do, as well as recreational activities to engage in, but had no schedules or clocks to determine the time they went to sleep or got up. The sleep and wakefulness would be completely determined by when they felt sleepy and when they wanted to get out of bed. In addition, suppose we could also eliminate the daily environmental fluctuations in light levels that accompany day and night and act like a sort of clock that controls our daily sleep–wakefulness cycles. How long would we sleep then?

Dr. Peter Suedfeld of the University of British Columbia in Vancouver, Canada, describes a place where these conditions can be met: "While many people might occasionally wish for an endless summer day, very few, it seems, would care to travel to those places where such a day is possible. The polar environments [the arctic and antarctic regions] are the only place on this planet where 24-hour daylight is a naturally occurring event, and we can report that the beaches are not crowded."

Suedfeld has done research at both poles of the earth and has helped establish the multinational Polar Psychology Project. With the assistance of people like Dr. G. Daniel Steel of Lincoln University in New Zealand and Dr. Lawrence Palinkas of the University of California in San Diego, Suedfeld was responsible for setting up the first Polar Psychological Research Station. It was established at the site of a decommissioned weather station called Isachsen, on Ellef Ringnes Island in the North West Territories of Canada. It is at about 79 degrees of latitude north, which places it some 13 degrees above the arctic circle. The experiment of interest to us took place in the summer.

Owing to the high latitude and the time of year, during the summer months the station has continuous daylight. Actually, if you were at the station, you would see the sun moving in the sky but in an odd fashion; it is continually above the horizon during any 24-hour period. Instead of dipping below the horizon at night, it merely performs a stately clockwise circle dance, with the circle being always well above the horizon. This means that the light level never changes, except for local weather conditions, such as overcast days.

Seven researchers (four men and three women) arrived at the Isachsen Research Station and gave up all of their watches, clocks, and other timekeeping devices. The station's computers were even specially programmed so that although they monitored the time of all activities, participants could not obtain the actual clock time. (Even the flight crew of their one resupply plane had been instructed to pocket their watches before getting off the plane.)

The people at this station had lots of activities and duties to perform. Each was a researcher who had scientific projects that needed attention. In addition, the group was part of an environmental project that was involved in the cataloging and preparation for removal of equipment and materials that had been left when the base was decommissioned. (This material had to be removed because it was feared that some of it might damage the fragile arctic biological environment.) Everyone at the station also contributed to camp maintenance and survival activities, including melting snow for water and cooking. There were also opportunities to spend a reasonable amount of time in indoor and outdoor recreational activities. All of these endeavors were designed so that they could be pursued alone or in groups of various sizes. Neither work nor recreation was scheduled; rather, all activities, including meals and sleeping, were left to the discretion of the individuals. This meant that momentary whims and inclinations often determined the next activity to be engaged in.

Although these polar researchers were working and carrying on normal daily activities, they could, and did, sleep whenever they felt they wanted to. Since the light levels did not dim according to the usual 24-hour cycle to provide a clue as to when "normal" sleep time might occur, most of the participants simply covered their eyes with a cloth pillow or the top of their sleeping bags or blocked off the light coming into the windows when they wanted to sleep. Whenever a person went to bed or awakened, appropriate entries were made into a computerized activity log.

For the first few days of the project the participants tended to follow their previous sleep length schedule of about 7 to 7½ hours. However, in a very short time all seven of the participants adopted a pattern of sleeping that was longer than their usual sleep time. By the end of the experiment the overall average sleep time was 10.3 hours for each 24-hour day. All the participants showed an increase in sleep time, with the shortest sleeper still sleeping 8.8 hours a day and the longest sleeping almost 12 hours a day. Dr. Suedfeld himself, who claims that he is normally a very short sleeper, ended up sleeping an average of 11.25 hours a night. In most cases the longer sleep pattern was the result of a longer single sleep per day. However, on more than one-third of the days, participants tended to have a short nap as well as a longer sleep episode. These naps tended to be around 1 to 2 hours long.

The important result of this study is what it tells us about sleep time in individuals who are living normally (except for the absence of clocks and the usual social cues to tell them when to sleep and when to awaken). The data from the Polar Psychology Research Station suggest that our natural sleep needs might be closer to the 10 hours a day that is typical of monkeys and apes living in the wild than to the 7 to 7½ hours typical of the denizens of today's modern cities, with the clock-driven high-tech lifestyle we have all come to accept. This suggests that we may actually be getting 2½ to 3 hours a night less sleep than our bodies and minds were designed to have.

Several studies conducted by Wilse Webb and H. W. Agnew have confirmed our need to sleep longer under very controlled conditions. These researchers tested people who were sleeping in experimental chambers designed to eliminate any hints as to the time of day. Volunteers were placed on a rigidly controlled sleep schedule that allowed them 8 hours in bed each night for 10 nights, followed by 10 nights when they could sleep as long as they liked. This group ended up sleeping approximately 9 hours each for the entire second 10-day period, clearly confirming that 8 hours of sleep is not enough as a regular sleep diet.

It makes some sense for our sleep time to be programmed to be around 9½ or 10 hours. One reason is that it keeps us out of trouble. In the equatorial and temperate zones of our planet, where man seems to have originally evolved and flourished, the dark hours of the night can last between 10 and 14 hours. During these hours it would have been hard for early man to find food. Furthermore, a creature blundering around in the darkness has a greater chance of being taken unawares by another creature with larger jaws and claws, or of falling from cliffs or getting into trouble in other ways; sleeping through the night, though, afforded protection from such dangers. Once evolution adopted that strategy, this quiet time could be used for physical or psychological maintenance or for other activities that could be accomplished while the body was asleep. With an average of 12 hours of darkness available, spreading sleep-related activities over a 10-hour period makes sense—and still gives a 2-hour safety margin to make up for random disturbances (such as a noisy young infant) that might disrupt normal sleep.

Let's consider an alternative explanation. It could be argued that people actually sleep longer than their bodies need, when given a chance, simply because it is a pleasant activity. This is similar to eating more food than you need to because it tastes good. However, we are actually programmed to overeat, since by adding a reasonable layer of fat we are really storing reserves for times when food is not available. In times of food scarcity (such as when game was not plentiful) it would have been our hominid ancestors who had reserve energy in the form of accumulated body fat who were most likely to survive.

It is possible that we have been similarly programmed in terms of sleep. Research has shown that we cannot store excess sleep the way we store excess calories as fat, at least not over the long term. However, over the short term, things are different. Sleeping a couple of hours longer the night before a period of sleep loss *does* improve overall performance. Many of the negative effects on mood and judgment are ameliorated and have reduced impact when we have rested an additional time before going through a period with less sleep. Thus, people who have the option to do so might actually be sleeping an additional amount just to offset a possible short-term "sleep famine," just as we have a tendency to eat too much to offset a longer-term food famine.

According to this reasoning, sleeping less than, say, the 10 hours that people might want to sleep may not do us any actual harm. A 7½ hour sleep might be quite adequate to meet our daily needs but might remove our safety net. If we are now called upon to meet some emergency where we must be awake for 24 or 36 hours continuously, we might be considerably less efficient than we would be if we had previously had 10 hours of sleep. On the other hand, for a normal daily cycle of activities involving only 16½ hours of wakefulness, the 7½ hours that we usually get may be enough.

Some researchers have tried to see if the extra sleep we take when we have the opportunity to do so is really useful or just "insurance," as suggested above. If we need more than 7½ hours of sleep, then increasing normal sleep length for people who have no complaints about daytime sleepiness ought to show some daytime benefits. This was demonstrated by Timothy Roehers and Thomas Roth and their associates at the Sleep Disorders Research Center of the Henry Ford Hospital in Detroit. In one of their experiments, for example, they extended the time in bed for their volunteers to 10 hours a night, which has 2 hours longer than their previous sleep time. This extended sleep length was continued for 6 days. The daytime alertness of the participants in this test was measured using the Multiple Sleep Latency Test, which is a measure of how long it takes a person to fall asleep under quiet conditions at various times during the day. Increasing the sleep length immediately increased the daytime alertness of these male volunteers, with the greatest improvement coming for those individuals who initially showed the greatest amount of sleepiness.

The improvements that came from extended sleep times were not just in terms of daytime alertness. They also showed up on a number of psychological tasks. These men were tested on a vigilance task that required them to focus their attention and look for small differences or changes in signals over long periods of time. This is the psychological process required of people who work at an inspection station on an assembly line or monitoring a radar screen for hours at a time. The men were also tested on their ability to divide their attention, the equivalent of the psychological task required of a technician in a nuclear power generation plant who has to continually watch several different monitors and dials, each of which might indicate a problem with the reactor. Both experimental tasks were designed to be difficult and wearing, and most research subjects have difficulty with them. The interesting thing about the results of the sleep extension was that it resulted in an improvement in the subjects' performance on both of these tasks. Remember, these were individuals who had no previous sleep complaints. They were sleeping the 7 to 8 hours that our culture deems normal. Yet extending the length of time that they slept still improved their alertness and their ability to process information.

Improved performance and feelings of well-being have been shown by a number of laboratories that have tried extending the sleep period of subjects above the usual 7 or 8 hours. For example, Dr. Mary Carskadon, now at the E. P. Bradley Hospital at Brown University, teamed up with Dr. William Dement of Stanford University to run a research facility called the Stanford Summer Sleep Camp. Their results were very similar to those found by the Henry Ford Hospital research team. They found that extending the sleep time of Stanford undergraduates to 10 hours (of which they actually slept about 9½) produced an immediate improvement in their daytime alertness and functioning. The same findings were found when the group tested was made up of preteen youngsters aged 10 to 12. Neither group had been getting enough sleep at 8 hours a night to sustain them through the day without bouts of sleepiness. In one interview Carskadon summarized her findings by saying that most people "probably need at least an hour more sleep every night than they're getting to be alert in the daytime."

An interesting follow-up to the Stanford results, showing the benefits of extending sleep time, was described to me by a career U.S. Army officer:

I was an instructor at the——————training school. There are several cycles of training that go on at the school at the same time [the course is several months long; however, a new class, or cycle, is started every 4 weeks], *and there is also a similar training program at——————. The army tries to keep up a competition between the various classes cycling through the two schools. They compare phase scores to determine how well trainees are doing.* [A phase score is based upon tests and performance and is much like the midterm grade for a university class.] *They also look at these scores to evaluate the training staff. The students coming out of our cycle of training were okay. They tended to perform about at the average level expected of students in each phase of training. That meant that when the performance of the instructors was rated, we usually got a "satisfactory" or, occasionally, a "very satisfactory" rating. Command was always pushing us to improve the quality of graduates, but none of the minor changes that we could work into the program seemed to have much of an effect.*

I was trying to do some career upgrading at the time. I was taking some correspondence courses on command, human factors, and the like. When I finished a section that had to do with the effects of fatigue on combat effectiveness, it got me interested in the question of sleep. The course material that I had been working on said that for maximum effectiveness people needed 7 to 8 hours of sleep a night. Then I saw this New York Times article that talked about some studies at Stanford that had shown that students did better when they had 1½ hours more time to sleep. I suppose that this got me to thinking about what was going on at our training program. I looked over our own schedule. At this installation standard lights out in the student barracks was 2200, and reveille was 0530, when the troops then were put through PT [physical training exercises, such as running, calisthenics] *before they were released for cleanup and morning mess. That meant that if the troops were actually in bed when lights-out came, they were getting 7½ hours of sleep. Now, the army says that that is enough, but I decided to try an experiment. Most of the students in any one cycle are housed in the same barracks, in the same bunk area. These are large rooms at the ends of corridors, each of which houses about 24 people. The important thing is that there are separate light controls. I decided to conduct a sort of experiment using the quarters housing my training class. When I started the next cycle, I informed the men that lights-out would be at 2100 and reveille would be at 0600 starting with each Sunday night through to each Thursday night. This meant that they would have 1½ hours longer to sleep on nights before classes. I told them that their NCOs* [sergeants] *would be checking after lights-out and anyone not in their bunks would be dinged. I knew that the class would be ticked off about the earlier lights-out, but I pointed out that this would result in a half hour less of PT and also that we would extend lights-out limits on Friday and Saturday. That seemed to be a reasonable deal to them, and I heard very little grumbling afterward.*

The results were really gratifying. The class scored nearly 10 percent higher on their phase tests. That made them one of the highest-scoring classes that anyone could remember. I repeated the same sleep routine for the next cycle and got almost identical scores, with the class average 9.3 percent better than the average. Even more exciting was the fact that the trainees seemed to be so much more enthusiastic. We didn't get any midphase depression, which was common when the work begins to pile up on the class. My immediate CO [commanding officer] was really excited and asked me what I was doing. I explained that the increased sleep time was the only change. He was really hot on the idea. I think that he must have mentioned my "new technique" to the base commander. The next thing I knew, I was called to base headquarters to see the commander. He was "old army." He tore a strip off my hide—told me that I had no right to reduce the PT in my troops. He said that he didn't want to be surrounded by any "panty-waist, out-of-shape technicians." He said that I was "mollycoddling" my troops and that by giving them extra sleep I was "encouraging them to be fat and lazy." He told me that sleep was for "fat housewives" and that the army experts say that 7½ hours a night is plenty. When I tried to tell him about the improved performance of my classes, he just went through the roof. He accused me and my staff of faking the results just so that we could give our "baby-skinned asses an extra hour and a half of beauty sleep." He insisted that I immediately go back to the standard schedule.

My own CO told me that there would be no disciplinary action, since the classes had done so well, but that I had to drop the experiment at once. I did, and we went back to the way it was. My students went back to the Army-mandated 7½ hours, and things reverted to "normal." My next class hit the usual average, at least what had been the usual average before the extra sleep time. Well, there was a typical Army response to all of this. At my next evaluation, command then gave me an "unsatisfactory" rating. The reason they put in my records was that my class's scores had "dropped nearly 10 percent below previous performance levels with this instructor, for no apparent reason." They said that they wanted to see my trainees' performances "return to normal," which I took to be the new 10 percent above normal that I had established. I applied for transfer right away.

The same pattern repeats itself many times. Extending the sleep of people to something closer to the 10 hours that is typical of other primates seems to improve performance, psychological status, and mood. Now, if 10 hours is good, might 12 hours a night be better? After all, the gorilla sleeps 12 hours out of every 24. Actually, the data suggest that 9 to 10 hours may be optimal, since when all time cues are taken away and people are allowed to sleep as they please, they tend to gravitate toward this sleep length. A recent example of this comes from the work of Dr. Thomas Wehr and his colleagues, who are currently doing research at the National Institute of Mental Health in Bethesda, Maryland. The interests of this group actually have more to do with circadian hormonal influences that may change regularly over the course of the day and the influence that particular hormones have on our health. In their research they attempted to control their research subjects' biological clock by looking at the effects of 8 hours of darkness out of every 24 (typical of our electric-light-lit world today) versus the 14 hours of darkness more typical of what our earliest ancestors might have experienced in the winter season.

Two important facts came out of this research: The first was that the people who were given 14 hours of darkness a day did not use all these hours for sleeping. They actually slept between 9 and 10 hours out of the 14, suggesting that some sleep interval in this range is quite adequate and that we do not need to extend the amount of time in bed to more than 10 hours. Secondly, when these participants in the "extended night" experiment were given standardized tests measuring their mood and their daytime alertness, they were considerably happier and more energetic than they were with their standard 8-hour night. Wehr put these results in a historical context when he said, "There may have been a lot of rest going on that has been virtually abolished by our modern lifestyle." In other words, we *are* running a sleep debt. When this sleep is returned, the debt is abolished and within a few days we work better and feel better.

What Is Your Personal Sleep Debt? 👁

On the basis of all the data we have seen, it should be clear that many people in today's society are chronically sleep deprived. Are you one of these sleep-deprived people? The evidence shows that even with a large sleep debt, you may truly believe that you are wide-awake and not a bit sleepy. This is because the internal pressure to sleep can be offset by certain types of stimulation. Antisleep stimulation may come from internal sources, such as the operation of your biological clock or feedback from your muscles as you exercise. Antisleep stimulation may also be external. External stimulation that helps to offset sleep can include noise and light, as well as psychological stimulation from social interaction, increased motivation, excitement, or interesting and novel occurrences.

We have already seen that there are times when our biological clock winds down, such as in the early morning hours, around 1 to 4 A.M., and the midafternoon hours, between 1 and 4 P.M. It is when this happens that any sleep debt that you may have incurred is apt to catch up with you—unless there is some internal or external source of stimulation to offset your sleep urge. When you have a small sleep debt and are placed in a situation where there is not much stimulation, nothing much happens; for instance, sitting and listening to a boring speaker leaves you bored, and perhaps annoyed, but does not put you to sleep. If your sleep debt is large, however, lowering the level of stimulation allows the sleep urge to express itself. Thus, if you have a sleep debt, the lack of anything interesting to think about in the speaker's presentation will probably result in a noticeable pressure to fall asleep. There is obviously not much danger to you if you are sitting in a chair and dozing off during a lecture or conference talk (unless one of your superiors interprets this as a sign of lack of motivation or ambition on your part). In other cases, however, falling asleep can be quite deadly.

Suppose that you have been building up a sleep debt. Now you go off to spend a pleasant social evening. At this time (say, 8 P.M. to sometime past midnight) your biological clock is still in a fairly active phase of its cycle. You are receiving lots of intellectual, social, and emotional stimulation, and you feel quite bright and alert. The alcoholic drink that you had seems to have had only a relaxing effect. Once the party is over, you get into your car and start to drive home. Now, however, your biological clock is entering its lowest phase, that early morning time of maximum sleep pressure that will reach its peak between 1 and 4 A.M. The reduction in stimulation as you move from the social gathering to your automobile is abrupt and substantial. The world around you is suddenly dim and quiet. In the absence of the interesting conversation, noise, light, and psychological stimulation that social interactions provide, your sleep debt demands that it be paid—now! As you drive down the road, you are suddenly overcome with sleepiness and an irresistible urge to doze off. You are too tired to do more than rub your eyes, shake your head, or slap your face. None of this works, and you momentarily slip into a light doze just as the car reaches 55 miles an hour. It has only slowed to 50 miles an hour when your hands slide off the steering wheel and you veer from the highway into a lamp pole by the side of the road. You probably don't even awaken in time to learn that you have now entered into eternal sleep.

While the previous example may seem melodramatic, similar slips into sleep due to a gradually increasing sleep debt may cause other, nonfatal, problems. Adding up a line of figures while sitting quietly at a desk in the back of the store, the sleepy bookkeeper dozes off and reawakens only to continue several lines lower down on the page than when he slipped into his momentary sleep. The error is minor, and missed, until the income tax audit. Then, because of accrued interest and penalties, the bookkeeper learns that he has taken a thousand-dollar nap. The student who has been cheating on sleep nods off in class just as his physics professor notes, "Here is a trick for solving this kind of problem that isn't covered in your textbook." The consequences of this nap will only appear weeks later when the student is taking the exam and a problem requiring exactly that solution costs him 25 percent of the test total. Then there is the sleep-deprived medical intern, listening to a patient explain his symptoms. As she sits there, she dozes off; it is only a microsleep lasting around 10 or 15 seconds, but it is long enough to allow her to miss two sentences' worth of the patient's narrative. One of those sentences, if it had actually been heard, could have told the intern that the drug she was getting ready to prescribe was inappropriate for this patient and could do him much harm. Examples like these can be multiplied in many different realms of activity. Since errors associated with the consequences of sleep debt can be costly, or even have life-or-death implications, it is important that we each understand whether or not we are running a sleep debt.

Some of us are aware of our daytime sleepiness; when this is the case, we have clear proof that our sleep account is not being paid in full. For others, the situation is less obvious because the reality often differs from what our feelings are telling us. Our feelings and momentary perceptions are often extremely poor reflections of what conditions really are. For example, on the basis of your own personal impressions you would never conclude that the world is a round ball hurtling through space at a speed of thousands of miles an hour. Scanning the horizon, your eyes provide sensory evidence that the world is as flat as a table top. Incontrovertible evidence of the shape and movement of the planet was eventually provided by photographs taken by various space missions. These proved, visually, that the earth is round. This evidence was so convincing that the *Society for Preservation of the Flat Earth* finally disbanded in 1970. It had survived for more than 400 years after Ferdinand Magellan proved that the world was round by sailing around it.

Determining the physical nature of our planet and ascertaining your own sleep status have much in common. This is because the degree of sleepiness you feel at any given moment in time is not always a reliable indicator of your sleep debt. The uncertainty about our state of sleepiness, however, is in one direction only. If you are feeling sleepy at this moment, the chances are good that you are currently running a sleep debt. If you are not feeling sleepy right now, you may or may not have a sleep deficit.

The relationship between sleep need and feelings of sleepiness is not simple. Your sleep need can be defined in physiological terms. The greater your sleep need, the more likely it is that you will fall asleep, regardless of the situation and regardless of what is going on in the environment around you. Sleepiness, however, is the subjective or psychological feeling interpreted by the person as meaning that sleep is required at this time. Your sleep need and your feelings of sleepiness are related to each other in much the same way that hunger and starvation are related. Starvation reflects the physical need for food, and hunger is the subjective feeling that you need to consume some food as soon as possible. Thus, after you have just eaten a large rich meal, your food need is completely satisfied and you don't feel hungry. When you have a food deficit, however, things are different. If you are starving to death, it is clear that your body needs food, yet you may or may not feel hungry at any particular moment. Your feelings of hunger will depend upon many things, including the present circumstances. If, for example, you are currently running for your life because you are being pursued by an angry bear, feelings of fear will dominate your thinking. You will not feel hunger or think about food. Even after you safely escape, there will be an extended period of time in which your feelings will be dominated by your sense of relief and perhaps by feelings of fatigue from the run or by aches or pains from muscle strains or bruises. All this while, however, when in effect you have "forgotten" or suppressed the feelings of hunger, you are still in the physiological state associated with starvation. It is even possible to go without food for such a long time that you virtually go beyond hunger and no longer feel these subjective pangs of hunger anymore.

When it comes to measuring our sleep debt and sleepiness, we have a situation similar to the one we just discussed for starvation and hunger. If you feel sleepy, this is definitely a sign of sleep debt, but not feeling sleepy does not mean that your sleep needs have been met. Because of this, it is important to develop an introspective and personal sensitivity to your sleep needs. To assist you in this, I have developed a simple questionnaire that will indicate just how big your sleep deficit is.

HOW LARGE IS YOUR SLEEP DEBT?

The following questionnaire is designed to determine whether you have a sleep deficit. Answer each question by circling *yes* or *no*.

1. Do you usually need a loud alarm clock to wake you up in the morning?   Yes   No

2. Do you usually hit the snooze control to get a few minutes more of sleep when the alarm goes off in the morning (or simply turn off the alarm and try to catch a bit more sleep)?   Yes   No

3. Do you find that getting out of bed in the morning is usually a struggle?   Yes   No

4. Do you sometimes sleep through the alarm?   Yes   No

5. Do you usually find that a single beer, glass of wine, or other alcoholic drink seems to have a noticeable effect on you?   Yes   No

6. Do you sleep longer on weekends than you normally do during the week?   Yes   No

7. On vacations and holidays do you sleep longer than you normally do on regular workweeks?   Yes   No

8. Do you often feel that your "get-up-and-go" has gotten up and gone?   Yes   No

9. Do you find that it is more difficult to attend to details or routine chores than it used to be?   Yes   No

10. Do you sometimes fall asleep when you had not intended to?   Yes   No

11. Do you sometimes find yourself getting very sleepy while you are sitting and reading?   Yes   No

12. Do you sometimes find yourself getting very sleepy or dozing off when you are watching TV?   Yes   No

13. When you are a passenger in an airplane, car, bus, or train and the trip lasts over an hour without a break, do you commonly find yourself getting very sleepy or dozing off?   Yes   No

14. Do you usually feel extremely sleepy or doze off when you are sitting quietly after a large lunch without alcohol?   Yes   No

15. Do you tend to get sleepy when you are sitting quietly at a public meeting, lecture, or in a theater?   Yes   No

16. Have you sometimes found yourself getting extremely sleepy with the urge to doze when you drive and are stopped for a few minutes in traffic?   Yes   No

17. Do you drink more than four cups of coffee or tea (containing caffeine) during the day? (Remember to count refills; also count extra large take-out cups as two cups).   Yes   No

To score this test, count the number of times you circled *yes.*

The interpretation of your scores is as follows:

4 or less: You are obtaining an adequate amount of sleep and are not showing significant signs of any sleep debt.

5 or 6: You are probably getting an adequate amount of sleep on most days, although there are some days when your sleep account is a bit short, which may cause you to be less than 100 percent on some activities.

7 or 8: You are showing evidence of sleep debt that may cause a noticeable reduction in your efficiency at work and your ability to finish all your required activities on time. Things to watch for are little errors and short episodes of inattention. You will occasionally just "slip up," act clumsy, reach a wrong conclusion, or miss an important detail. Usually at this level you will catch the errors if you have the chance to recheck your work, although the ones that get through may be embarrassing or costly.

9 to 11: With a score at these levels you definitely have a large sleep debt. There is a possibility that you may commit large, random errors or omissions in your work or that you may miss small errors even when you go over your work a second time. Things to watch for are missed appointments and not remembering that you were given particular information or instructions, although others remember telling you. Other telltale symptoms that you might notice are episodes of minor clumsiness, such as dropping or knocking things over more frequently. Sometimes there are mood changes. Especially watch for feelings of reduced motivation (a "Why bother?" attitude) or brief bouts of depression or annoyance. There may also be times when you just feel swamped or overworked because of all the tasks you have to do.

12 to 14: With scores at this level, sleep debt may be taking a major toll on your life. In addition to the symptoms that were outlined for scores 7 to 11, your general quality of life may be suffering. You may have inexplicable instances where you make a major mistake on a task or leave out an important item and just don't notice it until things are well along. Your patience for doing detailed and close work may be starting to disappear. You may find yourself less interested in many of the things you formerly found fascinating. You may also be less inclined to spend time socializing. All this is often accompanied by attitudes such as "I don't go to the movies (or watch TV programs) much anymore because they are getting so dull, boring, and predictable" or "I just don't have the time and patience anymore to sit and listen to music (or read a book)." You may also be a bit more accident prone. You may be noticing more near misses when you drive or finding that you cut or burn yourself, spill things, or bump into people and things more frequently. You may have occasional crises in confidence, such as misgivings about your overall competence. There may even be some temporary memory effects, such as momentarily forgetting or being unsure that you correctly remember your home or business address or phone number or some other familiar detail.

15 and above: Scores like this suggest sleep debt is a major problem. In fact, your levels of sleepiness are in the range often found in people with clinical levels of sleep disturbance (such as sleep apnea or severe insomnia). If your score is this high, you almost certainly need a marked change in sleep behavior to ensure your physical and psychological safety. You should definitely start by increasing the amount of sleep you get. If this doesn't lower your scores back below 7 within a few weeks, then you should seek professional help.

A simple way to interpret your scores on this questionnaire is this: With scores above 7 you will begin to notice the effects of your sleep debt in terms of reduced efficiency and feelings of well-being. With scores above 12 your reduced effectiveness and changes in your disposition and mood will also be quite apparent to other people, including fellow workers and family members.

Death on
Daylight Savings Time 💀

$\mathcal{S}$cientists are, in many ways, merely storytellers. It is their goal to tell a consistent tale that sums up a series of isolated facts in a neat fashion. They call the conclusion of their story a theory. The word *theory* comes from the Greek word *theoria*, which has to do with the act of looking at something and is the same source for the word *theater*. This is appropriate since every theory, no matter how sensible and lovely it appears to be, must be viewed, examined, and tested before it can be accepted.

Up to now I have given you a lot of information that can be formed into the theory that most of us in today's world are probably running some form of sleep debt. We sleep anywhere between 1½ to 5 hours less than evolutionary forces designed us to. Although there are lots of data from other researchers that suggest that this is a sensible conclusion, the mind of the scientist always wants one more test, just to make sure the theory works. Someone once suggested that we probably just want one spectacular experimental result that is interesting enough and that can sum things up simply enough so that we can convince people at cocktail parties that we are right.

I have suggested that if we are living with a sleep debt, there should be noticeable consequences of this problem. We know that sleepy peo-

268

ple make errors in judgment, process information less efficiently, and have poorer ability to sustain their attention on routine tasks. While it may be the case that we are making many errors in our work and home lives due to our sleep debt, it is difficult to determine whether any one error or any particular misjudgment was due to our loss of sleep or to some other factor. Is there any way to demonstrate that sleep loss is a major culprit that has an effect on our everyday lives? This was the question that followed me for several years. Sadly, there are times when finding the way to test a particular theory is elusive, and this was one such time.

Some sleep laboratories are filled with beds, EEG machines, and complex electronic equipment. Some are filled with animals. My laboratory is not like either of these. There is a little sign next to the door, which says HUMAN NEUROPSYCHOLOGY AND PERCEPTION LABORATORY, that at least tells you that you are not entering an office suite. There are two rooms that look "scientific" because they are filled with test equipment to measure aspects of seeing and hearing. The rest of the laboratory, however, looks much like what you might see in the work-rooms of a company that takes political opinion polls for newspapers or political parties. There are tables heaped high with survey and ques-tionnaire forms. Some are being prepared for administration to various groups in the university and the surrounding community, and some are already filled out. At a number of tables in two of the rooms you will find perhaps a half dozen people sitting quietly and filling out similar questionnaires. In the next room you might see several people taking a test in which they have to show how well they can visualize objects in three dimensions; a research technician patiently sits near them, occa-sionally looking at a stopwatch. In the rest of the lab you might find, at any point in time, research technicians sitting in front of computers and scoring questionnaires and survey forms, entering data for further analysis, or processing hospital records or data supplied from various governmental or other sources. There are no beds, no complex elec-tronics, no caged animals, and no smell of operating room disinfectant. Just pieces of paper being processed or written on and a bunch of com-puters. For most of the questions I want to answer, this is enough.

The data collected by my laboratory and by other labs had already convinced me that we are a sleep-deprived society. I wanted to know what the implications of this sleep debt are for the average person. Are we running a sleep debt large enough to put us at risk of some disaster, or are we just a little bit below our optimal level? Is there any way to answer this question using the kinds of resources available in a laboratory setup like mine? What I wanted was a real-world situation, where the influence of sleep loss would show up in everyday events and not just on specially designed, very sensitive laboratory tests. The way to test this question eluded me. I knew what I needed to answer it but not how to get there. Obviously, what I needed was some way in which I could get a large group of ordinary people to all lose some sleep at the same time, or to sleep a little longer.

The answer came one April evening. I was getting ready to go to bed when my wife asked me, "Did you remember to reset the clocks?"

"Why?" I asked.

"We're shifting to daylight savings time," she said, "You know, 'spring forward, fall back' and all of that."

Daylight saving time, which is also called "summer time" in some countries, is a system that is in use by around 30 nations in the world today. It involves advancing clocks in the spring or summer, to extend the hours of natural daylight obtainable during our usual waking hours, and then returning to standard time in the fall. The idea was first suggested in a lighthearted essay by Benjamin Franklin in 1784. He noted that by moving the clock forward people could utilize more of the available hours of sunlight each day—and be the richer for it since they could then avoid wasteful and unnecessary use of expensive candles. The tone of Franklin's essay was whimsical, and the idea was not really taken at all seriously until the outbreak of World War I. During the war, Germany, the United States, and Britain all adopted summer daylight saving time as a measure to reduce the amount of artificial light needed. This conserved fuel, which was not only expensive but in short supply. The practice was reinstated in World War II, when England used "double daylight savings time," which involved advancing the clock 2 hours in the summer to maximize use of natural light.

Following World War II, most countries kept daylight savings time. However, different governments have selected different sets of starting and ending times. In the United States, daylight savings time used to begin on the last Sunday in April and end on the last Sunday in October. Following heated (and often bizarre) congressional debates on the issue, Congress mandated that, starting in 1987, daylight savings time would begin on the first Sunday in April and continue to the last Sunday in October. In Britain the start time is a week earlier, and in some European countries the return to standard time is at the end of September.

"Sometimes God smiles on researchers," I thought to myself. Daylight savings time was exactly what I needed. It was a situation where the entire population of North America would all lose 1 hour of sleep on the same night in April and would all have the opportunity to sleep 1 hour extra in the fall. If an hour's worth of sleep loss caused noticeable negative effects in the population, we would know that our sleep debt as a population is large enough to mean that we are potentially teetering on the edge of major problems.

Before we can go any further with this, we must first determine whether people actually alter their sleep patterns as a result of that 1-hour shift in April and October. The answer to that came from clever sleep researchers—Dr. Timothy H. Monk and his associate Dr. Simon Folkard at the University of Sussex in Brighton, England. These researchers viewed the daylight savings time shift as something similar to jet lag, where you move one time zone to the east or west, thus gaining or losing an hour of sleep.[1] They had 65 volunteers keep a sleep diary that noted the time they went to sleep and the time they awakened. The diaries were started 6 days before a daylight savings time shift and continued for 11 days after. The data showed that people's sleep patterns were disrupted immediately following the time shift and that, in fact, their sleep patterns continued to be slightly off for the next 5 days. This is clearly consistent with the idea that the daylight savings time shift alters people's sleep, as I had suspected.

Once I knew a time when there would be a systematic sleep loss or gain in a population as large as that of the United States, I next needed some measure of inefficiency or error or lack of judgment. This again brought me to a halt. In the laboratory it is easy to set up situations where we can measure how well people perform. However, I wanted a measure from the real world. My reasoning went as follows: In the lab if a research subject makes an error in judgment or fails to pay attention, he or she gets a wrong answer or a computer beeps to indicate that a target has been missed. In the real world the consequences are much more drastic. If you are inattentive because you are sleepy, you may miss a traffic signal turning red and end up in the middle of an intersection with oncoming traffic. If you are inattentive when carrying materials up a ladder, you may miss a rung and end up falling. If you are not attentive while you are removing a pot of hot soup from the stove, you may trip over your 3-year-old child who has come quietly up behind you, resulting in bad burns for both of you. In other words, errors in the real world can hurt people. What I then needed was a database that contained accident information. This turned out to be much more difficult than I thought it would be. There are many sources of information on accidents, but most present only summary data; that is, the data are grouped by year, month, or week. To be useful to me such data would have to contain not only the notation of the accident itself but also the exact day on which it occurred. This turned out to be virtually impossible for me to find in public data banks.

I realized that what would suit my research requirements perfectly would be a daily registry of all serious accidents. There is, however, a registry of all *fatal* accidents: data is collected each year by the National Center for Health Statistics (NCHS), a division of the U.S. Department of Health and Human Services. I learned that the NCHS collects data from every registered death certificate in the United States and that it lists the cause of death and also the day of death, which means that we can isolate accidental deaths that occurred after the change to daylight savings time.

I should say that the NCHS *used to* code the deaths by the actual day. After 1988 this information about the date was removed. According to the NCHS, this was done to preserve the privacy of the people whose deaths they are recording, since information on the exact location and date could be used to identify a specific individual. I almost cried when I encountered this restriction. I am not a politician, so I do not know what political pressures brought this change around. However, as a researcher I know that this greatly reduces the usefulness of this data bank for many scientists. For the question I am interested in, this change in policy makes the data bank completely useless. What is saddest about this is that the new policy fails to accomplish any protection for the deceased individual at all. By law, death certificates are public records and may be requested directly. If you want to know what your neighbor died from, you can simply go down to city hall and request a copy of the death certificate. This would be a lot more efficient than combing your way through millions of recorded death certificates from the whole country and trying to guess which one was your neighbor's on the basis of place and date. There is something truly odd in the political mind if it is willing to damage a data source that costs taxpayers millions of dollars a year to produce simply to effect some cosmetic changes.

Still, we did obtain data tapes for all deaths from 1986 to 1988, which were made before the policy change and hence contained the actual date of death.

These records represented information stripped from 6,405,922 death certificates. The data were first limited to only those deaths that occurred due to accidents and to specific days around the daylight savings time shifts. The perfect data set would list the day the fatal accident occurred. These data were "next best" since they list the day the person died, not the day the accident that killed the person occurred. According to the *Oxford Textbook of Medicine,* however, more than 80 percent of deaths directly caused by accidents occur within 4 days of the actual incident. None the less, this means that even with day-by-day records, there will be a little blurring of the data, since any particular accident-related death could have occurred several days earlier than the date of death. For this reason, we considered all of the deaths occurring on the Monday through Thursday following daylight savings time changes. I tabulated all the accidental deaths for this period and compared the result to the same 4-day period of the week preceding the week of the shift as well as of the week following it.

If sleep debt makes us susceptible to the effects of any small additional sleep loss, then the hour of sleep we lose in the spring following the daylight savings shift should make us more clumsy, inattentive, and accident prone—and maybe more likely to die. In the fall, getting the extra hour back might make us a little bit more alert and might improve our safety record. Thus, an analysis of the data should reveal more deaths the week of the spring shift and fewer deaths the week of the fall shift. Analyzing this mass of data was a much larger job than I had expected. It totally overwhelmed the computer I usually use for

FIGURE 2

Number of accidental deaths in the United States in the first 4 working days for the weeks before, during, and after the shifts to and from daylight savings times for the years 1986 to 1988. Notice the increase in deaths for the period during the week of the spring shift, immediately after we lose an additional hour of sleep.

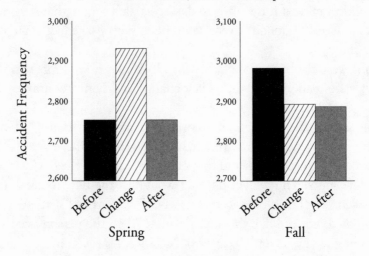

data analysis. When we finally assigned the task of analyzing the data to my fastest laboratory computer, the analysis took 96 hours of continuous processing. The results are shown in Figure 2.

The results for the spring shift to daylight savings time are really quite informative. In the 4 days after we lose just 1 hour of sleep, there is a 6 percent increase in accidental deaths compared to the week before and the week after. This is exactly what I predicted. In the fall, however, there is no definite improvement in safety; this is not devastating for our hypothesis, but it is a bit worrisome. I thought that a possible explanation was that the blurring of the actual times—since death can occur several days after an event—may have helped to wash out any indication of an improvement in safety, but I was still concerned enough to want further information if it was possible to get it. The data thus far seemed to say that additional loss of sleep is clearly a hazard but that adding additional sleep is not necessarily a proven benefit.

What I really needed was day-by-day data on accidents. Where could I get that kind of information for a sample of accidents large enough to make it worthwhile to do the analysis? I spent more than a month trying to track down such data. Eventually, as sometimes happens in science as well as in the rest of life, a friendly contact led to another and finally to someone who was willing to take the time to help. The major spadework was done by my university's data librarian. After a long and tedious search she learned that data in the form that I needed did not exist in public access information banks. However, somehow she found the one person in the Canadian Ministry of Transport who could provide appropriate data on traffic accidents. But, I was warned, his job doesn't require him to release this kind of information. With only a faint flicker of hope I contacted his office in Ottawa, feeling that even if he would not give the data I needed, perhaps he could at least point me in the direction of another data source. I explained that I was a university-based researcher trying to answer a particular question about safety. I also explained that I didn't have a lot of research funding (which, is, unfortunately, true of most researchers in the current economic situation). I described the minimal amount of information that I needed to get the answer I was looking for. There was a brief pause at the other end of the line. Then the voice said, "Well, if that's all you want, I think I can give you some printouts covering a couple of years. I'm pretty busy now, but I'll try to get to you in a few weeks."

Eight weeks later a large manila folder with fanfolds of computer printouts arrived. For the next several weeks everyone in the lab who could run a computer was typing the data into computer files. It turns out that what I had been sent was data representing every reported vehicle accident in Canada in 1991 and 1992, with information as to the province and the specific date that the accident occurred. There would be no blurring of the time of the accident here since we had the actual day of each incident. We had a total of better than a million and a half accidents from all over Canada. There was one minor quirk, however. We had to leave out data from the province of Saskatchewan, which never accepted the concept of daylight savings time. After that, the analysis was quite simple. I looked at the number of traffic accidents on

FIGURE 3

Number of traffic accidents in Canada for the Mondays before
and after the shifts to daylight savings times for the years 1991 to 1992.
Notice the increase in the spring, immediately after we lose an hour of sleep,
and the decrease in the fall, when we gain an extra hour of sleep.

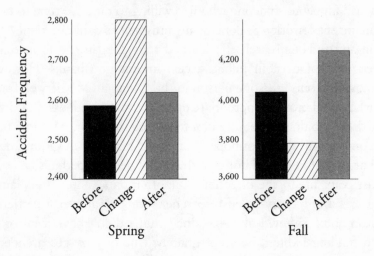

the Monday immediately following the shift to daylight savings time
and compared this to the Monday before and the Monday after. Figure
3 shows the results.

I was ecstatic. I don't believe the results could be more clear. Immediately following the spring daylight savings time shift, when we lose an
hour of sleep, there is approximately a 7 percent increase in traffic accidents, and this increase is gone a week later. Presumably, the increase
comes about simply because the additional hour of sleep debt makes us
that much more inattentive and clouds our judgment a bit more. In
the fall, when we gain an additional hour of sleep, the pattern is reversed. Immediately after the daylight savings time shift there is a decrease in the number of traffic accidents of approximately 7 percent,
but a week later things are back to "normal." Presumably, the decrease
is because that extra hour of sleep nibbles away at our existing sleep
debt and makes our attention a bit better and our judgment a bit more
accurate.

These data tell us a lot about our current sleep debt status. As a society, we must be running a fairly heavy sleep debt if the loss of 1 hour

more of sleep can make it 7 percent more likely that we will have a mishap on the road (and 6 percent more likely that we will die from injuries sustained in an accident). Remember, these are only the events we can count and tabulate. How many bad investment decisions were made that day because of sleep-fogged judgments? How many minor accidents happened at home or on the job because of a microsleep or lapse in attention? How many flawed widgets rolled past the inspection station on the assembly line because attention could not be sustained? How many design errors were missed, computer program steps miscoded, and prescriptions improperly filled? All of these events and possible problems resulting from them were occurring, all caused by the same underlying factor. That factor is a mind fogged by its sleep debt and less than 100 percent efficient. It is a sleep debt so high that just a single hour added to it causes people to die. The fall traffic data summarized in Figure 3 gives a clear indication that this sleep debt *can* be paid and that payments against it have an immediate effect. One additional hour of sleep reduced highway accidents by 7 percent. This shows that our alertness increased and our judgment improved with just that small increase in sleep. In the unmeasured events of that day, doubtless many other accidents were avoided, better judgments were applied to business and research, and perhaps, lives were even saved. Sixty minutes more in bed seems like a small investment, but these data make it clear that in our current sleep-debt-ridden state, it does pay large dividends.

A Wake-Up Call ☎

According to Greek mythology, Night gave birth to twin sons. (We do not know who fathered them, since Night never gives up her secrets easily.) One of these sons was named Hypnos (later renamed Somnus by the Romans). Hypnos was to become the god of sleep. He would wander the earth in many forms—sometimes a bird, sometimes a small child, but most often a handsome young man armed as a warrior or carrying a horn or poppy stalk from which he could drip a liquid that could cause people to slumber. He was always viewed as the health giver and a helper to man. Not so, however, his twin brother, Thanatos, who is Death. Hypnos and Thanatos were eternal adversaries. Thanatos hated all men, and Hypnos loved and cared for them.

Although Hypnos was known as the friend of man and as a great healer of body and mind, no cult ever grew up to worship or sacrifice to him. There are no temples to Hypnos and no songs of worship to thank him for his good deeds and his charity. Even in classical Greek and Roman times, sleep was accepted as a need, but it was never honored. So it is today.

Although many historical and legendary figures were said to have had unusual patterns of sleep, my search for those with a longer than normal sleep time has come up virtually empty. There appear to be social and cultural reasons for this. Society expects their heroes to be resilient and tough. This includes the expectation that great figures will be able to get along with less than the amount of sleep normal people need. Thus, a heroic character (like one played by John Wayne in the movies) will, for example, stand guard all night so that the rest of his troops can get their needed sleep, and he will still be fresh and ready to lead them into battle the next morning.

Whenever a longer than usual sleep pattern is found in a respected person, it is almost always apologized for, as if the biographer were ashamed of its existence. Consider the case of Charlemagne, who was emperor of the Holy Roman Empire for 14 years, beginning in 800 A.D. Biographers note that in addition to his regular sleep he was in the habit of taking a nap after his midday meal, a nap that would usually last about 3 hours. However, virtually every source that mentions Charlemagne's siesta will follow it with an apology stating that the emperor also tended to wake up an average of four times each night, hence implying that the nap was merely replacement sleep for the fragmentation caused by his insomnia.

The British mathematician Abraham De Moivre was one of the groundbreaking workers in the fields of probability theory and trigonometry. He was said to have always been a long sleeper, and the length of his sleep seems to have increased in his old age. De Moivre's biographers are always quick to point out that he was a genius who made many mathematical discoveries *despite* his long sleeping habits. Thomas Edison—who, as you will doubtless recall, felt that sleep was a waste of time and that too much sleep was harmful to a person's health—even used De Moivre as an object lesson. The story he told went as follows:

In his old age Moivre was sleeping 20 hours a day, which only left him 4 hours for his science and the rest of his life. Shortly before his death he declared that he was finding it necessary to sleep around 10 minutes longer each day than he had the day before. Soon his sleep got longer, and he was sleeping over 23 hours. Then it happened. One day he slept right up to the limit of 24 hours, and that finished him. He died in his sleep. Too much sleep is unhealthy, and Moivre proves that it can kill you.

Of course, Edison and his biographers always pointed out that Edison, himself, was a very short sleeper, which is given as a positive and laudable characteristic. Long sleepers are considered to be lazy and un-motivated. If they fail at something, those in charge will often criticize them with comments like "If you spent more time on the job, instead of sleeping, this never would have happened." Short sleepers, however, are protected by society's values. Faced with the failure of a project, they can always point to the long sleepless nights they spent working on it, so that success can then be seen as eluding them despite their best efforts.

Given the data that we have discussed showing that inadequate sleep is probably at the source of many errors, misjudgments, accidents, and deaths, it is a truly odd feature of our society that short sleepers are idolized. We are continually reminded of the great figures who slept very little, including Napoleon, Winston Churchill, John F. Kennedy, Salvador Dali, and Leonardo da Vinci.

The case of Leonardo is an interesting one, since it has received a lot of attention and several research projects have been based upon it. Leonardo da Vinci is noted for his paintings, sketches, sculpture, engineering ability, inventions, and his studies of anatomy. He was a prolific writer and appears to have made investigations involving mathematics, mechanics, ballistics, medicine, botany, astronomy, ge-ology, and biology. His diaries make interesting reading since they contain the precursors of such contemporary ideas as the helicopter. Despite the extensive writing and investigation that have focused on Leonardo, many aspects of his life remain a mystery. Much of what is believed about his work patterns and lifestyle comes from secondary sources and casual commentaries. One of the more interesting claims about Leonardo has been offered to explain his high level of produc-tivity. It deals with his sleep pattern. Supposedly, Leonardo would sleep 15 minutes out of every 4 hours, which would give him a daily sleep total of only 1½ hours. The net result of such a sleep pattern is a gain of 6 additional productive hours in each day. If Leonardo fol-lowed this regime over his entire life it would have effectively added 20 years of productivity to his 67-year life span. It has been suggested that this might, in addition to his genius, explain the vastness and richness of his work.

Leonardo's odd sleep schedule has been studied by the inventive re-searcher Claudio Stampi, who is now with the Sleep and Alertness Research Unit of the Institute for Circadian Physiology in Boston.[1] When Stampi was a young doctor in Bologna, he became interested in sleep–wakefulness patterns. He ultimately decided to seek out real-world situations in which normal sleep patterns cannot be followed and people are forced to adopt alternate sleep arrangements. What eventually caught his attention was the sport of solo yacht racing across long spans of the ocean. During a solo yacht race the sailor has many jobs to do. Some are routine and occur regularly, some are unpredictable. Some may make major demands upon the yacht racer, such as when steering and trimming the yacht are required to meet constantly changing and sometimes threatening conditions of wind and sea. The sailor must always try to set the optimum course and keep up the maximum speed. Sleep is clearly a danger here: while the yacht racer sleeps, the craft can go off course, losing time and risking collision with other boats in the area. In addition, even with self-steering and automatic control devices, if the sailor is asleep and conditions change, the yacht may not be moving at the best speed or be on the best possible course.

Stampi has studied several different races, including the Observer Single-Handed Transatlantic Race, usually just called OSTAR. This race covers a distance of 3,000 nautical miles. The first OSTAR was won by Sir Francis Chichester in 1960. He took 38 days to complete this race. In 1988 the fastest yacht racer took only 10 days to complete the same distance. Most yacht racers admit that the factor that limits the speed of the race is no longer the boat itself—since most are of high technical design and the latest innovations are continually applied to improve performance—rather, the limiting factor today is the sailor. The individual's sailing skill, mental and physical endurance, and stamina are what count the most. Winning the race will finally be determined by how the yacht racer's physical resources are allocated as well as by how the racer utilizes the wind and currents.

What Stampi found was that certain patterns of sleep were associated with better performance in these yacht racers. The best-performing racers completely abandoned the traditional sleep pattern, in which we take all our sleep in one large block at night. Instead, the better racers took their sleep in short naps, some as short as 10 or 20 minutes and almost all shorter than an hour. In addition, the better-performing yacht racers cut their sleep time down to a total of around 4 or 5 hours.

The idea that total sleep time can be shortened and that sleep can be taken in short naps throughout the 24 hours of the day got Stampi to thinking about Leonardo's sleep schedule. In a controlled set of experiments Stampi demonstrated that a 4-hour work–rest cycle can be achieved and maintained over a period of nearly 2 months. The total amount of sleep on such a schedule is only around 25 minutes every 4 hours, for a total of around 2½ hours sleep per 24 hours. Some research participants seemed to be able to function on such a schedule—at least for the duration of the experiment.

The longest experiment of this sort was attempted by Giancarlo Sbragia, a playwright and actor who lives and works in Rome. He decided to try to live using Leonardo's schedule in order to increase his own productivity. He was about 30 years of age at the time, and it took 20 to 25 days for him to finally establish his schedule. He monitored his time with an alarm clock, which was reset every 4 hours. Whenever the alarm sounded, Sbragia would immediately lie down to sleep for 15 minutes. The entire study lasted for 6 months. At first, Sbragia found the experience of living a 22½-hour day exhilarating. However, his mood began to gradually deteriorate and he admitted, "After a few months I felt psychologically a wreck." He began to notice a loss in his creativity and in the quality of his artistic work: "My imagination and my artistic activity started to suffer. I felt like I was using the power of a battery without ever recharging it (not a physical battery, but a sort of creative one). I was suffering a kind of imaginative damage." This worried him, and he terminated the experiment. "I then went back to sleeping for 8 full hours. I recovered my dreams, and best of all, I was at peace with myself."

Considering his own experiences while on Leonardo's schedule, Sbragia suggested that it may be possible to continue on this regimen if one is engaged in routine technical activities. On the basis of his own sense of what happened, however, he feels that artistic invention and creativity may depend upon an adequate sleep length taken in the traditional long, continuous interval rather than fragmented into short naps.

How, then, did Leonardo manage to keep this schedule up and still maintain his creativity? The answer is that he probably didn't. It is possible that he occasionally used such a schedule when he was under time pressure to complete a task. For example, we know that Leonardo's detailed studies of anatomy, which resulted in a series of marvelous drawings, were the result of the dissection and observation of at least 30 cadavers. During Leonardo's era the techniques for preservation of biological tissues were very primitive, to say the least. In such a situation, it might have been to Leonardo's advantage to adopt this short sleep schedule in order to finish the work before the bodies began to decompose. Afterward, he may well have returned to a normal sleep schedule.

When the historical record is checked, however, we actually have no hard evidence that Leonardo ever really used this schedule at all. Moreover, there is evidence that suggests that, at least in his later years, he may actually have been a long sleeper. In the last years of his life Leonardo accepted an invitation from the young king of France, Francis I, to enter his service. A letter written at the time notes that special attention was to be given to Leonardo's quarters since "he values his sleep and spends considerable time in bed."

Could we have been wrong? Is it possible that Leonardo was not such a short sleeper? This may well be the case. There seems to be a great deal of image management that people engage in to make themselves appear to be more ambitious, energetic, and committed, and this often involves creating the appearance of being a short sleeper, one who can "tough it out" with very little sleep. For example, Samuel Johnson, the famous British writer and lexicographer who put together the first English dictionary, once admitted, "*I have, all my life long, been lying* [in bed] *till noon; yet I tell all young men, and tell them with great sincerity, that nobody who does not rise early will ever do any good.*"

The Soviet leader Joseph Stalin also was involved in image management. He frequently exhorted the Russian population to work harder and to put in longer hours, and he cited himself as an example. "Look up at my office in the Kremlin," he would say. "Even in the middle of the night you will see the lights on because I am at my desk working for Russia." It was true that at virtually any hour of the night you could see the lights on in his office. The lights were on because he left them burning when he departed his office at night. Stalin himself was at home getting a full night's sleep.

Former British prime minister Winston Churchill reportedly slept only a few hours a night. Members of his household confirm that he actually spent about 6 hours in bed each night. However, those 6 hours were far from his total sleep for the day. As Churchill himself noted:

You must sleep sometime between lunch and dinner, and no halfway measures. Take off your clothes and get into bed. That's what I always do. Don't think you will be doing less work because you sleep during the day. That's a foolish notion held by people who have no imagination. You will be able to accomplish more. You get two days in one—well, at least one and a half, I'm sure. When the war started, I had to sleep during the day because that was the only way I could cope with my responsibilities.

Churchill's naps were usually 1½ to 2 hours long, giving him a normal complement of sleep totaling around 8 hours.

If often seems to be the case that when they are carefully looked at, many of the stories of short sleepers are quite exaggerated. For example, Napoleon was said to be a short sleeper, who claimed that he only needed 4 hours a night. Contemporaries, however, report that he tended to underestimate the actual amount of time he spent sleeping. In addition, numerous witnesses at some critical meetings and battles reported that he was often quite fatigued and complained about insufficient sleep. Some historians even suggest that in several important instances he may have performed badly because he was running a sleep debt.

The tendency to underestimate the hours of sleep one actually gets seems to be quite common. Consider the case of Nikola Tesla, a Croatian electrical engineer who became world renowned for his invention of the rotating magnetic field, which he used as the basis for alternating electric current systems, and also created the basis for radio and television broadcasting, with the Tesla coil. Tesla had the reputation for being a very short sleeper. Some people even suggested that he slept as little as 2 hours a day. It was certainly the case that he did research late into the night. The local police became quite accustomed to getting phone calls about weird noises and strange lights emanating from Tesla's lab in the small hours of the morning. However, Tesla actually got considerably more sleep than he reported. His lab staff reported that he would often take several naps during the day, with each sometimes lasting for several hours. He would also have spontaneous sleep attacks. When he lived for several years in a hotel, the staff reported that they often saw Tesla sitting in a chair with his eyes half open, as if he were staring straight ahead in a trance. The staff claimed that when Tesla was like this he was totally unaware of his surroundings and that on such occasions it was possible to clean his room around him and to make up his bed without disturbing him in the least.

It is interesting to note that Tesla worked with Thomas Edison for about 2 years. The two men did not get along well because their work styles were so different. However, when a reporter once pointed out that the two inventors had in common a reduced need for sleep, Tesla scoffed at the claim and made the following observation of Edison: "Although he needs only 4 sleep hours at night, he needs two 3-hour naps each day." Given the fact that Tesla and Edison were business and scientific competitors, perhaps we ought to reserve our judgment. Tesla might simply have been trying to damage Edison's reputation by casting doubt on an aspect of Edison's lifestyle that both men prized. After all, wasn't it Edison who believed that sleeping 8 hours a day was a "deplorable regression to the primitive state of the caveman"? Wasn't it Edison who created the electric lightbulb so that we could make sleep virtually unnecessary—and in so doing placed us on the pathway to our current level of sleep debt?

The truth of the matter is that Edison, like most of the short sleepers in history, probably had such a strong work ethic that he simply repressed or underestimated the length of time he spent napping to make up for his shortened nighttime hours of sleep. The auto maker Henry Ford once made an unexpected visit to Edison's lab. One of the technicians stopped him from entering Edison's private office, noting that "Mr. Edison is taking a nap."

Ford thought this was a bit amusing and said, "I understood that Mr. Edison didn't sleep very much."

"Oh, that's true," said the technician. "He doesn't sleep very much at all, he just naps a lot."

So here we are. We have traveled full circle and found that the very people who insisted that we do not need very much sleep, the people who instructed us to cut down on our sleep time to increase our productivity, the people who asked us to follow their example, were themselves longer sleepers than they either knew or were willing to admit. Sleep is simply not dispensable, regardless of the attempts in today's society to treat it as if it were simply unproductive "downtime." The desire to get more sleep is not a sign of laziness, nor does it represent a lack of ambition. The need for sleep is real.

The idea that one can go without sleep is wrong. The data seem to be quite clear about this. It is probably the case that we may need 9½ to 10 hours of sleep a day for optimal performance. This sleep can be had in one continuous nightly session, or it can be divided into something like 7½ to 8 hours at night and 1½ to 2 hours in the afternoon. With this amount of sleep we seem to be obtaining the quantity that evolution programmed us for. With this amount of sleep we also seem to be building up a bit of a reserve or a cushion, which will allow us to better handle times of stress and short-term sleep deprivation.

If we need 10 hours, why have we always seemed to be able to get along on the 8 hours of sleep that is traditional? Many of us can do fine on 8 hours of sleep for most purposes. As we pointed out earlier, what we lose is our safety margin. If we now encounter a short period of time when our sleep is restricted, we go downhill faster. Our normal efficiency, alertness, and creativity is not as good with 8 hours of sleep as it is with 10, and a significant segment of the population is still sleepy and fatigued with this amount of sleep. So 8 hours of sleep a day is survivable, over the long term, but 10 is better.

When we try to sleep less than the 8-hour minimum, things start to deteriorate. First of all, the effects of less than 8 hours of sleep a night seem to accumulate as a sleep debt. If you lose 2 hours today and 2 hours tomorrow, on the third day your efficiency is as low as if you had lost 4 hours in one night. This is the way our sleep debt builds up. Eventually, if the sleep debt becomes large enough, we become slow, clumsy, stupid, and, possibly, dead. This is not an exaggeration. Remember, the national death rate by accidents jumps 6 percent as a result of simply losing 1 hour more of sleep as we shift to daylight savings time in the spring.

Perhaps it is time for policymakers, health workers, and all the rest of us to wake up. The data is now quite clear that sleepiness, the direct result of not enough sleep, is a health hazard to individuals. It also may be a danger to the general public, because of the possibility that a sleepy individual might trigger a catastrophic accident such as those associated with Chernobyl, the *Exxon Valdez,* and the space shuttle *Challenger.*

As a society we attempt to exert controls on personal behavior that constitutes a personal health hazard or has the possibility of affecting the health and safety of others. Many places in society today restrict tobacco smoking because secondhand smoke may cause cancer in others. We restrict alcohol use because public drunkenness has been shown to be associated with outbreaks of violence and drunkenness on the highway may kill other drivers. We do, however, permit both drinking and smoking in private, where no harm can be done to anyone except the individual. At one time smoking was considered a sign of sophistication; later it was a sign of toughness. The ability to drink large amounts of alcohol has been viewed as a sign of strength and of self-control, especially in certain groups of males. Today, however, heavy drinkers and heavy smokers are not viewed very favorably in our society.

There are parallels between sleep deprivation and drinking or smoking. Today, the person who runs on little sleep is seen as being mentally tough, ambitious, and admirable. Perhaps as society recognizes the harm that building up a sleep debt does to the sleep-deprived person and to those around him or her, this situation will change. Perhaps someday society will act to do something about sleepiness. It may even come to pass that someday the person who drives or goes to work while sleepy will be viewed as being as reprehensible, dangerous, or even criminally negligent as the person who drives or goes to work while drunk. If so, perhaps the rest of us can all sleep a little bit more soundly.

Notes ✿

Edison's Curse

1. T. A. Edison in *The Diary and Sundry Observations of Thomas Alva Edison*, edited by D. D. Runes (New York: Philosophical Library, 1948), quotes from pp. 52 and 178.

Sleep and Consciousness

1. For example, D. Hutchins, *American Journal of Clinical Hypnosis* 4 (1961): 106–114.

What Is Sleep?

1. R. D. Olgivie and R. T. Wilkinson, *Sleep* 11 (1988):139–155.
2. I. Oswald and C. Adam, *British Medical Journal* 281 (1980):1684–1685, quotes from p. 1658.

Evolution's Mistake?

1. R. Meddis in *Sleep mechanisms and functions in humans and animals: An evolutionary perspective*, edited by A. Mayes (Berkshire, UK: Van Nostrand Reinhold, 1983).

No Sleep at All

1. J. J. Ross, *Archives of Neurology* 12 (1965):399–403.
2. H. A. C. Kamphuisen, B. Kemp, C. G. S. Kramer, J. Duijvestijn, L. Ras, & J. Steens, *Clinical Neurology and Neurosurgery* 94 (suppl.)(1992):S96–S99, quote on p. S98.

3. P. Suedfeld (ed.), *Psychology and torture* (New York: Hemisphere, 1990).

Cutting Down on Sleep

1. J. Horne, *Why we sleep* (Oxford, UK: Oxford University Press, 1988).

A Little Bit of Sleep

1. T. Reilly & M. Piercy, *Ergonomics* 37 (1994):107–115.
2. F. Mougin et al., *European Journal of Applied Physiology* 63 (1991):77–82.

The Clocks Within Us

1. L. E. M. Miles, D. M. Raynal, & M. A. Wilson, *Science* 198 (1977):421–423.
2. G. M. Brown, *Journal of Psychiatry and Neuroscience* 19 (1994):345–353.
3. H. Hoagland, *Journal of General Psychology* 9 (1933):267–287.
4. Some items adapted from B. Wallace, *Journal of Personality and Social Psychology* 64 (1993):827–833, and C. S. Smith, C. Reilly, & K. Midkiff, *Journal of Applied Psychology* 5 (1989):728–738.

Sleepy Children and Sleepy Parents

1. K. Busby & R. T. Pivik, *Sleep* 8 (1985):332–341.
2. R. E. Dahl, W. E. Pelham, M. Wierson, *Journal of Pediatric Psychology* 16 (1991):229–239.
3. *Los Angeles Times*, January 29, 1995.

Sleepy Teenagers

1. M. A. Carskadon & W. C. Dement, in *Sleep and its disorders in children*, edited by C. Guilleminault (New York: Raven Press, 1987), pp. 53–56.

Sleep Thieves in the Kitchen

1. T. Roth, T. Roehers, & L. Merlotti, *Alcohol Drugs Driving* 6 (1990):357–362.

Asleep at the Wheel

1. Cited in L. Dotto, *Losing sleep: How your sleeping habits affect your life* (New York: Morrow, 1990), p. 159.
2. Data from P. Lavie, in *Sleep, sleepiness and performance*, edited by T. H. Monk (West Sussex, UK: Wiley, 1991), pp. 65–93.

Asleep at the Operating Table

1. C. V. Ford & D. K. Wentz, *Southern Medical Journal* 77 (1984):1435–1442.
2. T. Lingenfelser, R. Kaschel, W. Weber, H. Zaiser-Kaschel, B. Jakober, & J. Küper, *Medical Education* 28 (1994):566–572.
3. I. J. Deary & R. Tait, *British Medical Journal* 295 (1987):1513–1516.

4. L. I. Goldman, M. T. McDonough, & G. P. Rosemond, *Journal of Surgical Research* 12 (1972):83–86.

Asleep on the Night Shift

1. T. Åkerstedt, in *Sleep, sleepiness and performance,* edited by T. H. Monk (New York: Wiley, 1991), pp. 129–154.
2. M. J. Paley & D. I. Tepas, *Human Factors* 36 (1994):269–284.
3. P. J. Sparks, *American Journal of Industrial Medicine* 21 (1992):507–516.
4. W. C. Dement, *The sleepwatchers* (Stanford, CA: Stanford Alumni Association, 1992).
5. D. R. Gold, S. Rogacz, N. Bock, T. D. Tosteson, T. M. Baum, F. E. Speizer, & C. A. Czeisler, *American Journal of Public Health* 82 (1992):1011–1014.
6. B. Phillips, L. Magan, C. Gerhardstein, & B. Cecil, *Southern Medical Journal* 84 (1991):1176–1184.

The Cost of Sleep Debt

1. D. Leger, *Sleep* 17 (1994):84–93.

Are We Chronically Sleep Deprived?

1. J. M. Taub, *Journal of Cross-Cultural Psychology* 2 (1971):353–362.

Death on Daylight Savings Time

1. T. H. Monk & S. Folkard, *Science* 261 (1976):688–689.

A Wake-Up Call

1. See C. Stampi (ed.), *Why we nap* (Boston: Birkhäuser, 1985).
2. Quoted in W. Graebner, *My dear Mister Churchill* (New York: Simon & Schuster, 1965), p. 172.

General Bibliography ◉

Aronoff, M. S. (1991). *Sleep and its secrets: The river of crystal light.* New York: Insight Books.

Carskadon, M. A. (1993). *Encyclopedia of sleep and dreaming.* New York: Macmillan.

Dement, W. C. (1992). *The sleepwatchers.* Stanford, CA: Stanford Alumni Association.

Dinges, D. F., & Broughton, R. J. (1989). *Sleep and alertness: Chronobiological, behavioral and medical aspects of napping.* New York: Raven Press.

Dotto, L. (1990). *Losing sleep: How your sleeping habits affect your life.* New York: Morrow.

Ellman, S. J., & Antrobus, J. S. (1991). *The mind in sleep: Psychology and psychophysiology.* New York: Wiley.

Horne, J. (1988). *Why we sleep: The functions of sleep in humans and other mammals.* Oxford, UK: Oxford University Press.

Kryger, M. H., Roth, T., & Dement, W. C. (1989). *Principles and practice of sleep medicine.* Philadelphia: Saunders.

Mayes, A. (1983). *Sleep mechanisms and functions in humans and animals: An evolutionary perspective.* Berkshire: Van Nostrand Reinhold.

Meddis, R. (1977). *The sleep instinct.* London: Routledge & Kegan Paul.

Monk, T. H. (1991). *Sleep, sleepiness and performance.* Chichester, UK: Wiley.

Moorcroft, W. H. (1989). *Sleep, dreaming and sleep disorders.* Lanham: University Press of America.

Peter, J. H., Penzel, T., Podszus, T., & von Wichert, P. (1991). *Sleep and health risk.* Berlin: Springer-Verlag.

Stampi, C. (1992). *Why we nap: Evolution, chronobiology and functions of polyphasic and ultrashort sleep.* Boston: Birkhäuser.

Index ◇